KILLER WIVES 5
MORE DEADLY WOMEN---MORE DEAD HUSBANDS

MATTHEW KELL TAYLOR

For Chrissy
My Constant Companion

INTRODUCTION

They were wives first, mothers, breadwinners, Sunday-smile neighbors, long before they became killers in the headlines. This book is the fifth volume in a chilling series about women who crossed the final line, and the nine wives you'll meet here did it in the one place meant to be safest: home.

Some struck in white hot rage, after years of humiliation, bruises, or betrayal. Others planned calmly and carefully, turning marriage into a ledger and a husband into a payout, killing not for freedom, but for cash. A poisoned drink. A staged accident. A hired gun.

Each chapter follows one wife, from vows to verdicts: the secrets they hid, the stories they told, the juries they faced. Together, their cases ask a single, unsettling question: when love and resentment collide with greed or fury, how far can an ordinary woman go, and how many red flags will everyone else ignore?

CONTENTS

1. Linda Lou Charbonneau	1
2. Lydia Sherman	23
3. Teresa Lewis	46
4. Josephine Gray	72
5. Amber Cummings	101
6. Susan Smith	129
7. Larissa Schuster	153
8. Shana Parkinson	179
9. Melinda Harmon-Raisch	208
About the Author	235
Also by Matthew Kell Taylor	237

CHAPTER 1
LINDA LOU CHARBONNEAU
BURIED HUSBAND ALIVE

Sussex County sits at the southern end of Delaware, a patchwork of small towns, secondary roads, and fields that run to tree lines and drainage ditches. In the late twentieth century the county balanced farming traditions with newer trades. Houses stood back from the road behind mailboxes that carried family names across generations. One of those names was Charbonneau, and for a long time it attached itself to a man named John and to a woman who would, by turns, live with him, leave him, and return to him. Before the events that later placed her in courtrooms, Linda Lou was a daughter, a partner, a mother, and then a figure known in two households set miles apart on the same peninsula.

She was born on 9th February 1948 Her first years were not recorded in newspapers or formal biographies. Neighbors and relatives recalled the ordinary beginnings of a life that would spur attention much later. The most stable notes in those early accounts draw attention to the first deep loss. Her first husband died in a car accident. That sudden death left Linda Lou with two children and a small circle of relatives who helped as families do in

Sussex County, with food on the stove and rides where needed and brief prayers at the door before night came down. The practical reality of single parenthood shaped her next choices. She needed money coming in. She needed a household that could hold together.

In time she formed a partnership with John Charbonneau. John was older, steady in his habits, and tied to a house that had the small efficiencies that long occupancy brings. He kept tools where he could reach them and had settled into patterns that people in Bridgeville recognized. Linda Lou moved in with him and the home became a place where her children grew. The arrangement lasted not months but years. Two decades is the span most often described when people mark the length of that shared life. Over that period a third child was born, a daughter named Mellisa. The family grew in the way many households do, with the slower pace of a rural county that often measures itself by seasons and school calendars rather than by office schedules.

The relationship between Linda Lou and John lived through the ordinary stresses of long familiarity. They argued about the things that people who share a home argue about. Money, who owned what, when a job should be done, whether a neighbor was right in a dispute, how to raise a child who had a different opinion from a parent, whether a relative should be tolerated at the table or turned away for a while. None of that would have drawn public notice in a place where couples have disagreements on front porches and then sweep the steps together. What marked the household was the length of the arrangement and the complicated web of relatives that stretched between the adults.

By the late nineteen nineties the relationship had frayed to the point where Linda Lou chose to leave. In 1997 she married another man, a younger member of the extended family, a nephew of John. His name was William Sproates the third. He was in his forties, energetic, and related to John through the line that tied uncle and nephew. The marriage drew attention because of that family connection, but people in the county understood that relationships can bend in complex ways. The couple did not move far. They built a life in another Sussex town and brought along the patterns Linda Lou had made in her first long arrangement, the attention to household management and to what she saw as her share of decisions.

The marriage to William did not sever every tie to the Bridgeville address where she had lived for so long. Over the next few years she spent time with John again. The periods of return and departure reflected a push and pull that people close to the family saw as a kind of pendulum. When life with William grew tense, she visited John. When life with John grew tense again, she returned to William. The geography of the peninsula made that movement simple. The route between Magnolia and Bridgeville is the sort of drive that does not need a map once a person has done it a few times. Children grew into teenagers. The older children sought their own balance with change. Mellisa moved toward adulthood with her mother as a constant presence even as the household around them shifted.

The homes where Linda Lou spent her days during that period carried the marks of her hand. In the Bridgeville house, she arranged rooms for functionality rather than display. A kitchen needed to serve meals. A living room needed to hold visitors without fuss. In Magnolia, William kept his own routines and tolerances, and she negotiated space there as couples do when a new partner moves into established rooms. She had a way of claiming responsibility for the flow of daily life. Who cooked, who cleaned, who paid for a repair, who called about a billing mistake, who decided whether a lawn ornament was worth keeping. These may sound like small matters, but they are the matters from which power and resentment grow in any house.

Across these years the county remained constant around them. Sussex County's public life revolves around school sports, church schedules, the work of volunteer fire companies, and events that anchor the calendar, from spring plantings to fall festivals. People meet at diners on the highway where the coffee is reliable and the waitress knows which regular takes sugar and which does not. In that setting a figure like Linda Lou could be both visible and unremarkable. She was known in two neighborhoods, recognized by store clerks, and part of a loose net of acquaintances who could place her face and name without needing to know more than that.

The line between the houses in Bridgeville and Magnolia ran through extended family as well as through geography. John as an uncle and William as a nephew belonged to the same larger tree. That overlap heightens both affection and friction. Gifts and loans cross that line, and so do grievances. In small communities where people measure worth by thrift and by keeping a promise, a borrowed tool returned late or in a different condition can start a quarrel that lasts months. A disagreement about who owns a particular piece of furniture can become more than a question of wood and cloth. It can stand for the larger question of who commands the house.

By 2000 those property tensions appeared in a way that left records beyond neighbor talk. A uniformed officer from the state police visited the Bridgeville house in August of that year to calm a dispute over possessions. The guidance he gave was simple. Items that were in question should remain in the house until the matter was resolved. That kind of official instruction is common in domestic property disagreements. It acknowledges that the people involved might act out of anger and seeks to stop immediate movement that could worsen the fight. The visit did not lead to arrests or charges. It did signal that the disagreements inside the house had reached a level that drew in outside authority.

The next year added more complexity. Linda Lou's relationship with Mellisa remained close. They exchanged confidences that sometimes excluded others in the family. Mellisa was in a period of change herself. She had left a marriage, secured custody arrangements for her child, and begun to build new ties. She met Willie Brown, a younger man from outside their long standing circles. He was not related to the Charbonneau line. He came into the family through a personal connection with her. That connection brought with it new possibilities and new stresses. When a new person is added to a family network, the net tightens in some places and loosens in others. The effects travel in directions that are not always easy to predict.

Money stood behind many of the arguments in these years. Cash from regular checks offered stability. It also created friction if more than one person believed they had a claim to it or to the property it supported. Social Security benefits arrived on a schedule that the household could count on. Who counted on them and for what purpose depended on who held the checkbook and who saw themselves as entitled to make decisions about spending and saving. Any household with thin margins knows the power of a steady monthly deposit. It eases a week and can settle a bill that a neighbor or a cousin has been quietly asking about. It can also pull people into conflict when loyalty and entitlement do not match.

The tone of the Bridgeville house in this period reflected the stress of these questions. Some visitors described tidy rooms and a host who could be warm when it suited her. Others described a colder atmosphere when a subject came up that she wanted to control. Her manner could change quick enough to surprise a guest not familiar with the family currents. In the Magnolia house William managed his own resources and watched new arrivals with a careful eye. He cared about order. He noticed when a box came in from somewhere else that did not belong in his space. He was the kind of man who looked at a detail and began to worry about the larger picture it suggested.

Linda Lou's identity in these years became a thread drawn taut between two places and two men. She was the mother in the Bridgeville house and the wife in the Magnolia house. She was the daughter to her own aging mother. She was the grandmother to a child who played on carpets that had seen several generations of feet. She made calls to relatives to ask for favors and to offer help. She borrowed a van when a move required it and offered rides when someone needed to get across the county. Those gestures created obligations in both directions. In a small place people keep mental ledgers of who owes whom. She knew how to balance those ledgers in her favor when she could.

People who observed her over time noticed that she favored a direct style. She told people what she wanted done and expected them to do it. That quality can be useful in a crisis. It can also harden into a controlling habit that strains the patience of those around her. In family gatherings she preferred to guide the conversation. She sometimes used the language of sacrifice to bolster her case, reminding others of what she had carried in earlier years when her first husband died and she raised two children alone. That story was true. It was also a tool, as any personal story can become when someone uses it to steer an argument in the present.

The children in her life learned to read her moods. They knew when to bring a request and when to wait. Mellisa in particular mirrored some of her mother's assertiveness. She learned that in a dispute above all one should not be the first to concede. That lesson would matter later when she faced serious questions in a formal setting and chose first to protect herself and then to adjust her account as pressure mounted. For the moment it simply meant that mother and daughter presented a united front in family matters. They handled decisions together and often informed others after facts had been set.

Outside of family circles, Linda Lou interacted with neighbors and clerks as any resident does. She introduced herself by first name and left an impression as someone who could be friendly if the exchange went her way. People who cross her in small matters sometimes heard sharp words. People who agreed with her decisions found her pleasant. She did not volunteer personal history unasked. She told the parts of her story that seemed useful in the moment. A widow left with children. A long time partner who had kept a house running. A new marriage that she was trying to make work. These versions of herself were all true in their core facts. They were also framed to elicit sympathy or support as needed.

As the summer of 2001 turned toward fall, the households that set the stage for the events to come presented the outward look of normal life. In Bridgeville, there were chores on a small property where a man had lived for years. In Magnolia, there were the daily tasks that attach themselves to any occupied house, from trash pickup to the care of a yard. Vehicles moved between the addresses. Boxes moved between them as well. People who live in rural places get used to the sight of trucks loaded with strange mixtures of items, the contents of sheds and basements where objects have been accumulating since the seventies. That movement did not draw special attention until much later, when people looked back and tried to remember exactly when the flow of goods had changed direction.

The only official call that summer that left a mark on paper was the property dispute visit in August. It placed an officer in the Bridgeville home as a neutral voice and established that there had been disagreement about what belonged to whom. The directive he gave left a trace in memory. If there is a question about ownership, leave the item where it is until the question is settled. That kind of advice becomes important later because it defines reasonable behaviour at the time. People who carry possessions out of a house after such advice know they are moving against an expressed rule.

Looking across the background of these years, the most important features for readers who want to understand what followed are these. Linda Lou had endured an early loss and built a long partnership afterward. She managed a blended household for two decades and raised a daughter to adulthood within it. She left that partnership in 1997 to marry into the same extended family. She later spent stretches of time back in the house she had once run, while remaining in the new marriage. Her sense of control within a home was strong. Property disputes were real and had drawn official attention even before the events at the center of this book. Her bond with her daughter was close and practical. A new young man entered their orbit through that daughter. And in the late summer of 2001, boxes and furniture began to move between houses in ways that would matter to investigators, though the investigators were not yet involved.

This is the frame through which the reader should view the next months. It offers context without reaching ahead to recount the crimes or the investigation, which are addressed in later sections. The picture here is of a woman who built influence over daily life in two linked households, who managed money and possessions as levers, who placed a high value on loyalty within her chosen circle, and who lived in a county where the distance between a living room and a field is thirty paces and the distance between rumor and fact is often only a day's walk.

THE MURDERS

The fall of 2001 brought with it a chain of grim events that would later be unpacked in courtrooms, grand jury rooms, and police interview suites across Sussex County. Two men vanished within weeks of one another. Both were intimately tied to the same woman. Both died violently. Both were concealed in ways that suggested someone understood how to erase a person's presence from a house and a neighborhood and possibly from memory. What could not be erased was the physical story in the ground and the physical story on floors and boxes. The record of what followed does not rely on rumor. It rests on bodies recovered, on autopsy findings, on photographs taken at the scenes, and on the statements of those who admitted participation.

The first disappearance preceded the first grave. In late September John Charbonneau dropped out of sight from his place near Millsboro. John had spent years entangled with Linda Lou Charbonneau in a long and stormy union that included separations and reconciliations. By September of that year he was living in a home where Linda still came and went. People who knew him expected to see him on errands and at the edges of his property. When they did not, questions started to gather. The questions would soon matter because signs of unusual activity at his house accumulated in his absence. Rooms were stripped. Items that did not typically travel were suddenly in motion. It was as if a move was being carried out without the mover.

Investigators later testified that the first killing unfolded inside John Charbonneau's residence and that the method was simple and brutal. A blow to the head with a heavy object is the kind of assault that leaves an unmistakable pattern. It fractures the skull, it produces spatter on nearby surfaces, and it leaves blood where the body falls or is dragged. That is exactly what the later investigation found when the case was finally opened. The story told was that John had been lured from routine into alarm. A ruse about a break in was used to pull him toward danger. The assailant waited. When John appeared he was struck and overpowered. The assault was not a struggle in a crowded place with many witnesses. It was a private attack that relied on surprise and force. He was bundled into a vehicle while still alive or recently grievously injured and driven away from his own front door.

The drive was not long. The Sussex County landscape offers plenty of narrow lanes and concealed spots where a body could be taken from a vehicle without interruption. According to the version of events later laid out in court, the assailant used a blunt instrument again at a secluded site to finish the killing. The blows were sufficient to cause catastrophic head trauma. The body was then concealed, not with care taken to dress a grave, but with speed and the confidence that distance from the house would cover the act. The earth received the body and the killer returned to familiar rooms.

What followed at John Charbonneau's residence was a removal of his things so extensive that it did not resemble ordinary tidying. Entire fittings were taken down to bare surfaces. Floors and cabinets went as if a contractor had been hired to renovate. It was a stripping that made more sense after the second crime came into focus, because the items moved from Millsboro to another address served an additional purpose. The relocation concealed evidence, and among the belongings moved was a box stained in a way that could not be explained by ordinary wear or storage. Only later would people tell police that the stains looked like blood and that the box had come from the house where John had vanished.

Weeks passed and the second of the two men at the center of this story was reported missing. William Sproates the third, John Charbonneau's nephew and the current husband of Linda Lou Charbonneau. He lived near

Bridgeville. He had become wary and vocal about what he found among the goods moved from his uncle's house. By mid October he was gone as well.

The second killing was carried out in a setting that seemed, at first, to offer shelter and safety. A domestic doorway is an easy place to step through if the person at that door is known to you. Investigators later stated that the plan to remove William from the list of those asking questions was set in motion after he discovered troubling evidence among the property that had been hauled from John's home. The plan required timing, access, and a familiar touch. The account accepted in court described how William was expected back and how someone was in place to meet him when he came inside. There is nothing elaborate about the kind of ambush that waits in a dark interior. There is no need for complex gear. What the autopsy and the testimony pointed to was a combined assault that involved stabbing, beating, and an act that closed the airways. The medical examiner would later record multiple stab wounds, blunt force trauma, and signs of asphyxiation. Dirt was discovered in William's lungs, a finding that means he was breathing when he was placed under soil. That detail, offered in a sterile report, says everything about the violence and the haste. He was attacked, he was subdued, and he was taken to a place where a pit had been prepared. He was still alive when the earth began to cover him.

The grave dug for William was not far from the daily paths of the people responsible for his burial. It would eventually be found in a backyard, not in a distant wood or a forgotten field. That placement speaks to the confidence the killers had that discovery would be avoidable. It also speaks to a degree of control over the property where the grave lay and the expectation that curious eyes would not be allowed to search the soil. The backyard grave told a story as soon as it was opened by officers. The soil layers showed the fresh disruption. The body told the rest. Wounds on the torso and head, ligature marks or pressure evidence on the neck and face, and the inhaled dirt explained the sequence likely followed that night.

The concealment did not stop with burial. There was a story told to anyone who asked where William had gone. It was a story about a man who had driven off with someone else or left town for a time. That kind of tale might hold for a day or two. It cannot hold against the relentless pressure of family members trying to reach a loved one, or against the routines of the postal service, or the constant presence of neighbors who expect to see a man step out in the morning. Silence at a dwelling where there used to be footsteps and conversation is noticed. Vehicles that do not move are noted. Lights that do not switch on at customary hours are noticed. So the story wore thin quickly and suspicion took its place.

When the second grave was uncovered it contained a man still dressed for the ordinary business of the day he had expected to finish. The items found with him were the common objects a person carries without thinking. None of those things could answer a single question. For answers officers had to look for the tools of the crimes and for the people who might have been near them. The objects used were not elaborate. A heavy object capable of causing a skull fracture. A knife capable of deep and repeated penetration. Something that could constrict breathing or compress the airway. The house where the second killing occurred contained the ordinary version of those items. The scene inside told its own story, even after attempts were made to wash and reorder things. Cleaning a place where a violent assault has occurred is never complete. Under furniture and behind appliances and in the pores of wood and grout there are traces. Investigators documented those traces, photographed them, and collected samples. Those materials would later help build the order of operations for the night William died.

The connection between the two crimes was both human and logistical. Human, because both victims were bound to the same woman through long and complicated relationships. Logistical, because items removed after the first killing became visible again in the orbit of the second before the second killing had even taken place. Boxes and household pieces traveled a familiar route from one address to another, and in that movement the seeds of the second murder were sown. When the second man spoke of his alarm concerning what he had seen, he made himself a problem for those who knew where the first man had gone. The decision to silence him was a decision to close a circle of risk.

Much of what we know about the movements of those two nights comes from the people who were there. One of them took police to the place where John lay. Another addressed the details of the second assault and the burial behind the house. In each case the accounts were accompanied by physical proof that aligned with the admissions. In the case of John, the remains were located where the guide said they would be found. The cause of death was consistent with a beating in a secluded place after an initial assault in the home. In the case of William, the grave was exactly where it was alleged and the injuries were consistent with a combined attack followed by a hurried burial.

The geography of the crimes was small. Millsboro to Bridgeville is not a long drive by Delaware standards. The roads between them run through farmland and stands of trees. At night they can feel very empty. The burial for the second man was not in a lonely field but in a yard. The burial for the first man was in a secluded area where no one was expected to be at the hour the work was done. Both sites were chosen because control over the ground could be exerted afterward. That control did not last. The ground at one site was disturbed by law enforcement shovels after the second body was found. The ground at the second site gave up its burden when an individual led officers there.

The tempo of the murders was fast. The first man was killed on September 23. The second died on October 17. That is less than a month apart. The short distance in time meant that the actions set in motion after the first killing were still visible when the second killing took place. Items remained in transit. People were still calling and asking for John when William vanished. The state of agitation and secrecy required to hide one body was still humming when the second was being buried. That kind of noise draws attention, even if the voices are speaking softly.

The methods in each murder shared the same features. There was no lengthy confinement or elaborate restraint. There was no use of firearms. The weapons were close quarters tools. The violence was personal and messy. The concealment aimed not at deep deception but at short term delay. In the first case the delay allowed for removal and redistribution of property. In the second case the delay seems aimed at simple avoidance of the first crime coming into full view. If the nephew was convinced to keep quiet or if he vanished without alarm, then the first death might remain a missing person case. That calculation failed.

The final element common to both crimes was the reliance on familiar spaces and familiar hands. The person who opened the door to William knew him. The person who moved comfortably around John's space knew the layout, knew which switches controlled which lights, knew where a heavy object could be found. Outsiders do not empty a home of cabinets and fences without help. Outsiders do not bury a man behind a house without knowing who might look over the fence at night. These were inside jobs, and the inside nature of the crimes became the path investigators followed toward their suspects.

To describe the murders is to describe sequence and means. To understand them is to look at motive, and in the context of the record that would later be made public the motive for the first killing, as argued by the state, combined money and control. The motive for the second killing, as the state also argued, was to remove a person who had become a witness to evidence that could collapse the fragile story explaining away the first disappearance. Whether one accepts those motives or not, the timeline invites that conclusion. The uncle is killed. The nephew finds a stained box among the belongings taken from the uncle's house. He raises questions. He is killed three weeks later and buried behind the former house of the uncle.

The injuries sustained by both men were described in language as stark as it comes. Skull fractures do not heal. The combination of multiple stab wounds and evidence of asphyxiation indicates an attack that not only intended to kill but ensured it. The dirt in the lungs of the second victim means that the burial was not an afterthought. It was part of the killing itself. The act of covering a still breathing man with soil is intimate and horrific. It was performed in a place where clothes lines and lawn chairs stood within view.

Everything that happened in those four weeks had a practical dimension. A ruse at a kitchen doorway. A heavy blow. A drive at night to a spot already chosen. A shallow grave. A return to a house where items were waiting to be loaded. A back door unlocked for the person who would confront a man with questions. A second beating. A knife used to finish a task that did not finish quickly enough. A second grave in a yard where dogs bark and neighbors pass by. Then the quiet that follows when a house is empty.

The murders of John Charbonneau and William Sproates the third were not mysteries created from thin air. They were crimes shaped by proximity and by the belief that neighbors will mind their own business and that family members can be managed with plausible stories. In the end the earth itself undid that belief. A shovel turned the truth over. A second shovel turned over more. From there, words began to fill in the gaps around the dirt and the blood. The words formed confessions, accusations, and explanations. But the material proof of what happened in late September and mid October of that year lay exactly where it had been left. One man buried after being driven from his home. One man buried behind a house where a small back gate swung open and closed on a hinge that squeaked.

ARREST, TRIAL AND SENTENCE

The arrests came after weeks of quiet surveillance and methodical interviewing, not as a single dramatic sweep but as a steady circling of suspects until the circle closed. Detectives had two missing men, two sets of relatives pressing for answers, and two properties that kept producing threads to pull. When the first grave yielded remains and the second grave was opened in a yard, the conversation changed from speculation to homicide. The list of persons of interest had always been short. It now narrowed to three names that kept appearing together in witness recollections and in the movement of vehicles and household goods. It ended with three sets of handcuffs.

On the final day of November the state police moved. Officers brought in Linda Lou Charbonneau, her youngest daughter, and the daughter's partner. The tenor of the interviews shifted from open ended to accusatory. One of the young people began to talk in a way that suggested he understood what the discovery of the graves meant. In measured stages he set out the path to the first body, a path that took investigators to a site away from the home where the older man had lived. It is one thing to hear a second hand account of a burial. It is another to watch a person guide officers to a precise spot where a human body lies beneath a few feet of soil. The spades turned, the earth gave way, and the man who had vanished in September came back into the case in the only way he could. The man who led officers there had just placed himself inside the crime. From that moment the investigation became not only a search for proof but a sorting of roles and motives among the three people now in custody.

Prosecutors began the deliberate work of building an indictment that would hold when challenged. That meant more than naming counts. It meant deciding whom to try for what and in what order, and it meant extracting full accounts from those willing to bargain. The calculus for each defendant was stark. The evidence placed them in the orbit of not one but two killings. There were traces in the homes, there were statements by neighbors and relatives, there were the graves, and there were the movements of property that connected the two houses. The state used that weight to press for cooperation.

The first to be offered a path out of a potential death sentence was the younger man, Willie Tony Brown. In the spring after the arrests he agreed to plead guilty to two counts of murder in the first degree. The terms required him to tell what he knew in writing, to sit for a recorded statement, and to testify truthfully at future trials. In return the state agreed to forgo a capital hearing and to recommend life in prison. His written proffer implicated himself and the two women in both killings, and it presented a version of how the crimes unfolded that would later conflict with the account offered by his partner.

Months later the state extended a different arrangement to the daughter, then known as Mellisa. She would plead to murder in the second degree for the death of her uncle and to conspiracy in the first degree in the matter of her mother's husband. Her obligation, like Brown's, was to provide a full account and to testify truthfully when called. The contents of her proffer disagreed with several significant statements offered by Brown. In her telling she placed herself away from the location when the younger man died and stated that he had acted alone at her mother's behest. She also described a sequence for the killing of her uncle that put the older woman in a supervisory role while the younger man executed the plan. These contradictions did not derail the plea agreement. They did, however, create a problem that would later surface at trial when the state had to decide which narrator to place before the jury.

Against that background the case against the central figure moved forward. The state prepared to try Linda Lou Charbonneau for the murder of her former partner John Charbonneau, for the murder of her husband William Sproates the third, and for the associated conspiracy and weapons charges that attached to the two homicides. There was no direct physical evidence that placed her hand on either weapon. The case against her turned on admissions by the two younger codefendants, on the physical trail the killers left behind, on the testimony of family members about threats and statements of intent, and on the totality of the movements in the weeks when both men vanished. It was a case that would live or die on whether the jury believed that she engineered both crimes and enlisted others to carry them out.

Jury selection took place in the spring. The pool was probed for views about capital punishment, domestic conflict, and the credibility of witnesses who stood to gain by testifying. The state previewed a straightforward theory. Linda planned the killing of John to take control of his money and property, and then arranged the killing of William when he began asking pointed questions after discovering a stained box among the items carted away from the first house. The defense previewed a different narrative. It emphasized the violence of the younger man, argued that the daughter had a powerful incentive to shift blame, and maintained that the older woman was convenient to accuse but not proven guilty beyond a reasonable doubt.

The trial opened with photographs that fixed the jury's attention on the earth that had been moved to swallow both men. Scenes from the recovery locations were shown in measured sequence. Officers described how the soil was cut, how the remains were documented in place, and how the bodies were transported for autopsy. The medical examiner did not dramatize. He described traumatic injuries to the head in the first case and a combination of stab wounds, blunt trauma, and signs consistent with asphyxiation in the second. He noted the presence of dirt in the airways of the younger victim, a finding that underscored the ferocity and haste of the burial. These clinical voices did more than offer conclusions. They set hard edges around the cause and manner of death.

Investigators then walked the jury through the houses. The Millsboro residence of the older man had been stripped in a way that suggested more than a simple move. Entire fixtures had been removed. Boxes were stacked and transported. Among them, witnesses recounted, was one with apparent blood staining. The Magnolia area residence of the younger man showed signs of a struggle and signs of later cleaning that did not erase what seeped into wood and grout. The state presented samples, photographs, and chain of custody forms. That part of the case was not about emotion. It was about the slow addition of small facts until a picture came into focus.

The state next brought in relatives. A sister spoke about unanswered calls and the growing conviction that her brother had not simply gone off. A cousin recounted a worried conversation with William after he found the stained box. A former in law described tensions between Linda and John over money and household contents, and recalled hearing the older woman float scenarios about getting him out of the way. The jury heard how these remarks were made at home and not in anger's heat. They were given as options, said the witness, not as outbursts. These recollections were supported by an officer who had intervened in an earlier property dispute at the Bridgeville house and later watched as items were loaded into a van.

Then came the daughter. It is one thing for jurors to listen to a pathologist. It is another to watch a child testify against her mother. Mellisa described a plan that had been talked about in stages, how she had been asked to drive on the night her uncle was taken away, and how the younger man waited to strike. She placed her mother in the house when the ruse was used to draw the older man toward danger and said that after the killing she returned to a home where cleaning had already begun. She then described escorting the younger man when he returned the following month to lie in wait for William. She testified that her mother set the meeting in motion and that the killer carried out the final blows in the house before the body was driven away and buried in the Bridgeville yard.

Cross examination zeroed in on the contradictions between her account and the earlier proffer by the younger man. The defense lawyer went line by line through the places where the two accounts differed. Why did the younger man say she was inside the house during the second killing when she now claimed she was elsewhere. Why did he say her role in the first homicide was more direct. She answered that he lied to protect himself and to spread blame. The defense pursued the point that she had her own reasons to minimize her exposure, that she had accepted a bargain the state had offered her, and that she had lied in earlier statements. She acknowledged lying more than once before entering her plea and said she was now telling the truth. The jurors, who had watched her through the long direct, watched just as closely now. Their verdict would turn on whether they believed her.

The state did not call the younger man. The prosecutors informed the court that they did not intend to put him on the stand because they could not vouch for the truth of what he would say concerning the second killing. The defense wanted the jury to hear about his plea and about the contents of his proffer in order to undercut the credibility of the daughter. The court permitted limited use of the material to confront her with contradictions, but it did not allow the full proffer to come into evidence. The missing witness was therefore present only as a shadow in the trial, through the parts of his words that the judge allowed the defense to use against the daughter's assertions.

Other witnesses filled out the state's case. A trooper described the recovery of the second body in the Bridgeville yard and the steps taken to preserve the scene. A forensic specialist explained what can and cannot be concluded from traces on floors and fixtures after an attempt to clean. A banker and a representative from the social security administration traced the flow of check payments and withdrawals that continued after John's death. A neighbor sketched an ordinary evening at Magnolia that was interrupted by violence, listing sounds and movements that did not fit the usual rhythm of the house.

The defense called its own witnesses to try to reframe the events. Family members who remained loyal to the older woman spoke to her relationship with the two men, argued that domestic friction did not equal murder, and suggested that the younger man's capacity for violence under stress was underestimated by the state. The lawyers emphasized the absence of any eyewitness who could say that Linda struck either victim or that she wielded the knife. They argued that the state had taken a set of ugly facts and forced them into a single theory because it wanted a person to hold accountable and the person it chose was easy to despise.

Closing arguments reflected two entirely different ways of reading the same record. The prosecutor moved across the calendar. Two men tied to the same woman vanished a few weeks apart. The first was beaten to death after being drawn into a trap at his own house. His home was then stripped and his goods moved to another property. The second man discovered a stained box among those goods, confided his fear, and was then lured to his own door where he was killed and buried while still breathing. At each step, the state argued, the older woman planned and directed while others supplied the muscle. The defense invited the jury to distrust the testimony that made that structure stand. It pointed to the many lies the daughter admitted telling before she accepted a bargain. It asked the jury to see a volatile young man as an independent killer and not as an obedient agent. It urged the jurors to demand proof that did not rely so heavily on the word of people who had everything to gain by pleasing the state.

Deliberations were measured rather than hurried. The jurors had to agree on the counts concerning each killing and on the related conspiracy and weapons charges. They returned guilty verdicts on the murders of both John Charbonneau and William Sproates the third and on the companion counts. That meant the case moved to a separate proceeding to decide whether the defendant would be sentenced to life imprisonment or to death.

The penalty hearing asked jurors to weigh aggravating and mitigating circumstances. The state urged the panel to see the double homicide as a course of conduct that demanded the most severe response. It catalogued planning and manipulation, the use of other participants to carry out the violence, and the burial of a still living man. The defense asked the jury to consider age, health, and family ties, to consider the indirect nature of the involvement as shown at trial, and to consider the potential for a long life sentence without the possibility of parole as sufficient punishment. The jurors voted by strong margins to recommend death for the murder of John and again to recommend death for the murder of William. Under Delaware law at that time, the judge made the final decision but was required to give great weight to the jury's recommendation.

Judge Richard Stokes addressed the courtroom at sentencing in a tone that was grave without being theatrical. He reviewed the record in the manner of a careful clerk. He noted the way the killings were planned and carried out, the roles of the people the state had called agents, and the purposes served by each death. He described the first killing as calculated and the second as a means of silencing a witness. He stated that the defendant had engineered the crimes and then employed the two younger participants to do the physical work. He pronounced two sentences of death and added terms of years on the conspiracy and weapons counts. The older woman did not display emotion when the judge finished.

The courtroom sounds after a capital sentence are subdued and strange. A murmur of voices, the scrape of a chair, the controlled movements of deputies. Outside the courthouse the focus shifted to the mandatory review by the state supreme court. A capital sentence in Delaware did not become final until the higher court examined the record for legal error. The defense team filed notices of appeal and began to assemble the issues. Those questions concerned the handling of the missing witness, the use of parts of his proffer to challenge the daughter, the admission of statements by relatives recounting threats and plans, and the overall sufficiency of the evidence. The prosecutors prepared to defend their choices and to argue that even if the trial court had misstepped on an evidentiary ruling, the verdict could stand because the proof was overwhelming.

In that moment between verdict and appellate review, the families of the two dead men stood outside the courthouse in the late afternoon light to answer questions from reporters. They spoke about relief and about pain that no sentence could erase. Inside, the formality of the docket moved on to the next case, but in Sussex County the names and graves and photographs that filled those weeks in court remained vivid. The law had reached a conclusion. The next stage would decide whether that conclusion would hold.

AFTERMATH AND PUBLIC OPINION

The verdicts in Sussex County did not settle the Charbonneau case so much as shift it into a long and complicated second act. The courtroom drama of 2004 had ended with the most severe penalty the state could impose, and for a time it appeared that would be the final line written under the names of John Charbonneau and William Sproates. Yet homicide cases rarely end cleanly, especially when the evidence turns on the words of accomplices and the prosecution's strategy is braided through plea promises. What followed was years of motions, appellate argument, and a re calibration of punishment that would alter Linda Lou Charbonneau's future and reshape how many people in Sussex County viewed the case.

In 2006 the High Court reviewed the record and focused on a narrow but powerful issue. The State had struck plea bargains with two central figures. Each deal required a full account of events and a willingness to testify if called. The problem was that the accounts did not match in several material ways. At trial the State elected not to call one of the two, a choice disclosed late in the process. The trial judge then barred the defense from placing that absent witness's sworn proffer before the jury to test the credibility of the witness who did appear. The justices concluded that excluding that material denied the jury a fair chance to weigh credibility where credibility was the spine of the case. The convictions were reversed and the matter was sent back for a new trial.

For the families this was not a technical point. It meant that the certainty they believed they had won two years earlier dissolved. Relatives who had attended every hearing and watched the sentence pronounced were now told that the case would start again. Some had spoken publicly of closure only when a sentence was carried out. Others, exhausted by years of grief and the retelling of violent scenes, simply wanted to stop appearing in courtrooms. The reversal did not answer the original questions about who planned what or who struck which blow. It asked the county to do something even harder, to repeat a trial that had taken a heavy toll on everyone involved.

Post remand negotiations began. The State weighed the logic of a second capital trial against the appellate court's instructions and the age of the case. The defense assessed risk in light of the opinion and the record the prosecution could still present. In March 2007 Linda Lou Charbonneau entered a plea to a single count of murder in the second degree in the death of John Charbonneau. The State dismissed the remaining counts, including those connected to the death of William Sproates. In May 2007 the court imposed a twenty year sentence at Level Five. A later request to modify that sentence was denied.

The legal posture changed, and with it, the public conversation. The earlier death sentence had drawn strong views across the county. Some in the gallery had praised the decision as proportionate to the brutality proved at trial. Others, while accepting the verdict, were uneasy with executing a woman and argued that life confinement would protect the public without crossing a line they believed the state should not cross. When the appellate ruling came down and a plea followed, those camps did not disappear, but the emphasis shifted. For the families of the dead the central point was not the legal doctrine. It was that the system had first promised finality and then replaced it with compromise. A twenty year term for one killing, even at maximum custody, did not feel to some like an answer equal to two graves.

There were quieter voices. People who had sat through earlier testimony remembered the dependency that ran through the case and the desperate bargains made by all involved. They saw some wisdom in a resolution that avoided another full trial built on contested statements. Still others, including residents who had never met the people at the center of the story, read the appellate opinion and took from it a civic lesson about what juries must hear when liberty or life is at stake. Even if they approved of the outcome in 2004, they accepted that a fair process demanded the jury be allowed to measure conflicting accounts side by side.

The plea also reframed how the co defendants were discussed. One had admitted to two counts of murder in the first degree years earlier and faced life terms, while another had admitted to lesser counts connected to the Bridgeville killing. Those outcomes remained distinct from Linda Lou Charbonneau's revised sentence, and that asymmetry fed new rounds of commentary in coffee shops and on courthouse steps. Was the architect of the plot the person who planned or the person who wielded the weapon. Should the planner receive the severest outcome because the crimes could not have been staged without a guiding hand. Or should the law reserve its longest punishments for the one who delivered the blows. The 2007 disposition did not settle those arguments, but it brought them forward again in a different key.

Within the law enforcement community there was a pragmatic acceptance of the end point. Investigators had spent months locating remains, reconstructing timelines, and documenting the removal of property and the forging of narratives to conceal absence. Detectives had walked the same routes again and again to fix distances and times. They had watched as juries listened to testimony that shifted under cross examination. They understood how fragile any case becomes when proof rests on the memories of people who were both actors and witnesses. From that perspective, a plea to a serious felony and a long term of imprisonment looked like a responsible way to preserve accountability and spare surviving relatives from reliving photographs and pathology reports in a second capital trial.

The victims' relatives navigated those currents in their own ways. Some continued to attend hearings each time the case came on for status, unwilling to let official silence stand in for their presence. Others chose to step back, preserving the good memories they still had rather than opening more boxes of evidence. What united them was the knowledge that two men were gone and that they had been asked by the system to sit with that fact through multiple legal seasons. When the court declined to modify the twenty year term later in 2007, it signaled that the post plea bargain would stand. There would be no sudden return to the penalties argued in 2004.

Outside the courthouse, the case found a quiet second life in classrooms where students parse appellate opinions. The ruling has been taught as an example of how trial courts must handle conflicting co operator statements and the limits of excluding impeachment material when the State itself has created the conditions under which those conflicts arise. It is cited to show that fairness is not a vague idea but a set of rules about what a jury may weigh when a witness speaks and another witness's sworn account diverges. The lesson is not about leniency. It is about the integrity of verdicts.

In Sussex County the physical places remain. The home in Bridgeville long ago returned to ordinary use. The Magnolia address lost its notoriety to time. The shallow place in the ground where one victim was buried became part of a narrative rather than a visible scar. Yet for those who knew the men, the details do not recede. They recall the laughter of a holiday, the way a room used to sound, the scent of cut grass in late summer when families were intact. They measure the years by birthdays missed and by the awkward sentences children learned to say about uncles and grandfathers who did not come back.

As for the woman at the center of the case, the sentence fixed her future within concrete routines. A life once spent moving between households narrowed to schedules and counts, to letters written and received, to visits arranged under supervision. The notoriety of being the only woman on the state's death row at one point dwindled into the anonymity of a number on a cell door. Those who believed the original sentence was deserved have not been persuaded otherwise. Those who were uncomfortable with an execution will note that the state did not carry it out. Between those positions is a plain reality. Two men are dead. Three people admitted roles that ensured those deaths occurred. The law answered, first one way and then another.

The community's final opinion is not unanimous because communities rarely speak with a single voice. What you hear depends on which kitchen table you sit at and how you view the job of the courts. But there is one common thread among the people who followed the case closely. They will tell you that justice is not a single event at the end of a trial. It is a long practice of returning to what the evidence proved, honoring what families lost, and accepting that sometimes, in the interest of fairness, even the hardest won decisions must be done again.

CHAPTER 2
LYDIA SHERMAN
THE DERBY POISONER

The woman the newspapers would later call the Derby Poisoner began life without either notoriety or the protection that steadies a child. Lydia Danbury was born on 24th December 1824. Within a few short years she was an orphan. There were no inheritances to cushion that loss and no grand relations to fold her into a wealthy household. The task of raising her fell to an uncle, a farmer named John Claygay, who lived by the rhythm of seasons and stock and the careful counting of coins that small farms required in that century. His house was no place for idleness. Children old enough to carry a pail were old enough to contribute. Lydia learned early that dawn called for motion and that the day belonged to work.

That work took many forms. In a farmhouse intention is a kind of law. The same hands that fed chickens and scrubbed a wooden floor also kept the hearth supplied and the family mended and presentable. Lydia proved handy with needle and thread. A seam finished cleanly and a button that would not pull free mattered in a world where garments had to last and most families could not simply replace what wore thin. By her mid teens she was doing paid work as a tailor. Those wages were modest but they brought with them something more valuable than money. They brought entry into rooms beyond her uncle's farm and into the circles that form wherever people exchange goods and news and notice one another.

Faith and work braided together in those years. The Methodist church drew in the devout and the hopeful in villages from New Jersey into New England and along the rails and roads that carried young men and women to bigger towns where wages might better a life. Lydia joined that stream. The church offered fellowship, a sense of belonging, and an introduction to others whose lives were as hard working and as earnest as her own. It was within that community that she met a young man named Edward Struck. He was a laboring man with expectations that matched hers. The promise of a steady marriage and a home of their own was no small thing to a young woman with an uncertain past.

They married when she was barely seventeen. The record does not dwell on their courtship. It records the fact and moves on, as records do. The newly married couple joined the tide that pulled ambitious and hopeful people toward New York City. The city in the middle decades of the century offered work to those who had the constitution to endure cramped rooms, loud streets, and air laced with smoke and dust. In return it promised a wage that a smaller town often could not. It promised markets where a capable woman could choose food with an eye not only to price but to quality. It promised a network of churches and mutual aid groups that helped families face the common turns of fortune that arrived without warning.

The marriage began in a place that would have looked familiar to many couples of their class. A rented room or a small set of rooms. Furniture pieced together from what could be bought cheaply and what could be made by a husband who understood a plane and a saw. A small trunk that held the better clothes. A box for the tools Lydia used when she took in mending to ease the strain on the household account during lean spells. Routine asserted itself. And routine is what makes a young family.

Children came. The exact dates are recorded in certificates and in notices in church registers where a minister's hand made its careful strokes across the page. They were baptized into congregations that kept a watch over their members, a watch of kindness and care when illness visited or when work was lost. Lydia knew that world well. She fit within it. She joined other women at sewing circles where charity was stitched into shirts and gowns for those who had none. She mastered the arts that make a house run. In kitchens where coal or wood controlled how quickly a pot could be brought to a boil she learned to judge heat by the look of flame and the sound of a simmer. She knew which stores were fair on a Monday and which cheated on weight on a Saturday evening when crowds were thick and clerks careless.

New York in those years was noisy with promise and with disappointment. Dock work ebbed and flowed with ships and seasons. Small shops closed as quickly as they opened. A run of bad luck could strip a man of hope in a fortnight. Sickness was common. The water was not always safe. Milk was sometimes diluted and sometimes worse. Fever traveled through rooms that were crowded and warm in winter and stifling in summer. Children died. Not because any hand meant them harm but because the century had not yet worked out how to keep them safe from the diseases that stalked families with a regularity that now seems barbaric. That repeated grief trained an entire class of women to nurse. Lydia learned what many women learned. She learned how to keep a patient clean and fed, how to lift a cup to a mouth that could barely swallow, how to coax calories past a body that believed it had no appetite left.

Those skills made her valuable. They also gave her a role that extended beyond her own household. A neighbor called when a baby failed to thrive. The woman who had a reputation for patience came to sit through the night with a man whose cough would not let him sleep. The church committee knew who would bring broth unasked to a widow whose grief was too raw for company. That person often found herself sitting alone with the afflicted while the family caught necessary sleep. In that quiet she learned where the medicines were kept and what their labels promised. She learned to mix powders into water and to stir drinks that soothed a throat or calmed a stomach. She learned to measure and to time and to wait.

Those habits shaped Lydia. They taught her to appear unhurried even when the day ran short. They taught her to keep her voice even when children were fretful and a husband cross. They taught her to plan tomorrow's work while finishing today's. The church likewise taught her the rhythms of prayer and the power of the composed face in rooms where anxiety and sorrow were ordinary. No one who watched her in those years would have called her idler or meddler. She kept her place. She did what women in her station did. She balanced accounts written in chalk on a scrap of slate by the pantry door. She bought soap and starch and flour according to cash on hand. She knew how to stretch meat in a stew so that a family left the table a little hungry but not unsatisfied. She knew that sometimes the line between a dignified supper and humiliation was as thin as a failure on a single purchase made unwisely.

She also learned the economy within an economy. Households at that time bought what we now would call poisons as readily as they bought sugar or tea. Rats made free with cupboards. Flies swarmed when the heat gathered. Every housekeeper kept a drawer where fly papers and ratsbane were stored. Apothecaries sold those as freely as they sold cough syrups and bitters. Clerks were used to seeing women in aprons leave with small parcels wrapped in brown paper and tied with string. There was no prying into motives. There was only the assumption that a clean house did not come without such instruments. In that setting a woman could acquire familiarity with the look of powders that promised to kill vermin without attracting much notice. It is part of the frank record of those years that arsenic was a tool in an ordinary householder's kit.

Those facts along with the rest fill the landscape of Lydia's early life. She was no stranger to labor or to thrift. She managed illnesses as a matter of course long before any coroner uttered the word arsenic in connection with her name. She kept faith with the church that had organized her social world and given shape to her weeks. She moved through rooms with a quiet competence that both reassured and kept others from asking questions about how things were done. The plain truth is that the skills that make a household run well are the same skills that grant a person nearly complete command of what those in that household eat and drink when they are too sick to cook or too weary to stand. That command is ordinarily a mercy. In the life we are about to recount it became the foundation of a calamity. But for the period we mark as early life, it was simply what a capable woman in that century did and was.

It is important to hold that portrait in mind because it tells us what a community saw when they looked at Lydia in the years before the arrests and the headlines. They saw a woman for whom the words steady and prudent and helpful carried their real weight. They saw a person who embodied the virtues that the clergy praised and that neighbors said made a town humane. If later events made those words bitter in the mouth, that bitterness does not erase the fact that for a long span of years she lived a life that would have drawn no special attention. She married young as many women did. She kept house under hard conditions as many women did. She bore children as many women did. She learned to nurse as nearly all women of her class did. The strangeness to modern readers is not in those facts but in the ease with which a woman of that time could come to handle substances that now sit in locked cabinets. In that ease lay the seed of the disaster that followed. But in these years, that ease was no more remarkable than a needle and thread resting on the arm of a chair while a pot simmered nearby.

THE MURDERS

To understand the murders that later came to be linked to the woman born as Lydia Danbury, one must walk slowly through rooms that at first looked like any other working household in the middle decades of the century. There were the same small economies, the same hard choices about what to buy and what to mend again, the same unending attention to food and to the sick. The difference, which no one grasped in time to prevent a cascade of deaths, was a decision taken in private to turn the ordinary tools of housekeeping toward ends that homes are supposed to fear and resist. The record of that turn begins in New York and ends in Connecticut. Along the way it passes through the lives of husbands and children who trusted the hand that prepared their meals.

The first husband, Edward Struck, met the young Lydia within the fellowship of a Methodist congregation. Marriage followed when she was still a teenager. They joined the stream of couples who sought work and a future in New York City. There the rhythms of a striving life were their portion. He worked when work was available. She kept the rooms and took in sewing when a neighbor could spare a coin for a hem that needed finishing or a shirt that needed repair. They had children. Then the city that can make a man felt like it was unmaking him. Work faltered. Edward grew despondent. Employers who once had called him toward the docks or into a warehouse ceased to do so. The savings, such as they were, vanished at the pace any housewife of that time could have predicted. One day there was a few dollars in a teacup in a cabinet. The next week there was almost nothing. Men react to such turns in different ways. Some grow angry and drink. Others grow quiet and drift through days like figures already half absent from their own homes. Edward's spirits failed in a way that frightened the wife who had bet her life on a marriage.

What happened next is the hinge on which the whole tale turns. In a house where ratsbane or fly paper sat in the same drawer as spices and salves, where arsenic was a common tool to keep vermin at bay, a decision was made to administer that substance to a grown man in small and repeated doses until his body failed. The method used by those who choose this path is part of the common literature of that century's criminal courts. The poison is mixed into food and drink. It is given at mealtimes, often in porridge or broth or tea. The first doses are not large enough to trigger a panic. They are enough to make a person unwell and to make him or her depend all the more on the nurse who is doing the cooking. The nurse in this household knew precisely how to maintain that balance. She could ease symptoms when she wanted the patient to recover enough to eat again. She could allow the symptoms to intensify when she wanted the decline to resume. Arsenic has a way of imitating the fevers that terrified families in those years. Vomiting, cramping, diarrhea, thirst that cannot be satisfied, weakness that grows by the day. When such a cluster of signs appears in a city where cholera had often swept entire streets, most people think first of disease. That is how Edward's end came to be understood. The year was 1864. The certificate did not name poison. It named a natural illness.

The death of a husband throws a working family into crisis. In that era many men carried no insurance at all. Those who did often carried a policy so modest that it helped for a month or two and no more. A widow had to find a way to keep a roof and to feed any children left in her care. Some remarried quickly. Others lived on the edge, taking in washing and sewing and what nursing work their neighbors required. Lydia did all those things in turn. She had another choice before her, darker than the first and more terrible to recount because it extends the same decision into the lives of children. Within six weeks of Edward's death, three of her young children sickened with the same pattern of symptoms and died. In 1865 two more followed. The official story called these deaths typhoid fever. The houses of the poor and even of the middling often bred such deaths. There were no modern sewers. Water carried disease from one address to another with an ease that defied conscience. Many mothers buried babies in those years and nobody ever suggested that a hand had helped the disease do its work. Here the later record would insist that disease had been used as disguise. The nurse who once calmed fevers had learned how to bring them on.

There is no way to make the passage of those six weeks less terrible by changing the words used to tell it. The widow tended her small children. She controlled the food they ate. She soothed their foreheads and told them stories to pass the long hours. She called the doctor when a case needed official notice to make it possible for a certificate to be issued and a burial to proceed without questions that might delay the family from making arrangements. In a city where death was common, no clerk leaned forward and said that a pattern was forming. No neighbor registered suspicion that cut through the air like a chill. The woman had a reputation as a careful nurse, and nothing invites blind trust more than a reputation for patient care offered without complaint. In that trust the work continued, child by child. When the fifth little coffin had been lowered into the ground, the house stood silent.

It is striking to note that during this same span the woman at the center of the story drew herself up, wrapped herself again in the duties that defined a respectable life, and resumed the outward signs of the caregiver. She nursed for pay in other houses. She did this in a city large enough for memory to fade and for neighbors to accept a tidy woman with calm hands as a blessing again and not a threat. Some of those she nursed recovered. That fact belongs to the record, too, because it shows that her purpose was not to poison as a matter of ideology. It was to secure control in the one place where she must have felt it most deeply. That inner reckoning is beyond the reach of any court. The outward facts are enough. A husband dead in 1864. Five children in quick succession, three within weeks and two in the following year. All the while a woman with a serious face filling spoons and stirring broths.

After some years as a widow, Lydia remarried. The second husband was Dennis Hurlburt. He was a widower himself. The match made sense to those who knew both households. He needed a woman to run his home. She needed a man whose wage would keep a roof over her head and whose companionship would mask both sorrow and the whispers that sometimes follow any woman whose house has seen too many funerals. They married in 1868. Once more the pattern unfurled. At first the house must have felt like a chance to begin again. But the same quiet command of the kitchen and the sickbed remained. When Dennis began to feel unwell, the nurse inside the wife rose to take charge. The symptoms followed the same path. Cramping, vomiting, diarrhea, waves of thirst, and then exhaustion that made a man accept help he might otherwise have refused. The doses mounted or fell away according to a plan that only one person understood. The pace of the decline can be set by the one holding the spoon. Dennis died, and once more there were no fireworks of suspicion. There was a death in a house where there had been too many deaths, but the law did not move at the speed of rumor in those years. A second husband gone. No charge. A widow again.

A woman twice widowed could expect attention from men and concern from women. Both come for reasons that have nothing to do with love or malice. Men require housekeepers. Women understand loss and offer companionship in rooms where silence sits like a weight on a chest. Lydia moved in that world with the assurance of someone who had learned to balance her face between gratitude and reserve. Before long there was a third marriage. The man was named Horatio Sherman. They married in 1870 and settled in Connecticut. He brought with him standing in a town where reputation mattered. She brought skills and a manner that presented as the ideal of sober competence. It is possible Horatio believed he had beaten the odds and found a partner who would anchor the remainder of his days.

The same pattern returned in a new house. There is no titillation to be wrung from the record. The story is the same rectangular room, the same table, the same stove, the same cups and bowls. The difference is in what was placed in those bowls. Arsenic, whether bought as ratsbane or extracted from fly paper, does not announce itself with exotic perfumes or colors. It is a powder easily disguised in foods that are dull to the eye and that rely on spice or sugar for taste. It is impossible to know whether the third husband ever suspected that what he took from his wife's hand contained more than kindness. The record did preserve the detail that by the spring of 1871 he had weakened. A doctor came and did what doctors in that time could do. He attempted to ease symptoms. He signed his name at the end. Horatio died in May 1871.

What changed after that death was not the substance of the acts but the attention that others gave to the cluster of tragedies that had formed around

Lydia's name. A doctor who had attended Horatio could not quite reconcile the speed of the decline with the explanation that satisfied him in other cases. Men who kept insurance ledgers noticed that claims connected to one household or one woman had become too frequent to be easily explained as bad luck. Clerks in county offices who knew how many births and deaths to expect in a given season now saw in their books a concentration around a single set of rooms. That kind of attention did not form in an instant. It collected as rain collects on bricks through a long storm. One morning a man looks up and sees that water is running in a place where it should not. Suspicion broke its banks in that way around the time of the third husband's death.

What did not change was the method. She reached for the same white powder and hid it again in the same foods. She continued to present to the world the appearance of a nurse doing exactly what a nurse should. There is a cruel logic in that. People grant a generous margin to those who take on the burden of care. Ask any woman who has sat through the night with a dying child what she has had to ignore in order to maintain a steady face for her family. She will tell you that care requires a kind of performance. Nothing throws a room into panic faster than the nurse confessing that she is frightened. Lydia made use of that performance. She kept her voice level even when a husband moaned. She moved between kitchen and bed with the solemn competence of a wife who means to be commended by ministers and by neighbors. In that competence she placed doses and waited for the next day to tell her whether to ease or to press on.

Children died in connection with the second and third households as well. The base of facts that scholars have assembled names eight children, six born to Lydia and two in her care by marriage, who did not survive. The cause written on their certificates was the same cluster of illnesses that had stalked families across the region for years. The cruel twist is that those natural causes stood ready as a mask. Fever and flux were common enough that a house with poor luck could see more than one child lost in a season without raising official alarm. A woman who moved easily within the roles of nurse and mother could multiply that bad luck and still be seen as stalwart and long suffering. The same neighbors who praised her for her patience were describing the very thing that allowed her to carry out further acts under cover of piety.

The starkest way to say what must be said is also the simplest. Between 1864 and May1871 three men who had married Lydia died after illnesses in which she presided at table and at bedside. Within that span eight children in her care died after similar illnesses. The means was arsenic. The pattern was careful dosing over time to mimic the common fevers of that era. The disguise was the role of nurse performed with persuasive dignity. The households were in New York City and in towns in Connecticut where a calm face and a busy set of hands can hold off suspicion longer than a modern reader might believe possible. No trumpet sounded. No confession was whispered under a cloak. No accomplice boasted in a saloon. The silence that surrounded these deaths was the ordinary silence of private rooms where families tend to their own.

When a modern mind searches for motive it often seeks a single answer that will bear the whole weight of a story. Money is the first possibility. Insurance claims did find their way into ledgers after some of the deaths. Money alone does not explain the order of events, the alternation between killing and nursing that saved some and doomed others. Resentment or fear or a craving for control fits the pattern as well. The nurse who controls when a person eats and when a person rests and how much comfort is given has in her hands a power that might for some become an end in itself. That does not excuse or explain away. It simply points to the very thing that made her valuable. In a century where medicine could not rescue everyone, the household nurse possessed nearly absolute authority in the rooms where the very sick lay. In this case that authority was turned to deliberate harm.

The murders ended not because the poison lost its power or because the method failed. They ended because the community's attention finally settled into focus. A third husband dying made too neat a diagram when placed alongside the New York deaths that had come before. Patterns suggested a question and the question demanded an answer more firmly grounded than another certificate with the same vague cause. The story of that attention turning into exhumations, into science entering a courtroom, into a verdict that carried the weight of years, belongs to another section. Here the record stands as the plain tale of a series of deaths enabled by the very habits and virtues that households and churches prized. That is what makes the murders so hard for some to accept even long after the facts were laid bare. The same spoon that feeds a fever can deliver a poison. The same hand that smooths a pillow can arrange a final breath. The same voice that says trust me can mean it, or it can mean something else entirely.

ARREST, TRIAL AND SENTENCE

Suspicion does not march down a street with a drum. It seeps under doors and pools in offices where clerks hold ledgers in their hands and sense that the pattern on the page does not align with the pattern they know by long habit. After the death of Horatio the quiet mathematics of death and paperwork shifted. A doctor who had made visits to the Sherman house could not shake the feeling that the final decline did not behave like the fevers he knew. An insurance agent found himself paging backward through entries, tracing the same name across years and towns. A clerk in a coroner's office, who had written so many certificates of cholera and typhoid that his quill could form the letters in the dark, realized that too many of those words had lately been written beside one woman's signature.

It began, as such cases often did in that era, with a conversation between men who generally had little to say to one another beyond the formalities their different trades required. The doctor mentioned his unease to a colleague. The colleague asked a question in a barber's chair where men gather and talk a little too freely. A city official heard a rumor that matched a rumor already set aside as uncharitable by an earlier listener. Gossip is never a court brief. But when a thread runs through several rooms, eventually someone tugs it to see what unravels. In this instance the tug led to a request that had to be made carefully if it was not to break the politics of the town. The authorities asked that the body of the most recent husband be examined again.

Exhumation in that century was a grim privilege. It required the permission of a court. It required the presence of a physician who could both observe and attest to what was found. It required the attendance of men who could keep order if a crowd gathered. The coffin was opened. The stomach and portions of the viscera that hold traces of certain substances were removed into jars that had been prepared in advance and sealed with care. There was no theatrics to the work. There was a grim economy and a sequence that had been laid down by the growing science of forensic inquiry. Those jars made their way to laboratories where chemists trained in the testing of minerals and in the detection of poison in the bodies of the dead could now apply their skill to a case that had shaken a town.

Arsenic was the suspect and arsenic is discoverable even after burial if care is taken in the testing. The chemists of that era used methods that are now quaint in their apparatus but that were then state of the art and respected across the Atlantic. They reduced the tissue with acids. They trapped gases in small glass bulbs. They looked for the metallic sheen that tells a practiced eye that arsenic is present in more than the tiny traces the human body can hold from food or water without harm. When the analysis was done, the chemists made their reports in the sober language of their craft. The stomach and the sections of the liver and bowels contained arsenic in quantities that could not be considered incidental. The conclusion was plain. Poison had been present in the body of Horatio Sherman.

Facts on paper gave permission for what officers of the law had been waiting to do. They arrested Lydia. There was no dramatic flight across rooftops or sudden attempt to vanish into a crowd that has not yet been named. She had lived so long behind a face arranged for calm that even the arrival of a sheriff at her own door did not break it. She was taken into custody and held while the court system made ready to hear a case that would not be simple. Rumors traveling behind the officers gathered other deaths beneath the same umbrella. A first husband in New York years earlier. Children taken one by one and called victims of fevers. A second husband dead after an illness that troubled the memory of his attending doctor. The law is not a net that can be thrown over an entire life at once. It takes one death and tries it. It tests the charge against the rules that govern evidence and proof. But the stories that swell around a trial shape how witnesses feel when they climb the steps to a courthouse and how a town waits for a verdict.

The indictment that followed the arrest named the murder of Horatio. It charged that Lydia had administered arsenic with malice and that the act had brought about his death. The form of the document belonged to the nineteenth century. It was formal and slow and brought the full weight of the state against a citizen in measured strokes. The prosecutor was a man accustomed to building a case out of details that might have looked ordinary one by one but that together built a form that could stand against cross examination. The defense was led by a lawyer with the experience to know how juries in Connecticut could be moved by the mixture of science and story.

Before the trial, more exhumations followed. Authorities obtained permission to open graves connected to the earlier households. They did not dig up every child for fear of the public's patience and the families' hearts. They chose strategically. They sought to test whether the pattern in the most recent case repeated in the others. Chemists repeated their procedures on those remains. Arsenic appeared again in quantities that exceeded what ordinary exposure could account for. These findings did not become part of the counts in the indictment. They became context. They became the background against which the prosecution would argue that the presence of poison in the last husband's body was not an accident or the result of contaminated water or vicious coincidence. It was part of a way of solving problems.

When the trial opened in 1872 there was already a name for the accused on the front pages. The Derby Poisoner. It was a tidy headline that folded a town's name and the alleged method of murder into a phrase that readers could pass from one mouth to another. Inside the courtroom the work was less tidy. Jury selection consumed days. Men were asked whether they could consider testimony about other deaths without treating those deaths as proof of guilt in the single case before them. They were asked whether they could accept the word of chemists whose instruments they had never seen and whose science, though fascinating, felt far removed from the work by which most of them fed their families. They were asked whether they could keep their minds still in the face of a woman who presented as a nurse and a devout person. In that era the presence of a woman in the dock for murder by poison stirred ancient fears and prejudices. The judge instructed the parties to keep the questions to the point. They did their best. The jury was sworn.

The state opened with a quiet narrative that did not reach for thunder. Horatio ate meals prepared by the defendant. He fell ill. He declined in a way that mirrored the course arsenic poisoning takes in the body. A doctor attended and did what medicine then allowed. The death came. The body was buried. An exhumation was granted. The chemists did their work. Arsenic in significant amount was found in the stomach and in organs that store traces longer than other parts of the body do. There was no evidence of a fire in the house or of accidental contamination from a known source. This was not a case of a single cup from a neighbor's hand. This was a case of repeated dosing. The state mapped the days on a chalkboard so the jury could see how appetite, weakness, and care had woven together. The phrase malice aforethought came late. It came only after the picture had been drawn with care.

Chemists then took the stand one by one and translated their craft into stories that twelve men could weigh. They described the apparatus. They explained why arsenic remains in certain tissues and how tiny quantities that occur naturally are dwarfed by quantities that point to deliberate administration. They displayed small glass tubes and the mirrors inside them that turn gas into a metallic record. They spoke the names of reactions and then set aside those names in favor of plain explanations with examples drawn from food and from ordinary household experience. The defense pressed them. Could the arsenic have come from embalming fluids. The chemists answered that the fluids then used in ordinary undertakers' practice did not account for the pattern observed. Could water contaminated by poor drainage be at fault. The chemists explained that the very distribution of the poison within the tissue argued for doses taken by mouth within a span of time rather than for a background contamination that would have poisoned more than one person in the house. Could fly paper or rat poison sitting open in a pantry have infected other food by mistake. The chemists conceded that household arsenic was common but returned to their central point. The levels were such that chance contamination was not a reasonable explanation.

Physicians testified to the course of the illness. They described symptoms and their progression. They admitted that symptoms of arsenic poisoning and symptoms of cholera can resemble one another in the early days of an attack. They stressed that in this case the pattern and the duration did not fit cholera as they had seen it over many summers. They spoke of the response to remedies they had used. They used the limited vocabulary of their time to describe what they observed, and they were careful when they explained where their knowledge ended and where the chemists' knowledge began.

The state brought forward witnesses who had lived near the Sherman house and who had seen Lydia in the days when Horatio's illness held the rooms in its grip. These neighbors offered little that would thrill a court reporter. They described a woman tending a husband. They were moved by her calm. They remembered that she insisted on preparing every cup and every bowl with her own hands. The state leaned on that detail. Control of the kitchen means control of doses. It was an argument of circumstance, but the totality of the circumstances framed the poisoning in a way that the jury could grasp without needing to master every chemical test described earlier in the day.

When the defense rose it leaned on two planks. The first plank was the resemblance of the illness to the fevers that had haunted cities and towns for decades. Jurors who had buried children did not need to be convinced that nature can be as cruel as any human mind. The defense pointed to the era's regular outbreaks and argued that medicine's limited power left room for honest error in diagnosis and therefore for reasonable doubt in a courtroom. The second plank was character. Lydia had been for years a nurse in her own house and in the houses of others. She had lowly means and was not a figure of extravagance. Why would such a woman poison the men and the children who gave her place and purpose. Faced with a jury in which many men carried conventional assumptions about women and about the virtues of caregiving, the defense leaned into those assumptions. It offered no alternative suspect. It offered instead a portrait of misfortune and an invitation to resist the urge to turn misfortune into malice in a city eager for a cautionary tale.

The state's reply was brief and firm. The chemists had done their work. The physicians had charted a course of illness that accorded with the deliberate administration of a known poison. The access and the control were established by witnesses. The pattern across years gave context and removed the case from the realm of coincidence. Motive could be debated. Means and opportunity were not in serious dispute. In a decade when courts were only beginning to accept scientific testimony as more than an exotic garnish, this prosecutor managed to seat science at the center of the table.

The judge's charge to the jury reflected that balance. He explained that the presence of arsenic alone did not convict. He described the law's requirement that the state prove that the accused administered the substance or caused it to be administered and that she did so with malice. He reminded the jurors that they were not to convict on the basis of rumor about other deaths but that they could weigh the repetition of circumstances as it shed light on intent and on the plausibility of accident. He directed them that the testimony of experts was admissible and should be weighed according to the credibility of the experts and the coherence of their accounts. He did not press them toward a result. He set the law before them and sent them to their work.

Deliberations lasted long enough to produce anxiety in a packed room. Some jurors were reluctant to convict a woman in a case in which the weapon could not be laid on the table. Others were troubled by the simplicity of the story the defense had offered in an age of frequent illness. Still others saw clearly that explanation by coincidence increased the moment a person took control of every spoonful of food and every cup of drink a patient consumed. Gradually the weight of the tests and of the pattern settled on those who still hesitated. When they returned, they found the accused and the court on its feet.

The verdict was not the maximum that the charge might have urged. The jury found Lydia guilty of murder in the second degree. The statute in Connecticut defined degrees in ways that reflected both intent and the circumstances in which the act was done. A first degree conviction would have meant the gallows. A second degree conviction recognized malice and intent but stopped short of the category that in that era always brought a rope. The judge received the paper, looked down the bench at the woman who had arranged her face for calm again, and pronounced sentence. Life imprisonment.

That sentence sent her first to New Haven County for formalities and then to the state prison at Wethersfield. The walls of that place had held men and women convicted of every kind of crime. The women's ward was smaller and older and managed with a strictness that was felt more in the absence of speech than in the presence of loud commands. The silent system was the principle that faltered in theory and yet persisted because wardens believed in its supposed virtues. Lydia entered those walls and submitted to the routines. Her head was shaved. Her civilian garments were exchanged for prison clothes. Her days were broken into stretches of work and prayer and sleep under supervision. The doctor examined her. The chaplain visited with a book and with sincerity.

In 1873 a pamphlet appeared that claimed to be a confession. It bore her name on the title page and promised readers an account of crimes written in a hand cooled by prison's enforced pause. Whether the text represents her voice or someone else's idea of what that voice should have said is something the press debated then and scholars still argue now. The state did not reopen the case. The families of the dead read the pamphlet and either threw it away in disgust or tucked it into a drawer where they kept other things they could not bear to show. For the purposes of the law the only words that mattered were those spoken in court and the few points the clerk had written into a ledger.

Five years into her sentence a piece of audacity tore a page from the prison calendar. She feigned a decline that required assignment to the hospital ward within the prison. It was not unusual. Middle aged women who enter prison after years of stress often suffer. The ward is less secure than the cells because its design must allow movement and access by nurses and doctors. One evening in 1877 she exploited a moment in which a door did not close according to habit. She slipped through, passed under a watch that failed for a single breath, and crossed the threshold into air that did not belong to the state. It was not a sprint through fields. She understood that ordinary bearing is a better cloak than speed. She traveled without fuss and without ostentation to Providence. There she took work under an assumed name in a new household whose widower master wanted exactly the qualities she could present. Tidy competence. A willing pair of hands. Steady nerves around sickness. The story might have repeated itself in a new city.

She did not vanish because the press had made her name too widely known and because lawmen have long memories when their mistakes become fodder for columns. Someone who had seen a drawing in a paper looked twice at the housekeeper in an otherwise unremarkable home. A whisper reached a patrolman who passed it along to an officer who remembered a notice posted after the escape. The circle tightened. She was arrested again without a struggle and returned to Wethersfield. The warden had to stand before the governor and explain how it had happened. The guards had to submit to questions about routine and about small lapses that had produced a breach. The prison corrected its practices. Lydia took up again the set of days that the sentence had required all along.

Her health did not permit the law to keep her very long. Cancer set to its slow task and would not be bargained with. In 1878 her decline became obvious even to those who had no wish to be fooled again. The prison physician tended her not because of who she had been but because of who he believed he was. A chaplain sat by her bed and prayed the way a chaplain prays when the company of the dying cannot be widened to include more kin. On 16th May 1878 she died in the women's ward at Wethersfield.

Looking back across the span from arrest to death, three notes sound again and again. First, the case marks a moment when chemistry left the lecture hall and took a seat at counsel table. Without the testing that revealed arsenic in organs that do not lie, the state would have had little more than rumors and a string of sad coincidences. Second, the law showed both its appetite for caution and its willingness to punish. A jury of ordinary men in a decade uneasy with female defendants accepted that a woman could administer poison with deliberation and judged accordingly. They chose second degree rather than first. Whether that choice grew from mercy given to a woman or from doubt that stopped short of the rope is a question the record permits but does not resolve. Third, the prison proved as fallible as any human institution. A breach opened. A prisoner stepped through. The breach was mended only when embarrassment forced change. In that fallibility there is a lesson that communities have to relearn whenever they imagine that stones and rules are enough to keep the worst of human decisions penned in forever.

When the cell door closed for the last time behind the woman the papers had named, the loudest part of the story quieted. What remained were the papers filed, the tests written down in the careful hands of chemists, the sentence in the clerk's book, and the long slow work of households learning how to trust the people who fed them without surrendering entirely the right to ask what had been placed in a cup. That long slow work is part of the aftermath. It belongs to the next chapter.

AFTERMATH WITH FAMILY AND PUBLIC OPINION

On the morning after Sherman's death, the women's ward at Wethersfield returned to its routines with the dull steadiness that follows any death inside a prison. A sheet had been drawn over the face of the woman the newspapers had named the Derby Poisoner. A physician signed the papers that recorded cancer as the cause. A chaplain wrote a brief line in his private book. Outside the walls the effect of her life and trial did not pass so quickly. It moved outward, first through the families that had known her and then through the towns that had read about her, and finally into the wider culture that shapes how a nation talks about the crimes of women and how it trusts the hands that pour a cup at a sickbed.

Families are the first historians of any crime. They tell the story to one another, they decide which parts to save and which to silence, and they carry the memory in ways that no public archive can fully capture. The houses that had been linked to Lydia's name had already seen too many funerals by the time the state took her away in 1872. Those who remained had to decide how to talk about the dead. Some refused any public part in that conversation. They closed their doors to reporters and would not be drawn into the court of opinion. Others found that the act of speaking brought a measure of order to grief that had gone unanswered during the years when doctors said cholera or fever and left a family to wonder whether they had done something wrong. After the verdict and sentence, some relatives spoke in a chastened way about the small signs that had worried them and that made sense only once the chemists' reports were read aloud in a courtroom. A cousin remembered that Lydia was insistent that no one else prepare a bowl or pour a cup for a patient. A neighbor recalled the way she stood gently between a visitor and the bed, as if to guard against interruption. These were not proofs of anything at the time. They were ordinary acts of care. Only after the fact did their meaning darken.

For those families there was also the matter of graves. Exhumations had disturbed the rest of some of their dead during the investigation. When the last testing had been completed and the remains returned, reburial was done quickly and with as much dignity as the moment allowed. In a century that placed great weight on the quiet of the grave, that disturbance felt like a second injury. It also brought a second kind of comfort. The reports that followed the testing gave a clear name to a cause that had previously floated between fever and bad water and fate. To place a loved one again in the earth with that knowledge, unkind as it was, allowed a family to feel that the final words on the matter had been spoken by fact rather than by rumor.

If families lived with the intimate shape of the story, the public shaped it into something larger. The arrest in 1871 and the trial in 1872 came at a time when city papers were eager for narratives that fed both fear and fascination. The figure of the female poisoner gave editors an image that could be framed with phrases about domestic treachery and about the dark arts of the kitchen. Sketch artists drew a composed face with tidy hair and calm eyes. Articles described the quiet of the courtroom as experts explained their tests and as neighbors described bowls of broth carried from stove to bedside. There were no spectacular weapons to display. No pistol was placed on a table for a jury to see. The drama lay in the idea that a household utensil could be turned into a weapon. That idea reached an audience far beyond the counties in which the events had unfolded.

Church talk took on the same theme but with a different goal. Ministers in Methodist meeting houses and in other congregations preached sermons about the moral obligations of caregiving and about the duty of husbands and wives to guard one another without surrendering the judgment that keeps a house honest. Some used the case to warn against the easy availability of arsenic in markets where anyone with a coin could buy a packet of ratsbane or sheets of fly paper and carry them home in a plain wrapping. Others used it to remind parishioners that the virtues of patience and gentleness, which are real virtues in a nurse, must be anchored in character and not merely in demeanor. The result was a season in which women who ran households found themselves observed more closely than before. It was not always fair. It was the natural consequence of a case that had asked a community to examine the most private of rooms.

Public opinion about the fairness of the sentence remains a study in how a people read gender into the law. Some readers congratulated the jury for refusing to bend to sentiment and for accepting the testimony of chemists in a time when science had not yet earned the trust it now enjoys. Others argued that a conviction for second degree murder reflected a reluctance to hang a woman rather than a careful distinction among legal elements. In taverns and parlors the talk turned on that point. Should the law treat a woman who uses a household poison differently from a man who uses a knife in a street. The judge had instructed and the jury had chosen. But the community kept talking because the case had asked hard questions about intent and about trust within a marriage and because the usual narrative of sudden violence did not fit the slow and deliberate method revealed in court.

The escape in 1877 stirred another wave of commentary. No institution likes to be made a fool of, and few things make a prison look more foolish than a prisoner who simply walks through a door unobserved. The newspaper coverage vacillated between mockery of the guards and alarm at the thought of a woman whose crimes had been described so fully taking up work in another household as if nothing had happened. That brief period in Providence during which she worked under an assumed name for a widower only deepened the sense that the line between safety and danger is thin where trust is the currency of domestic life. The recapture quieted the ridicule. It did not fully quiet the worry. In the months after her return to Wethersfield, more than one paper ran editorials urging closer control in hospital wards and better routines for the supervision of prisoners whose health required them to be moved from their cells.

Not all the aftershocks were cultural. Some were practical. Apothecaries began to keep a closer watch on the sale of arsenic. In some towns clerks kept a book that recorded the names of those who purchased certain powders. Grocery stores and dry goods houses that had previously stocked fly paper and ratsbane beside soaps and brushes moved those items into drawers behind the counter so that a customer had to ask for them rather than simply pick them up. These small changes did not amount to formal regulation. They were the self protection of vendors who had read enough scandal to know that public anger can fall on anyone who appears careless in the face of danger.

Insurance companies adjusted their practices as well. One of the quiet engines in the case had been the growing awareness among agents and clerks that too many small policies associated with one house had been paid within a short period. That awareness did not flow through a central office in those days. It lived in the heads of men who knew their books. After the trial, companies circulated memoranda within branches urging their people to note patterns and to report concerns to supervisors. This was the beginning of what would later become routine in that industry. It sat somewhere between prudence and suspicion. It is fair to note that such attentiveness cut both ways. It protected some potential victims. It also brought new scrutiny to families who had simply suffered a season of genuine disease.

The acceptance of scientific testimony received a lasting boost from the conviction. Jurors who had walked into a courtroom wary of apparatus and unfamiliar terms had walked out convinced or at least willing to sign their names to a paper that assumed the authority of chemistry to locate a poison in the organs of the dead. Judges who read the record saw that a careful presentation of tests could be made intelligible to laymen. Prosecutors across New England took notice. In the years that followed, coroners and police were quicker to request exhumations when similarity of symptoms suggested foul play. Physicians learned to preserve stomach contents and sections of the liver when a death raised even faint questions. This habit of preservation is the beginning of modern forensic practice. It owes as much to courtroom learning as it does to laboratory advance.

The image of the poisoner as a type took firm hold as well. From pamphlets to sermons to novels, the figure of the outwardly dutiful caregiver masking an inner will to control or to profit became a stock character. That is not fair to the hundreds of thousands of women whose skill kept families alive. It is a fact of cultural history that one notorious case can define an era in the minds of readers far from the facts. The result is a paradox. The same century that began to praise nursing as a vocation also began to fear the nurse as a figure cloaked in unearned power. That paradox shows up whenever a country has to learn who to trust in a crisis. This case contributed to that education in a way that bred caution, and sometimes bred suspicion, within the very rooms where trust is most necessary.

In the towns where Lydia had lived, people continued to argue about motive because unity on that point never arrived. Some thought money explained the sequence. Small insurance policies do not make a person wealthy. They can provide relief in moments of crisis. In houses where every dollar has to be made to do three dollars' worth of work, such relief can tempt those who have learned to live in constant fear of the next bill. Others thought the motive darker and simpler. Power in private rooms can become a drug. The nurse who decides when to ease a pain and when to let it climb, the housekeeper who insists on controlling every dish and every spoon, discovers that the house moves according to her will. That sense can become its own end. The law does not need a single motive to convict. The public, which lives with the story after the law has finished with its part, often insists on one. In this case no neat answer survived to carry the day.

There were other, quieter effects. Families learned to ask questions in kitchens. This learning was not aggressive. It sounded like a husband rising from bed to fetch his own drink rather than wait for a nurse to bring it. It looked like a sister offering to help in the preparation of a meal for a sick child rather than leaving one person to carry the burden alone. In better houses it looked like the provincial adoption of small etiquettes borrowed from hospitals. Medicines were kept in a box that others could see. Doses were written on slips of paper and left beside bottles. None of this guaranteed safety. It expressed a desire to make care a shared enterprise. That desire arose from fear, which is never the best teacher. It also arose from a wish to do better, which is the beginning of wisdom in any house.

Public opinion mellowed after May 1878, not because the facts softened but because new crimes demanded fresh attention. The name that once carried the shock of the new took its place alongside other names that later generations would learn when they read pamphlets about notorious women. The prison accounted for her death in its usual way. The grave closed. The wardens moved on to other duties. The doctors refined their tests. The insurers improved their ledgers. The shopkeepers shifted their stock and took down their notes in the books they kept behind the counter. The town clocks kept time.

From the vantage of distance, the case stands as a set of lessons rather than as a single moral. It teaches that the tools of care can be turned to harm if a person chooses to use them that way. It teaches that households that prize composure and patience must also prize the kind of transparency that makes composure trustworthy. It teaches that science, when careful and modest, can help a jury see what the eye alone cannot. It teaches that the state can punish without spectacle and still satisfy a community's sense that justice has been done. Finally, it teaches that the way a people remembers a crime shapes how they live afterward. The families closest to the events learned to grieve with knowledge rather than with vague dread. The neighbors learned to combine the praise of nursing with a small measure of watchfulness that keeps power from turning inward. The rest of us learn again, whenever we pick up a cup that someone else has poured, that trust is the most fragile and the most necessary ingredient in any room where sickness and care meet.

CHAPTER 3
TERESA LEWIS
MURDER FOR PROFIT

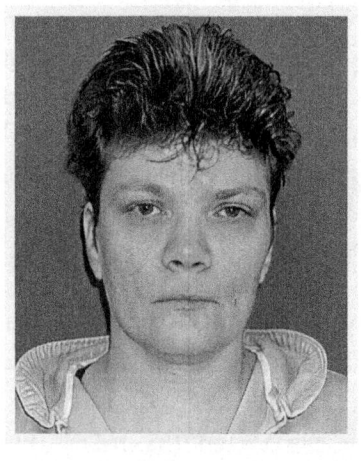

Teresa Wilson was born on 26th April 1969 in Danville, Virginia, a mill town that rose and fell with the fortunes of textile work. Her parents held jobs at the Dan River plant and measured their days by whistles and shift changes. The family's budget was always tight, and the house rules were simple. Work hard. Keep faith. Stretch every dollar. A local church shaped much of Teresa's childhood. She learned hymns by ear, sang with a clear voice, and absorbed the rhythms of sermons that promised grace in lean times. Neighbors remembered a quiet girl who liked to sing and who smiled easily when spoken to. Teachers saw a student who tried but drifted when demands at home mounted. Adolescence pulled her toward independence. By mid teens, school felt like a distant concern compared to the pull of adult life beyond the classroom windows.

At 16 she left high school and married a young man she met through the church. They began in a small place with secondhand furniture and the optimism that carries many young couples through the first months of rent and bills. A daughter was born and named Christie. The arrival brought joy and pressure in equal measure. Money was scarce. Arguments came easily. The marriage did not last. Divorce papers closed one story and opened another, and in the space left by that loss Teresa struggled. She leaned on pills that softened hard edges and reached for alcohol when days grew long. It was not the life she had imagined when she stood at the church steps as a teenager with a borrowed bouquet, but it was the life she had, and she pressed forward, taking any work she could find.

The next years were a patchwork of low wage jobs. Teresa stocked shelves, checked out customers, and cleaned rooms. She learned the routines of time cards and the steady fatigue that comes from standing on concrete floors. The people who hired her remember a worker who showed up early and tried to please, who sometimes seemed overwhelmed but not unwilling. Her plans narrowed to essentials. Keep a roof overhead. Feed a child. Pay the light bill. Her mother in law from the first marriage formed an unvarnished view, calling her not right, a phrase that would linger in family lore. Whether that judgment reflected long standing worry, the strain of post divorce behaviors, or a blend of the two, it mirrored a perception that Teresa did not think several steps ahead and could be easily moved by the wishes of others.

As she approached 30, she found steadier hours at the Dan River textile mill. Mills in places like Danville were more than job sites. They were social networks where friendships formed over machines and shifts, where families passed work from parent to child. In the spring of 2000 Teresa entered that world and met a supervisor named Julian Clifton Lewis Jr. He was older, had carried the responsibilities of a household for many years, and had known grief. He had three children, Jason, Charles, and Kathy, and had lost a spouse. To a woman who had been drifting across short term jobs, a man with a stable position and a settled home could look like an anchor in a choppy tide. To a widower, a woman who cooked and sang and paid attention to his children could look like a chance to rebuild what had been broken.

Teresa and her teenage daughter Christie moved into Julian's house in June 2000. The arrangement quickly became a marriage, and with that step Teresa went from single mother to wife and stepmother. The household mixed histories that predated her with new routines that required her care. She learned where the groceries were kept and which drawer held the good towels. She learned the moods of teenagers and the habits of a man who had set his life in grooves long before she entered it. She attended to the chores that fill a home with the quiet structure of meals and laundry. She drew strength from the church again, returning to pews and songs she knew by heart. Neighbors saw her as attentive and eager to please, quick to laugh, quick to defer. In the first months the house felt steadier than anything she had known in years.

The family suffered a terrible blow in December 2001 when Julian's older son Jason died in a car accident. The suddenness of the loss ricocheted through the house. Grief magnified stress. People in the circle of friends and relatives remember a father supporting his children while he tried to steady himself, and a wife trying to bind wounds that did not easily close. In the aftermath, Julian looked for ways to reset the family's environment. He bought a manufactured home and placed it on a parcel of land in Pittsylvania County. Moving promised a fresh start. New walls. New views. Fewer constant reminders of the accident. Teresa unpacked in the new residence and arranged furniture in a way that made the rooms feel familiar, a sign that the couple meant to settle.

The calendar turned to 2002 with the family trying to build new routines. Teresa baked more. Julian worked. Kathy moved through the steps of a young adult forging her own path. Charles, the younger son, wore his uniform with quiet pride and trained as a reservist, preparing for deployment in a world that had changed since the previous year. Friends noticed Teresa's blended qualities. She could be warm and generous, especially to church members and to people she wanted to please. She also craved approval and attention. Those who knew her best observed that she sometimes said yes simply to make someone else happy, even if the choice was not wise. Pills remained a presence. The painkillers that had once marked her low periods had never fully left the medicine cabinet. She took them in ways that smudged lines between treatment and dependence.

Those who later examined her mental functioning would write numbers on paper and frame her ability in clinical language, but during these months the indicators were much simpler. She was not an abstract case. She was a woman who made impulsive choices and was often guided by stronger personalities around her. In family discussions she rarely led. She followed. She found it hard to speak up when a decision carried the risk of conflict. She accepted what she was told by people she trusted and sometimes by people she barely knew. When confronted with a problem, she did not always grasp its long term consequences. Several relatives saw her as naive, particularly when praise or attention were involved.

Her relationship with her daughter remained close. Christie had grown up watching her mother juggle work and worry. In the new house the daughter helped as teenagers will help when they sense a parent is stretched thin. They shared errands and small confidences. The bond between them mattered in the months ahead, though in ways neither would have predicted. In the wider family Teresa worked to fit the roles expected of her. She attended family events. She sat quietly when the older children shared memories of their mother. She tried to be liked. That trait, harmless in ordinary settings, could become dangerous when the wrong kind of person decided to take advantage.

Around this time Teresa reached for something beyond domestic routine. The mill had offered stability, but it was repetitive work with little chance for advancement. She wanted to feel chosen, valuable, part of a story that placed her at its center. That desire led her to chat more with strangers in stores, to linger when someone paid her a compliment, and to accept invitations that promised excitement. In a small city where contact points are predictable, these small shifts increased the odds that she would meet people who did not share the values of the church community that had shaped her. The habits of deference and the need for attention formed a risky combination, especially for someone who had not learned to say no when a smiling face asked her for something she should not give.

The marriage itself was a mixture of real care and periodic tension. Julian managed money conservatively and measured decisions by long experience. Teresa grew up with very little and found it difficult to delay gratification when a bit of cash was on hand. Disagreements about spending were not unusual. In most households such disputes end with a compromise and a return to ordinary concerns. Here they sometimes left her feeling rebuked and him feeling exasperated. Still, to friends at church and to neighbors in the county, the couple appeared committed. They were present at services. They hosted family dinners. They talked about plans for the property, ordinary things like plantings and small repairs that signal intent to stay.

At the edges of this life were facts that would later loom large. Charles came home on leave at times, proud of his service and focused on obligations that were larger than family chores. The family had recently endured one devastating loss and was trying to adjust. Teresa's yearning for approval made her susceptible to flattery. Her use of pills dulled judgment. None of these points by itself marks a path toward calamity. Taken together, they mapped vulnerabilities in a woman who craved guidance, and in a household trying to heal while it absorbed change.

The portrait of Teresa in these years is therefore layered. She was a church singer who prayed. She was a mother who kept close to her daughter. She was a wife who cooked meals and learned to fold into a family that existed before she arrived. She was also a person who struggled with impulse control, who often deferred to others because it felt easier than disagreeing, and who measured her worth by how often she could please someone else. In the quiet of the manufactured home on a rural plot, those strengths and weaknesses coexisted. Friends might see only the friendly neighbor who lent a pie plate or the woman who sang loudly at the hymn that everyone loved. Only those inside the family saw the moments when her wish to be liked pushed aside better judgment.

Any account of her early life must also name the forces around her. The mill culture taught reliability but rarely encouraged independent thinking. Church culture taught obedience and humility. Poverty taught patience and endurance. Divorce taught loss and the sense that stability could vanish without warning. The sudden death of a stepson renewed that lesson with terrible force. These experiences do not excuse later choices. They form the context in which later choices were made. When the time came that a new voice praised her, promised her attention, and asked her for favors, she was ill equipped to resist.

Teresa did not expect the life that followed. Most people who stand at a kitchen sink in a rural county do not imagine that their names will one day appear in news stories and court orders. She seemed to believe that her ambitions were modest and achievable. A secure home. Approval from the people around her. A sense that she mattered. The story of the years leading up to the crimes is not a tale of a woman plotting grand designs. It is the story of a woman whose need to be wanted, combined with a long habit of deference and the numbing effects of pills, left her open to suggestions that would have horrified the girl who sang in church.

By late 2002 the household looked stable to outsiders. The new place was set on its acreage. The younger stepson came and went as his duty required. Teresa had a church to attend, a kitchen to manage, and a circle of acquaintances that reached beyond the family. Inside that calm were fault lines. Grief still sat at the table. Finances, while not desperate, were the subject of ongoing debate. Teresa's emotional dependencies were constant. A woman who lives to be pleasing will often do things that make no sense when measured by ordinary logic. That trait, harmless when a friend asks for a favor, becomes perilous if the person making the request wants something dark. Sadly, that is what the next chapter of the story reveals.

Teresa's early life in Danville and the years of struggle that followed did not write her destiny. They did, however, shape the choices she made when new people walked into her life promising excitement and admiration. Those choices were not born in a vacuum. They were the product of a background that blended poverty, religious aspiration, a longing to be loved, and a pattern of stepping aside whenever a stronger will pressed forward. When the time came that others would seek to use her, they found a woman primed by years of deferring to others and eager to hold on to any attention given to her. The consequences of that dynamic would be catastrophic, not only for those who placed trust in her but also for Teresa herself. The next section draws a line from the quiet rooms of a rural home to a night when two men entered through a door left open and everything changed.

THE MURDERS

The path to the killings began quietly, in the ordinary circuits of a small city where the same stores draw the same faces week after week. In the fall of 2002, Teresa crossed paths at a discount store with two young men, Matthew Jessee Shallenberger and Rodney Lamont Fuller. They were in their early twenties and full of the restless confidence that comes with youth and the belief that the rules can be bent. The first conversations were light. A smile. A joke. A suggestion to meet later. What followed was not a dramatic turn in a single moment but a slide built out of attention, flattery, and the thrill of being noticed. Teresa was drawn in. Soon she was meeting both men and blurring lines between friendship, romance, and manipulation. They talked about money, about dreams that needed funding, about needs that could be met if only a large sum could be found. The idea of easy money seduces in stages. First there is the wish. Then there is the plan that seems almost theoretical. And then there is the step from talk to deed.

By early October, the conversations had narrowed to one clear aim. Julian Lewis and his son Charles were the obstacles between Teresa and a significant sum that could be accessed through insurance. The stepson, a reservist preparing for deployment, had a policy that named his father as primary beneficiary and Teresa as secondary. The father, a careful man who had already weathered one son's tragic death, had funds and property that could be gathered by a surviving spouse. The talk among the three adults hardened into intent. Matthew and Rodney would do the violence. Teresa would set the stage, provide access, and handle the aftermath inside the home. It was not a sudden pact but the endpoint of weeks of reinforcement. Teresa provided money, praise, and encouragement. The two young men provided bravado and a willingness to take a life for a price.

On 23rd October 2002, Teresa pressed a stack of bills into Matthew's and Rodney's hands. It totaled approximately one thousand two hundred dollars. The cash was for weapons and ammunition. That exchange of money moved the conspiracy from a conversation to an active operation. The first plan focused on Julian's movements outside the home. There was to be an interception on the road, a forced encounter that would look like a robbery or a random act of roadside violence. For reasons that would only later come out in interviews and statements, that attempt failed. The failure did not end the plot. It recalibrated it. In the days that followed, the trio shifted to a simpler approach, one that required less improvisation and more reliance on a controlled environment. They chose the manufactured home on the rural plot where the family now lived. The idea was to strike at night while the victims slept, to create confusion about entry, to take a few valuables for show, and to disappear into the dark before neighbors noticed anything amiss.

The week between the failed attempt and the night of the killings moved with deceptive stillness. Teresa kept household routines, but she was also making preparations. She maintained her contacts with the two men. She sketched out the interior layout for them and told them where the bedrooms were. She agreed to leave a back door unlocked. That detail was small and devastating. It removed the primary obstacle to entry, and it allowed the intruders to slip inside without breaking glass or forcing latches. The lack of a broken door or a shattered window would matter later when investigators examined the scene, but on the night itself it meant only that two men armed with a handgun and a shotgun could glide into the house while the occupants slept.

The date was 30th October 2002. The day had been ordinary. The younger stepson, Charles, was home from training. The father, Julian, had settled into evening habits. The house grew dark. Somewhere around midnight, depending on which clock was used as reference, Matthew and Rodney approached the property. They came to the back door that Teresa had promised to leave unsecured. True to her word, the door opened under the lightest touch. Teresa waited in the kitchen. The men moved toward their targets. Julian slept in the main bedroom. Charles slept in a separate room down the hall.

The first shots came from the handgun. Matthew stepped into the bedroom where Julian lay and fired several times at close range. The sound in a small structure was deafening. In the hall, Rodney raised a shotgun and entered the room where Charles slept. He fired once, then again. The rush of noise, the suddenness of injury, the shock to bodies at rest created chaos. After the first blasts, the scene fractured. Teresa remained in the kitchen. Matthew and Rodney moved through the house making sure their assignments were complete. In Charles's room, it became clear after seconds that the first shot had not been fatal. He was still alive, struggling. Rodney fired again. The young man's body absorbed the force of the second shot. In the bedroom where Julian lay, the multiple handgun rounds had done terrible damage, but he was not immediately dead. His breathing was labored. He bled into the sheets. He attempted to speak.

Inside the kitchen, Teresa did not call for help. She waited. The waiting would later be measured as approximately three quarters of an hour. In that span of time, the two men collected a few items of value to create a veneer of robbery. They also expected payment. Teresa made sure they received cash, around three hundred dollars divided before they left. The amount was small compared to the figure they discussed when they first talked about insurance money and future splits. Money was tight in the house, and in any case, the larger payoff was never meant to come in loose bills. It would come, the plan imagined, once policies were paid and accounts were closed. The three conspirators understood this. The small cash that changed hands that night was a token, a gesture, and an incentive for the two men to leave quickly.

The minutes ticked by. In the main bedroom, Julian fought to breathe. He had enough awareness to understand that he had been shot at home. He had enough awareness to know who had been present. The man who had guided his family through one son's funeral now stared at a ceiling while life drained from him. When Teresa finally dialed 911, the call began a chain. First responders in rural counties often arrive within minutes if the call is clear and the address is known. At the Lewis residence, deputies reached the scene while Julian was still alive. He tried to speak. He managed words that would echo through the case. He said that his wife knew who had done this to him. In the immediate aftermath, Teresa spoke of unknown intruders and the terror of a home invasion. She told the dispatcher and the arriving deputies that she had been helpless. The narrative was sparse. Two men. A door. Shots. Her own account would be examined later, but in those first moments she stuck to a simple description that placed the attackers outside any circle of acquaintance.

While emergency personnel worked, while lights flashed against the siding of the home, Teresa did something that would be noted, recorded, and revisited. She removed money from her dying husband's wallet. The act was quick. She believed she had a window before anyone would begin the controlled tracking of items on scene. That window was shorter than she thought. Trained officers note such details. They notice who is near a victim. They notice where hands go. They notice what is missing when they begin to inventory a crime scene where a possible robbery has occurred. In a later interview, this detail would be one of several that undermined the story of strangers who came in the night. It revealed a person thinking already in transactional terms, even as a spouse lay mortally wounded a few feet away.

The scene inside the house bore the signatures of the night's choices. The back door showed no damage. A few items were disturbed to suggest theft, but valuable electronics remained. There was blood in the bedrooms and on bedding. There was no trail through the garage to suggest that attackers had exited that way. Outside, the property showed little sign of an approach other than footprints that could have been anyone's. The lack of signs of forced entry and the focused nature of the violence pointed to attackers who knew the interior and the routines of those who lived there. That is a pattern that experienced investigators read quickly. It does not prove who ordered a killing. It suggests familiarity, and it sharpens attention toward acquaintances and family.

The two young men left after the division of the small cash. They had entered through an unlocked door and left through the night in the same manner. They did not stay to ensure silence. Whether that was because they assumed their targets would not survive or because they wanted to be as far from the home as possible before emergency vehicles arrived does not change the result. Julian did not immediately die. He had time to speak. Charles, blasted by a shotgun at close range, could not be saved. Blood pooled on floors and soaked into sheets. The smell of gunpowder hung in the rooms. The neighbors slept through it, as neighbors often do in rural places where houses are spaced apart and night sounds are common.

Inside the kitchen that now functioned as a staging area for responders, Teresa looked shocked. People who describe her demeanor later use words like dazed and numb, terms that can hold both genuine trauma and an attempt to present emotion as a shield. Her story emphasized a door left unsecured by mistake, strangers entering, shots, confusion. She said she had been in the kitchen. She said she had hidden. The manner in which she told this account is part of the record. It contained pauses and overlaps, the sort of fractured speech that can come when a person is under stress. It also contained gaping omissions, the sort that appear when a person is trying quickly to build a structure of explanation over a sequence of acts that included decisions to let killers into a house and to wait before calling for help.

The timeline of the night is important. The men approached. They entered through an unlocked back door. They shot both sleeping victims. One of the victims lingered with enough awareness to speak a sentence that referenced knowledge on the part of the spouse. The conspirators divided a small amount of cash and left. Teresa waited for an extended period before dialing. Those points trace a path that would be followed in the next section by investigators. In this section the focus remains on the acts themselves. There was a decision to use the interior of a family home as the place of attack. There was a specific assignment of targets. There was prepared access. There was a staged robbery designed to misdirect. There was a delay after the attack which increased the likelihood of death. There was removal of money from a dying man's wallet. These are the factual elements of the murders that occurred in the early morning of 31st October 2002 if measured against the moment of the 911 call, but which began for the three conspirators as they put the plan into motion with an unlocked door.

In the days that preceded the night, Teresa had set other details in motion. She had sounded out financial institutions about access to funds that would be available to a spouse after a death. She had made mental lists of what property could be claimed under her name. These actions did not by themselves prove the existence of a conspiracy to kill. People make inquiries about finances for many reasons. But these actions, when aligned with the events of the night, formed a pattern that investigators would later assemble. In this section they are noted only to show that the night did not come as an isolated event. It was the culmination of a period in which the lines between an ordinary domestic routine and a criminal plot blurred and then disappeared.

After the shots, the trailer held a silence broken by radios and voices speaking in firm tones as paramedics and deputies did their work. If one were to stand at the kitchen doorway and look down the hall, one would see a bedroom strewn with the signs of a struggle under gunfire. Another room held the aftermath of shotgun blasts. The hall itself showed footprints and the tracks of hurried movement. It was a terrible scene. Most homicides in homes share this quality. They are both intensely personal and shockingly brutal. The victims have the imprint of the ordinary around them. A lamp on a bedside table. A partially full glass. A familiar blanket pulled by instinct in the moment before the shot. The intrusion of violence into such spaces is always jarring. In this case, that contrast was sharpened by the knowledge that the entry point was an unlocked door and that the person responsible for leaving it open stood in the kitchen and watched events unfold.

There was no gunfight, no chase, no dramatic confrontation. The murders were planned as executions. The choice of weapons matched that plan. A handgun at close range in a bedroom allows multiple shots without the long arc of a shotgun. A shotgun aimed at a sleeping person is devastating, and at close range it leaves little chance for survival. The two men used both. The sequence of shots and their placement demonstrated that the victims were not meant to be intimidated or wounded as part of a robbery. They were meant to be killed. The division of roles and the immediate payment afterward confirmed the essence of the plan. Teresa did not squeeze a trigger, but she provided the means and the access, and she took actions before and after that integrated her into the lethal sequence.

The trauma to the surviving stepdaughter, who would later walk into courtrooms carrying sorrow mixed with anger, cannot be captured by a crime scene report. On that night, she was not present. She learned by call and by the unfolding of events that her father and her brother were gone. In the separate quiet of her own home, she absorbed the first cold wave of grief, not yet aware of the details. Teresa remained at the scene as a spouse who had called for help after a supposed invasion. She was the primary witness to what had happened, and for the remainder of the night the house and the people in it were secured for processing and interviews.

The murders on that October night were not improvised. They were the result of planning that had become more determined after an initial failure a week earlier. They were carried out by men who had been paid to do it and who expected to collect much more when insurance proceeds cleared. They happened in the quiet of a rural home, using a door left open by someone inside, and followed by a delay on the part of that same person before anyone was called to stop the bleeding. These facts stand on their own. They draw a line that does not reach beyond this night into later investigations and court proceedings. They do not draw conclusions about legal responsibility. They show what happened. A wife let two men into a house. They shot a father and a son while they slept. Cash changed hands. An attempt was made to make it look like strangers had come to steal. A husband, bleeding, spoke words that indicated his wife had knowledge of the perpetrators. Those words hung in the air long after the blue lights faded from the walls and the house fell silent again.

The immediate aftermath inside the house included the movements of professionals who know how to read rooms and how to preserve evidence. It also included the first hints of the explanations that Teresa would offer, explanations that would strain under the weight of physical facts and the timeline of her own choices. But those elements belong to the next chapter, which follows the path from this violent scene to the steps of a courthouse.

For the purpose of this section, the story ends where the chalk measurements and the photographs begin, at a rural residence where two men entered through an unlocked back door, fired their weapons into sleeping bodies, took a few dollars and a promise of more, and left a woman in a kitchen to decide how long she would wait before she picked up a phone and asked for help.

ARREST, TRIAL AND SENTENCE

The investigation moved fast once the scene was secured. Deputies from the county sheriff office, assisted by state police investigators, began with the basics. They documented rooms, photographed patterns of blood, and compared what they saw with the first account that Teresa gave in the kitchen. The story she told involved unknown men who had entered and fled. The physical evidence suggested something else. Forced entry was hard to find. Valuables were in plain view. There were small disturbances that looked staged. None of that proved who was responsible, but it directed the next steps. The investigators decided to widen their lens beyond the image of strangers and to examine the relationships inside and around the home.

In the first round of interviews, Teresa gave a general description of fear and confusion. She spoke of an unlocked door and the terror of being surprised in the night. The detectives listened, then began to fill out a timeline by talking with neighbors, relatives, and coworkers. They learned about recent discussions of insurance. They learned about her new acquaintances, two young men who had entered her life only weeks before. They also learned that she had shown interest in accessing accounts connected to the victims. Bank employees later described interactions in which Teresa asked about withdrawals and balances around the time of the deaths. Those inquiries mattered because they showed a financial focus at a moment when most spouses are absorbed in grief. The contrast was stark and it did not escape notice.

Within days, a new incident sharpened the picture. Teresa presented a check for fifty thousand dollars drawn on her late husband account. The signature was not his. The bank flagged the attempt. That alone would have triggered questions. Combined with the circumstances in the home and the growing knowledge of her relationships with the two young men from the discount store, it gave investigators the leverage they needed for a deeper conversation. When questioned about the check, Teresa did not offer a credible explanation. The pressure was building. At the same time detectives were untangling bank transactions, they were also tracing the movements of Matthew Shallenberger and Rodney Fuller. Records showed the purchase of firearms and ammunition with cash on the same day that Teresa had made a withdrawal of more than one thousand dollars. Store clerks remembered the men. Those clerks remembered a customer who was older and who seemed to be in charge of the money.

Small details began to fuse into a pattern. One investigator noted that the back door had been found unsecured with no damage to the frame. Another noted that the home had been set up to look as if thieves had come for goods, but that the most valuable items had not been taken. A third noted that a modest amount of cash had apparently been taken from the victims, but that this removal seemed more like a token than the goal of a violent robbery. When these notes were placed beside the emerging financial story and the nascent trail leading to the two young men, the robbery story began to collapse. What remained was a picture of an inside job arranged by someone familiar with daily routines.

The interviews changed tone as a result. Detectives asked direct questions. They presented the banking incident. They presented information from store employees. Teresa was now a focus rather than a bystander. Within a week of the killings she acknowledged that she had offered money to have her husband killed. That admission ended the possibility that this would be treated as a random act. The next question was who had joined her. That answer did not take long. The names of Matthew and Rodney were already on the board. They were located and brought in. Their stories were not identical. They did however place themselves in the house that night and described a plan that matched the evidence.

The case then split into two tracks that would later meet in court. One track concerned the two shooters and the sentences they would face. The other concerned Teresa and the question of capital charges. In Virginia, a person who hires or orders a killing for financial gain can be charged with capital murder even if that person did not fire a shot. The prosecutors believed they had the elements necessary to file that charge. They had an admission that money had been offered to make the death happen. They had statements from the two men who described how the plan was born and what role Teresa played. They had financial behavior before and after the event that pointed to a clear motive. They also had telephone contact patterns showing that messages were exchanged around the time of the attack. Taken together, those points supported the theory of murder for hire.

On the day of her formal arrest, Teresa was not the public figure she would later become. She was a woman led from an interview room to a booking process in a county facility. The standard steps unfurled. Fingerprints. A photograph. Property cataloged. She was advised of the charges. At that stage they included capital counts because of the for profit element. She was appointed counsel. Those lawyers faced an uphill climb. The evidence had a simple logic and a paper trail. It also had corroboration from two codefendants who were already negotiating for life sentences in exchange for cooperation.

Counsel for Teresa evaluated the options and the probable reaction of a jury. The case involved the killing of a husband and a stepson in their sleep. It involved an insurance policy that named the father first and the wife second. It involved an adult romantic relationship with one of the shooters that would be easy for jurors to understand as manipulation. The lawyers concluded there was little chance of avoiding a conviction if the case went to a jury. They considered asking for a bench sentencing after entering a guilty plea on the capital counts. A plea would avoid a lengthy guilt phase. It would also present the judge with the image of a defendant taking responsibility. The defense hoped to build an argument for a sentence less than death based on background, remorse, psychological testing, and cooperation.

Before any plea, the court ordered a mental health evaluation. A board certified psychiatrist interviewed Teresa and administered a standard intelligence test. The score returned was in the low seventies for full scale, with a slightly lower verbal result and a higher performance result. The report concluded that she understood the nature of the proceedings, could assist counsel, and could enter a plea responsibly. The same report identified dependent personality traits and described a long history of substance abuse. The defense integrated those findings into a plan for the penalty phase. The mental health information did not bar capital sentencing. Instead it provided context that the defense hoped would persuade the court to impose life imprisonment.

Teresa entered pleas of guilty to capital counts related to both deaths. This decision meant that a jury would not be convened to weigh guilt or innocence. In Virginia at that time, a judge could impose sentence after hearing evidence in a structured proceeding. The hearing was held in 2003. It lasted long enough for the court to receive reports and hear testimony from witnesses for both sides. The Commonwealth presented a straightforward narrative about greed, betrayal, and lethal planning. It emphasized the payment of cash before the crime to secure guns and the promise of more later when insurance paid. It emphasized the manner in which access had been arranged and the delay before help was called. It emphasized the swiftness with which Teresa moved to secure money and property in the days after the deaths. The Commonwealth also presented victim impact testimony that conveyed the anguish of a family that had already lost one son in an accident and now had to stand beside two more graves.

The defense asked the court to step back from the harshest penalty. Counsel acknowledged the gravity of the acts but argued that Teresa was not the architect in the way the Commonwealth alleged. They described her dependent traits, her addiction, and her gullibility. They argued that she had fallen under the influence of a younger man and that she had been more a follower than a leader. They presented her cooperation with authorities in the days after her arrest and her expressions of remorse as indications that she was capable of conscience and change. They pointed to her family support and to her stated intent to spend the remainder of her life in prison in service and repentance if given that chance.

The judge listened to both sides and took note of the legal standard for murder for profit. The key question was whether the plan had been formed to obtain money through the deaths of Julian and Charles and whether Teresa had led or directed that plan. The court noted several factors as it explained its decision. It focused on the cash that had been provided in advance to secure weapons. It focused on the fact that the person with access to the interior had left a point of entry available. It focused on the steps taken after the deaths to secure funds and the fact that the attempt to move significant money began even before funerals. It focused on the reality that the lives had been traded for the promise of a payout. When the court summarized the case in open session, it characterized Teresa as the driving force behind the plot. The language was vivid and left no doubt about the conclusion. The court saw her as the leader who set the killings in motion and used the two young men as instruments.

On that basis, the judge imposed sentence of death for the two capital counts. The court stated this sentence was warranted because the murders had been planned to obtain insurance proceeds and because the defendant had recruited others to commit the violence. The order spelled out that the method would be lethal injection in accordance with state law. It also enumerated the statutory aggravating factors that applied and referenced the mitigating evidence presented by the defense, which the court found insufficient to overcome the gravity of the crimes.

After the verdict and sentence in the trial court, the case moved into the automatic review process required for capital cases. The Supreme Court of Virginia examined the record to determine whether the sentence was excessive or disproportionate and whether legal error had tainted the proceeding. In 2004 and 2007 the high court issued opinions that rejected constitutional challenges to the state capital scheme and declined to set aside the sentence. The court addressed the argument that the shooters had received life sentences while Teresa faced death by pointing to the statutory focus on the person who arranges a killing for money and to the trial court finding that she had directed the plan. The Supreme Court affirmed the judgment and sentence.

During this period, the two men who fired the weapons resolved their cases through separate proceedings. Matthew accepted a sentence of life without the possibility of parole as part of a plea that recognized his role and his agreement to testify if called. Rodney likewise received a life sentence. These outcomes created a contrast that would later surface in petitions for clemency and in public discussion, but at the time they were wholly consistent with a system that imposes the ultimate penalty on the organizer of a murder for hire while sparing the shooters when they accept responsibility and assist the Commonwealth.

Teresa was transferred to the women correctional facility at Troy and placed in the unit that housed inmates under sentence of death. There she lived under conditions set aside for capital inmates. She had limited movement, strict schedules, and intensive supervision. She communicated with counsel regularly as the direct appeal concluded and as the case moved into state collateral review. Her lawyers filed a petition for a writ of habeas corpus in state court that raised claims about trial counsel decisions and about the handling of mental health evidence. The state courts denied relief. A petition for a writ of certiorari to the Supreme Court of the United States was filed to challenge the refusal to halt the execution on the basis of intellectual disability claims and to seek review of other issues. The petition was denied in September 2010, with two justices recorded as voting to grant a stay. Those votes did not change the outcome. The legal road narrowed to a final request for clemency from the governor.

Throughout the appellate process, the same common themes appeared. The Commonwealth emphasized the clarity of the for profit motive, the preparation in advance, and the swift post crime pursuit of funds. The defense emphasized cognitive limits, dependent traits, addiction, remorse, and the disparity between the life sentences imposed on the shooters and the death sentence imposed on the woman who did not fire a weapon. The state appellate courts and the executive office of the governor weighed these themes in the context of settled law and the facts in the record. While the ultimate decision by the governor to deny clemency belongs to the next chapter, the framework for that decision was formed during the trial and the sentencing and the review that followed.

One part of the legal picture that mattered to observers was this. The trial judge had the discretion to impose life even after a plea to capital counts. The judge chose death. That choice meant that later reviewers began with the premise that a person with full authority had weighed aggravation and mitigation and had concluded that aggravation outweighed. All later review took place inside that frame. It is a high bar for a defendant to clear. Absent constitutional error or newly discovered evidence that creates a probability of a different outcome, appellate courts rarely replace the sentencing judgment of the trial judge.

In the years after sentencing and before the scheduled execution date in 2010, Teresa's case became a symbol used by both sides of the death penalty debate. That broad public discussion belongs in the final section of this chapter. Within the walls of the legal system, however, the case remained what it had been from the first morning. It was a murder for money carried out by two young shooters recruited and paid by a woman who lived inside the home. The sequence from arrest to sentencing was steady and direct. Investigators followed a trail of money and contacts from a rural kitchen to a courthouse. The court heard the evidence and entered a capital judgment. The appeals were filed and denied. The sentence was scheduled to be carried out. The next chapter follows what happened outside the courtroom and inside the final corridors of the state system as the date drew near and as both supporters and critics spoke in the public square.

AFTERMATH WITH FAMILY AND PUBLIC OPINION

The sentences pronounced in a quiet Virginia courtroom did not end the story. They opened a different one, played out across prison visiting rooms, church pulpits, editorial pages, and the private corners of families that had already endured more loss than most people face in a lifetime. The deaths of Julian and Charles were followed by arrests, guilty pleas by the gunmen, and a capital judgment against Teresa. What came next was a long reckoning. It involved the question that always follows a verdict in a capital case. Should the state carry out the sentence. Around that question gathered relatives who mourned, a daughter who had once shared the family roof, a community that had known all the principals, and a broader public that took up sides as the date grew near.

Inside the women correctional facility at Troy, Teresa settled into a routine unlike any she had known. Capital inmates live under strict schedules and their lives are measured in movements from cell to shower to small recreation enclosures and back again. Over time she developed ties with chaplains and with a small circle of women who looked to faith as a way to manage guilt and fear. Volunteers who ministered in the prison described a woman who sang during services and prayed with others. They remarked on a steady presence rather than the impulse driven figure whom prosecutors had depicted at sentencing. To those volunteers she was a person who made amends in the only way available to her, through contrition and service to fellow inmates. To the families of the dead, that image was at best incomplete and at worst an attempt to rewrite a life story that had included deliberate planning and a fatal exchange of cash for violence.

The division between those views ran through almost every conversation about the case in the years leading to 2010. Faith leaders who visited the prison or who corresponded with Teresa spoke publicly about mercy. They pointed to a life spent in poverty and to a set of cognitive limits that experts had documented during the court proceedings. They noted that she did not fire the shots in the bedrooms and argued that life without parole was sufficient punishment for a person who would die in prison either way. Some of those same leaders urged the governor to compare the life sentences of the two shooters with the capital sentence imposed on the woman who had recruited them and to ask whether proportionality had been respected. They gathered signatures from congregants and organized prayer vigils across the state in the months when the final legal petitions were pending.

Relatives on the victims side answered with their own moral language. They remembered a father and a young man who had faced danger abroad and who died instead under the roof they shared. They remembered the constant worry that came with military service, the pride of a deployment planned, and the terrible irony of a homecoming that became a funeral procession. They reminded anyone who would listen that Julian had lost one son to a wreck less than a year before the murders and that the double loss had emptied a family tree. For them, talk of forgiveness could not displace the fact that the plan had been born from greed and carried out in quiet rooms while the household slept. At public hearings and in interviews, they said that the sentence affirmed the value of the lives that were taken, and they urged the state to carry it out.

The wider public conversation drew in voices far beyond the counties where the crimes had occurred. Legal commentators used the case to discuss questions that had been debated for years. What role should cognitive testing play in decisions about capital punishment. How should the law judge a person with low measured intelligence who is nevertheless found competent to plead and who understands the nature of the proceedings. Advocates opposed to capital punishment noted that her full scale score placed her near widely accepted thresholds used in other contexts such as public school assessments or service eligibility. They argued that mercy should be extended not only for reasons of principle but also because her life experience of deprivation and dependency had combined with drug abuse to reduce her moral agency at the time of the crime. Those who supported the sentence countered that the legal standard was not a rough sympathy threshold but a carefully defined clinical and constitutional line. They stressed that state and federal courts had examined the evaluations and had concluded that she met the requirements for criminal responsibility and that the sentence had been lawfully imposed.

As the legal clock moved through successive stages of appeal, the case also became a touchstone in the enduring argument about how the death penalty is applied to women. Executions of female offenders are rare in the United States. The rarity itself gave the case a special gravity. Some critics of the sentence suggested that gender played a role in public reaction, cutting in two directions. On one side, they argued, a woman condemned arouses a heightened sense of outrage precisely because people do not expect women to order killings for money. On the other side, they argued that the law should not temper judgment simply because the defendant is a woman. Supporters of the sentence called that the correct conclusion. They said the response should be measured by the acts themselves and by the legal standard, not by the gender of the person who planned the murders.

The last year of litigation drew intense scrutiny. The defense returned to the subject of mental limitations and added accounts from people who had known Teresa in her youth. They described a girl who struggled in school and who left early, a teenage mother who attached herself quickly to stronger personalities, and a worker who held a series of small jobs without advancement. They asked the executive branch for mercy on those grounds and on the grounds of her conduct in prison. The governor office faced a choice that has no easy version. The file on the case contained a thick record assembled by courts over years. It also contained letters from families on both sides, from church leaders, from mental health professionals, and from citizens who had never set foot in Pittsylvania County but who felt compelled to speak.

Public figures stepped forward as the date approached. Some novelists and essayists wrote pieces arguing that the balance of responsibility had been weighed incorrectly and that the death sentence should be commuted to life. They pointed to statements by one of the shooters in which he described himself as the more dominant figure in the relationship. They argued that she was a person who sought approval and who had deferred to younger men who embraced violence. Those arguments did not persuade the authorities. The state pointed back to the original findings that placed her at the center of the plan and to the steps she took to finance it and to secure the benefits afterward. In the state account, she had not merely assented to violence. She had recruited it, funded it, and facilitated it in a place where the victims slept under the illusion of safety.

There were also international echoes. Officials in foreign capitals used the case to make rhetorical points about the rights and wrongs of capital punishment in general. In some corners of the world press the case was set beside others that had little in common beyond the presence of a female defendant and an impending execution. Such comparisons often flattened important differences. In Virginia, the debate remained grounded in the practical language of state law and the factual record. For supporters of clemency, the best argument was not a sweeping claim about global double standards. It was a focused claim that this particular woman, with these particular limitations and this record of good behavior in prison, should not be put to death.

Within the prison, the final months brought a familiar series of emotional scenes. Counsel met with Teresa to review options and to manage expectations. Clergy arranged additional visits and requested permission for extended prayer sessions. Family members made difficult decisions about whether to attend the execution and what to say if asked to speak. Her daughter, who had already served time for her own criminal exposure related to knowledge of the plot, struggled with the knowledge that a mother who had once tucked her in at night would now die in a state chamber. Members of the victims family prepared statements that would be delivered outside the prison gates after the sentence was carried out. Those statements focused on loss rather than on anger. They recalled the warm details that help relatives carry on. A favorite meal. A good joke. A day spent fishing. These intimate fragments framed the public act that was about to occur.

The final decision from the governor came in mid September 2010. He issued a statement that acknowledged the pleas that had arrived by mail and email and the vigils that had been held outside the executive mansion and the prison. He also acknowledged the legal opinions that had tested the sentence and affirmed it. He wrote that he found no compelling reason to set aside the judgment. With that decision the last official avenue closed. Petitions to the Supreme Court of the United States for a stay did not change the course. Two justices noted their dissent from the denial of a stay, but the order that mattered was the one that allowed the state to proceed.

The day of the execution was ordinary for most of the people across the state. It was not ordinary inside the complex at Greensville. The procedures there have been refined over decades. The warden circulates a schedule for the day. The inmate is moved to a holding cell and monitored closely. A final meal can be requested from a limited menu. A chaplain is present. A small group of witnesses from the press, from the victims family, from the defense, and from the state are placed in their assigned seats. The curtains are drawn back. In the minutes before the injection, the condemned may make a short statement. Teresa used her time to speak to the surviving stepdaughter and to express remorse. She asked for forgiveness. She thanked those who had supported her. There were a few moments of stillness and then the sequence began. The line was opened. The drugs did their work. At 9 13 in the evening on 23rd September 2010, the warden announced that the sentence had been carried out.

The immediate aftermath was quiet. Reporters filed brief accounts noting the time and place and including short quotes from official statements and from relatives on both sides. Supporters of clemency held a vigil outside the prison and sang hymns. Family members of the dead spoke of justice served. The body was released for cremation. By the next morning the story had moved from breaking news to analysis. Commentators returned to the themes that had occupied the airwaves for weeks. Did the sentence fit the person. Did the law apply fairly. What did the case say about the broader use of capital punishment in the state. For those who knew the family, the analysis did not matter. The practical work of grief is not improved by learned essays. It is done in kitchens where the chairs are now too many for the people left.

In the months and years that followed, the case remained a reference point. When Virginia later abolished capital punishment in 2021, historians noted that Teresa was the last woman executed in the state and the first female executed there since the early twentieth century. Opponents of capital punishment cited the case as an example of how the ultimate sanction can be imposed on a person with significant cognitive limitations and a record of abuse and addiction. Supporters of capital punishment responded that the case exemplified the narrow use of the penalty in the most aggravated circumstances. The public conversation did not produce consensus. It rarely does in matters that touch such deep moral chords. What it did produce was a shared recognition that an arrangement to pay for death in a family home can tear communities apart for a generation.

For the surviving relatives of Julian and Charles, the execution did not restore anything. It did however mark the end of formal proceedings. There were no more hearings to attend. No more statements to rehearse. No more sudden flashes of an old photograph on a nightly news broadcast. They still had to cross the parking lot of a grocery store where someone would remember the case and want to talk, but they no longer had to answer quietly to a clerk who asked whether another appeal would delay closure. In private, different family members reached different accommodations with the past. Some embraced a language of forgiveness without surrendering their sense of justice. Others closed the door on any further discussion of the woman who had arranged the deaths.

Within the faith community that had rallied to Teresa cause, the execution prompted reflection. Ministers who had argued for mercy used sermons to discuss the tensions between justice and forgiveness, between state power and individual sin, between the necessity of accountability and the possibility of redemption. Some parishioners felt relief that a painful story had ended. Others felt anger that the state had ended a life when another path was available. In letters and phone calls, volunteers who had visited the prison expressed sadness at the loss of a person they had come to know. They also described a resolve to continue prison ministry with the women who remained behind. Life in a correctional facility is measured in relationships. When one ends, the group must adjust.

More quietly, the case also altered the life of Teresa daughter. She had borne her own punishment for failing to act when she learned of the plan. Now she had to live with memories of her mother as both caretaker and condemned prisoner. Some journalists sought her out for interviews. She declined most of them, choosing to grieve in private. People in the region where she grew up respected that decision. They had watched the story unfold across a decade. They understood that not every part of it needed to be written down.

Legal scholars continued to examine the record as a study in the use of psychiatric evidence in capital sentencing. They noted that the courts had accepted the testing as valid but had concluded that the scores did not cross the legal bar that would remove a defendant from eligibility for the death penalty. They highlighted the gap that can exist between clinical categories and legal categories and the difficulty of communicating that distinction to a general public that hears numbers without the context of diagnostic manuals and case law. Some argued that the best way to avoid that confusion is to remove the death penalty altogether. Others argued that careful case by case attention could address the risk.

One last strand of reaction belonged to those who had investigated the case. Detectives and prosecutors rarely speak publicly after the work is done. When they did, they expressed a kind of weary empathy for everyone involved, even for the woman whose actions they had documented and whose conviction they had defended all the way to the high court. They had sat in the bedrooms where the shots were fired. They had listened to the first statements and seen the told you so scrawl of a cut window screen that never fooled anyone. They had watched a community shrink from the horror of betrayal in a family and then try to find itself again. In that experience they found little to celebrate. They found, instead, a confirmation of what had led them into public service in the first place. The work is not about catharsis. It is about honoring the dead by telling the truth.

The chapter of Teresa life that ended in 2010 leaves no easy moral lesson. It asks readers to hold conflicting truths at once. A woman who sang hymns with other inmates and wept over her past arranged deaths for money. A family that asked the state to carry out the sentence also struggled with the knowledge that nothing could give back a father and a son. A governor who rejected clemency encountered thousands of petitioners urging mercy and two justices who would have paused the process. The legal system that affirmed the sentence in final form later presided over the end of the death penalty in the same state. In that sequence can be found the great American argument about crime and punishment that never truly ends.

For true crime readers the case is compelling because it reveals how an ordinary place can become the stage for an extraordinary act. It shows how a simple financial instrument can be the hinge on which a lethal plan swings open. It shows how human weakness and calculation can coexist in one person in ways that do not fit easy categories. It shows how friends become strangers when a shared roof hides secrets. And it shows how the aftermath of a crime ripples outward for years, touching people who are many steps removed from the first violent act.

The last word in that aftermath must belong to the dead. Julian raised three children, put in long hours at a mill, and found contentment in routine.

Charles prepared to serve abroad and returned home for a visit to the people he loved. They died not because of a random act by strangers but because of a plan that grew in the very house where they napped and watched television and put away groceries. The public debate that followed their deaths may tell us something about law and politics and faith. Their lives remind us that the center of any case is not the arguments made around it but the lives lost at its core.

CHAPTER 4
JOSEPHINE GRAY

TWO DEAD HUSBANDS, ONE DEAD BOYFRIEND- THREE INSURANCE POLICIES PAID OUT.

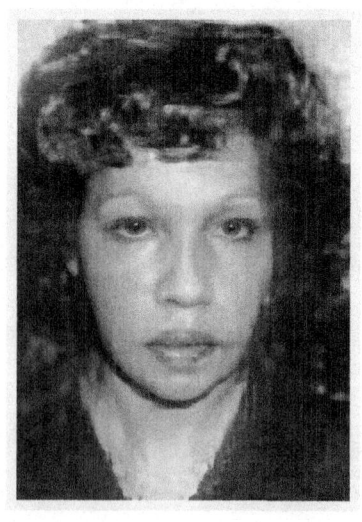

The story of Josephine Virginia Gray begins not in a courtroom but in ordinary neighborhoods where paychecks were stretched and families built their routines around schools, church calendars, and the long hours demanded by working life. Born in 1946, she came of age in a mid Atlantic corridor that was fast changing. Montgomery County and the city of Baltimore were drawing new residents from across the region as government and private employers expanded. Shopping centers and apartment complexes went up along major arteries. In the span of a few decades the quiet rural pockets diminished and commuter traffic grew into a steady hum. Against that backdrop Josephine formed relationships, raised children, and worked jobs that kept buildings clean and the lights on for others.

Those who would later investigate her life could verify a number of fixed points. She became a mother to a large family and a grandmother. She spent more than two decades as a custodian in the Montgomery County public school system, a job that placed her in schools before dawn and after the last buses had gone, mopping floors and stocking paper towels, knowing the schedules of teachers and coaches and the rhythms that come with a building that never fully sleeps. Coworkers remembered a woman who was often present and seldom idle, someone who could be found in hallways with a cart, a ring of keys at the ready, and a practiced awareness of who belonged in the building and who did not.

The work of a custodian is straightforward in description and demanding in practice. It is physical and quiet. In winter it means salt grit in the entry vestibules, water tracked in by boots, and heating systems that cough to life before students arrive. In spring it means wax, dust, pollen, and the strange mix of perfume and gym floor finish during awards nights. In summer it means scrubbing, moving furniture, and making sure rooms come back from the chaos of the year to a clean slate for the next class. Josephine knew these cycles. She earned a paycheck through them year after year, and that paycheck was an anchor for a household with many needs.

Family responsibilities extended far beyond her hours on the clock. The record shows that Josephine raised six children. Extended family visited and stayed. Nieces and nephews were part of the swirl. Grandchildren came along and the shape of her life widened to include school pick ups and holiday dinners, illnesses and celebrations. Anyone who has managed a large family knows the steady pressure to make ends meet, the constant churn of laundry, groceries, paperwork, and appointments. There were years when she balanced these demands while also maintaining friendships and romantic relationships that would later become the gravitational center of the public story about her life.

The neighborhoods where she lived mattered. In Montgomery County, census maps traced a landscape of subdivisions and garden apartments built along wide roads with turning lanes and service drives. In Baltimore you could move two blocks and the brickwork would change from rowhouses with marble steps to narrow streets where stoops sat almost on the curb. The traffic, the bus lines, the grocery stores, the corner carryouts, and the nearby churches gave shape to everyday life. Josephine lived in rentals and in houses that were bought with mortgages, typical of lives that rise and fall with work hours and credit reports. By the late nineteen eighties and early nineteen nineties she had lived long enough in the county to know the reputations of supervisors and the speed of rumor. She had relationships that went back years, and others that were new and charged.

In the early nineteen seventies Josephine married Norman Stribbling. Records of that union and the home they made in Montgomery County place her firmly in a community of working families. She moved through a network that included cousins and in laws, coworkers, and neighbors who shared fences and driveways. The marriage joined two lives with their own patterns and widened those circles. It also brought with it the challenges that many couples face when money is tight and jobs require sacrifice. The demands of shift work and the strain of competing obligations can wear on a household. Josephine understood what could be expected from a paycheck and what could not.

By the mid nineteen seventies, as public employment grew and the suburban footprint widened, Josephine became involved with a man named William Robert Gray. Their relationship did not begin in a vacuum. It unfolded in the familiar spaces of workplaces and neighborhoods. Over time the relationship deepened. After the end of her marriage to Stribbling, Josephine married Robert Gray. Marriage blended their families and finances and created a new center of gravity. They bought a house in Gaithersburg, a city that epitomized the county's rapid growth with its planned communities, shopping plazas, and access to major roads. Owning a home placed them squarely in a world of mortgage payments, homeowners insurance, and the steady math of monthly budgeting.

Insurance was part of that math. In the mid and late twentieth century life insurance policies were sold at kitchen tables and in modest office suites. Policyholders signed forms naming beneficiaries and listing addresses and occupations. The policies offered a promise that if tragedy struck, a policy payout could pay off a mortgage or bridge a gap for a surviving spouse. Josephine knew the language of premiums, beneficiaries, and riders. She had been on both sides of insurance paperwork as a spouse and as a beneficiary, and she understood the financial cushion these products were designed to provide.

Relationships within her household were layered. There were the ties between Josephine and Robert. Around them stood children whose needs were immediate and ongoing. Beyond them stood cousins and long time friends. Among those who passed through Josephine's life was a man named

Clarence Goode. He would become a romantic partner and a figure central to later events, but in these years his presence can be understood as part of the wider network of friends and relatives orbiting the household. He spent time with the family, ran errands, moved furniture, shared meals, and helped with the practical chores that mark close relationships.

This was a period when Josephine's public face was ordinary. She clocked in, clocked out, went home, and made meals. She looked after children and took calls. She knew the clerks at the local stores and likely could tell you which gas station had the better price that week. In apartment complexes she would have seen the same maintenance staff at work and known which neighbors kept to themselves and which were quick to ask questions. Her roots in the area deepened when she stayed, held jobs, and shepherded her children through school years. That continuity built familiarity and also allowed her to blend in without attracting undue attention.

To understand her place within her community it is useful to consider the moments that develop a reputation. A parent who brings snacks to a classroom party, a coworker who steps in to cover a shift, a neighbor who takes delivery of a package or keeps an eye on a child at the bus stop becomes known for reliability. Others are remembered for their temper, their gossip, or their flakiness. The record portrays Josephine as someone who could project assurance and control. People remembered a woman who could keep a straight face, maintain eye contact, and speak with authority about household and work matters. That demeanor helped her in everyday life and would later influence how those around her interpreted her words.

The spiritual and cultural elements that would later be described by witnesses were also part of the world she inhabited. In many communities in the mid Atlantic corridor, Christian practice was strong and closely woven into daily life. At the same time, strands of folk belief and ritual moved alongside formal religion. Stories about charms, candles, and rituals circulated through families. Some people believed in them. Others laughed them off. Within Josephine's circles there were acquaintances who believed she drew power from ritual acts and that crossing her could bring consequences. Whether these beliefs were accurate or exaggerated, they mattered because they shaped the willingness of people around her to speak publicly and to stand their ground. The idea that someone has hidden power can be as potent as any objective proof when the person believed to have that power carries herself with confidence.

The economic facts of Josephine's life are plain. A custodian's wages cover a household when other sources of money are present or when expenses are carefully managed. When children need clothes and teenagers ask for money and a car note comes due, the budget is a living thing that requires attention and sometimes help from beyond a single paycheck. Insurance money, tax refunds, overtime hours, and informal loans from relatives can become crucial. She knew the value of every dollar and knew how to extract value from relationships, whether by asking for a favor, pressing a point, or presenting a plan with the tone of someone who had already decided.

By the late nineteen eighties and early nineteen nineties, Josephine was not a young woman trying to find her footing. She was an adult with a long work history, a mother to grown and nearly grown children, and a person with deep connections through family and romance. Her living arrangements reflected that maturity. She lived at addresses that became known to friends and to the people who later investigated her life. She hosted relatives. She kept vehicles registered and inspected. She moved furniture in and out and maintained storage areas in basements and garages. These are the building blocks of a settled life.

The way Josephine navigated conflict also emerged over time. People in her orbit remembered long arguments, disputes over possessions, and fierce loyalty to those she favored. Disagreements over money or possessions could take on an outsized importance. Arguments that began with something small could grow. Those who knew her learned not to underestimate her will. When she set her mind on an outcome she looked for the leverage available. Sometimes it was charm and patience. Sometimes it was pressure applied through others. At other times it was a simple refusal to yield.

Her pattern of forming close ties with men who became central to her life is also clear. Norman Stribbling was a husband and a provider within the limits of his means. He represented a version of stability and obligation that came with a shared household and shared duties. William Robert Gray, known to friends and relatives as Robert, provided a different kind of partnership. With him came the purchase of a home and a new structure of bills and assets. Clarence Goode presented yet another kind of relationship. He was a partner whose presence in the household blurred family and romance, someone who could be counted on for help and also someone who demanded attention and loyalty of his own.

These relationships existed within a legal and financial framework that was not abstract at all. Mortgages were written with insurance requirements. Life insurance policies were sold with forms designating beneficiaries and conditions. When a policyholder died, the companies paid out in accordance with law and contract. If the policy language made a bank the primary beneficiary to satisfy a mortgage, the bank would be paid first. If there was an excess benefit beyond the mortgage balance, that amount would be disbursed to the spouse. With other policies that paid a lump sum to a named beneficiary, the company would verify the death and the identity of the beneficiary before cutting a check. Josephine had occasion to see how quickly money could move when the paperwork was in order.

By the mid nineteen nineties she had also experienced how suspicion collected around her. In workplaces, rumors can linger. In family networks, grievances accumulate. People talk. When a person projects confidence and insists on her version of events, some accept it without question while others grow more doubtful. Josephine's insistence and her ability to put on a composed front meant that even skeptical observers had trouble piercing her presentation. That quality would later be described by people who said she could sit for an interview without flinching, recounting events in a flat tone that discouraged interruption.

This section of her life story ends with a woman in late middle age who has built a reputation for being unflappable, who has raised a large family, and who has maintained an employment record that stretches across decades. She has owned and sold a house and kept close connections with men who knew her well. She has become the person others in her family call when something breaks or when news needs to be shared. She is the person who answers the phone late at night and assures the caller that she will handle it. People who admire her see steadiness. People who fear her see willpower with edges.

To understand the choices and events that would later define her in the eyes of the public, it helps to picture the rooms she inhabited. A kitchen with linoleum worn smooth by feet, a table piled with mail and school forms, a garage with a workbench and a vacuum cleaner, a living room with a television and family photos arranged on top of a console. Picture the keys on a ring and the calendar on a wall with bills clipped beneath it. Picture the trunk of a car loaded with groceries or boxes. Picture a purse with a wallet, a checkbook, and everyday items that become significant only when police later inventory them. These settings are where her life unfolded. They are the spaces where decisions were made, confidences were exchanged, and plans took shape.

When investigators later mapped the connections among the people closest to Josephine they found that the map resembled a family tree drawn over a neighborhood street plan. Names they had heard from one relative showed up at an address linked to another. Timelines overlapped not just in dates but in places where cars were seen and calls were made. In that web Josephine was usually at the center, the person whose schedule touched all the others. It is in that centrality that her power rested. She was the one who knew who had a key, who had a copy of an insurance statement, who had left a jacket in the hall closet with a pay stub in the pocket. She knew the value of these details and she used them. That is not speculation. It is the natural conclusion drawn from a pattern of conduct that those around her recognized and described.

These years formed the bedrock of what came next. A steady job, a network of family and partners, a home with a mortgage, and an intimate familiarity with the ways money arrives and leaves a household. A person with these elements in place is well positioned to manage crises and to profit from opportunities. Josephine's story would ultimately be told through the lens of criminal courts. Before that, it was the story of a woman who seemed to master the rules of everyday life so completely that others either leaned on her or learned to keep a careful distance.

THE MURDERS

The first death that would be linked to Josephine Virginia Gray happened on a cold morning in early March of 1974. A Montgomery County patrol officer working the pre dawn hours was sent to check a car parked at an odd angle along River Road. The vehicle's engine was off and there were no hazard lights flashing on the shoulder. When the officer approached, he found the driver slumped to the side with a wound to the head. The man was identified as Norman Stribbling. The medical examiner later documented a single gunshot wound to the right side of the head. There were no signs of a struggle inside the car beyond the sudden, violent end that the bullet made plain. The scene had the stillness that attends this kind of death. No shell casing was immediately visible in the dim light. The exterior of the car showed no collision damage. Personal items were in place in the passenger compartment. The first reports that morning read like many such reports across the country. A body. A wound. A call to detectives.

Detectives began with the facts they could secure quickly. They documented the position of the car, the direction of the front wheels, the state of the ignition, the placement of the victim's keys, wallet, and watch. They photographed the wound. They learned from family who the man was and from colleagues where he worked. They asked who had seen him last. They began the difficult task that homicide units undertake every day. They sought the chain of events that brought a living person to an abrupt stop on the side of a road. In the weeks that followed, two people would later tell authorities that, on separate occasions, Josephine had asked them to help her get rid of Norman. Their accounts described solicitations rather than spur of the moment anger. Those accounts would never be tested in a criminal trial at the time. What did happen is that an insurance company processed a claim and cut a check in the amount of sixteen thousand dollars to the named beneficiary on Norman Stribbling's life policy. That beneficiary was Josephine.

Years later, when federal prosecutors presented a sweeping financial case, jurors heard the bare facts of that first killing in the cadence of courtroom testimony. The autopsy was summarized. The shot to the head. The location along River Road. The insurance records showing the policy in force and the payment to the widow. Jurors also learned that witnesses had described earlier attempts to recruit help to murder Norman, but that state charges did not lead to a conviction. The reasons sat in the shadows of a world where silence can be purchased with fear and where those who might talk find reasons to avoid the witness chair. For the officers who responded in 1974, the file was a homicide without a defendant who could be brought to a verdict. It stayed that way for a long time.

The second killing nearly seventeen years later presented similarities and differences that would only become significant when investigators laid the files side by side. The victim was William Robert Gray, known to family members as Robert. He had left the Gaithersburg house he shared with Josephine in August of 1990 and had settled in an apartment of his own. He told relatives and friends that he feared for his safety. He told police that his wife had attacked him and that a man close to her had pointed a handgun at him. He went so far as to file criminal complaints that brought him into a courtroom and put those accusations into the record. On a day in October, after appearing in court on those complaints, he told police that he had been chased in a vehicle and that when Josephine pulled alongside his car the man in her passenger seat sat up and pointed a gun at him. A warrant issued for their arrest. The calendar ticked toward a trial date in mid November. Before that date arrived, Robert Gray was found in his new apartment, shot twice with a large caliber handgun. He had kept a detective's card in his pocket, a small paper square that said plainly that he expected to need police help again.

The scene at the apartment showed no evidence of a long struggle. He had been shot in the chest and in the neck. A homicide like that narrows possibilities. It argues an episode at close range. It suggests that the shooter was someone who knew the victim well enough to be in a room with him, or someone who surprised him at the door. Friends and relatives did not hesitate to tell investigators what Robert had said in the weeks before his death. He had told them he feared Josephine. He had described the earlier attack with a club and a knife. He had reported the brandishing of a handgun. He had gone to court to name names and he had asked for help. He had changed some of his life insurance beneficiary designations in an effort to cut Josephine out of those policies. On others, including a policy tied to the mortgage on the Gaithersburg house, the beneficiary arrangement could not be changed in the same way. That mattered.

Detectives interviewed Josephine. She denied involvement in the murder. She denied owning a handgun of the type that killed him. Witnesses recalled a different picture. They told police they had seen her with a 45 caliber handgun. Investigators eventually recovered a bullet of that caliber from her purse. She offered an alibi that others undercut. The case had the elements that prosecutors rely upon. Motive in the form of insurance proceeds and relief from an ongoing domestic battle. Opportunity in the form of access that comes with marriage and shared life. Evidence that linked her to a weapon of the type used in the killing. Yet as with the earlier murder, charges brought by county prosecutors did not lead to a resolution. Witnesses faltered. The case did not go to verdict. Outside the courtroom, however, the financial machinery moved. An insurance company that had issued a mortgage protection policy paid more than fifty one thousand dollars to the bank that held the mortgage on the Gaithersburg home. Once the mortgage was satisfied the house was sold at a profit. Another insurer that had issued an accidental death policy resisted paying benefits to Josephine because state law disqualifies a beneficiary who wrongfully causes the death of an insured. That company took the unusual step of filing an interpleader action in court to let a judge direct the funds to the proper party. Years later, after a contested legal process, that company sent Josephine a much smaller payment than the policy limits. Her pursuit of the money created a paper trail that would later be central to a federal prosecution.

The third killing occurred in Baltimore on the first day of summer in nineteen ninety six. The victim was Clarence Goode. His body was discovered in the trunk of his car. He had been shot in the back of the head with a 9mm handgun. He had told relatives that he was going to see Josephine. He had also reported to police months before that she had assaulted him and threatened him with a knife. When officers executed a search warrant at Josephine's home in the weeks after his death they found an alarming stain on the concrete floor of the garage. Testing indicated that the stain was blood. Near it sat a commercial grade vacuum cleaner. Small amounts of what appeared to be blood were collected from the vacuum. The scene suggested that a body had bled in that space and that efforts had been made to clean the area. It suggested a crime of planning and aftermath rather than an impulsive event that left visible chaos. In that same period an insurer had sent notices that a life policy on Goode carried a grace period before lapse for nonpayment. Mail to Goode was delivered to Josephine's address. Within that window of time the killing occurred. The policy named Josephine as beneficiary. A claim was filed. The company resisted payment because the circumstances were suspicious. Unable to secure an arrest that would settle the matter in criminal court, the company filed its own interpleader case. In the end it paid almost the entire policy proceeds to Josephine and the remainder to Goode's minor son.

These three deaths look different if viewed through separate windows, divided across decades and jurisdictions. A lone man in a car on the side of a road in the 1970's. An estranged husband shot in an apartment weeks after he had appeared in court to accuse his wife and her companion of violence. A boyfriend stuffed in his own trunk in the nineteen nineties, with blood in a garage and a vacuum nearby. The differences are clear. Yet the common threads are also plain. Each man had ties to Josephine. Each man had either told others of fear or had been the subject of accounts that pointed to threats and violence. Each man had an insurance policy with a beneficiary designation that placed Josephine in line to collect. Each death involved a firearm at close range. Each death generated insurance claim files and correspondence that would outlast the fear and silence that halted earlier local prosecutions.

The way the murders were framed to different audiences tells part of the story. In the immediate aftermath of Norman Stribbling's death, those who knew him were told that it looked like a robbery gone wrong. That phrase serves a purpose. It points attention outward rather than inward. It suggests a random crime committed by a stranger on a lonely road. In the months after Robert Gray's death, the picture was harder to paint as random. He had warned others that he expected to be killed. He had gone to police. He had placed a business card in his pocket as if to carry the presence of a detective with him when he went home at night. In the days after Clarence Goode was killed and left in a trunk, the message that filtered through some circles was that he had angered people in Baltimore and paid a price. That kind of story travels easily. It leans on stereotypes about city violence. It moves attention away from a garage floor forty miles to the west.

Physical evidence in these killings was both abundant and frustrating. The stain on the garage floor in 1996 was powerful. So was the presence of a vacuum with traces of blood. Those items told a story without words. Yet they did not point to a single person with absolute certainty. The bullet caliber in 1990 was specific and matched witness testimony that Josephine had possessed such a weapon. The cartridge later found in her purse made that match stronger. Yet it demanded that witnesses appear and withstand cross examination. The financial documents were clean and indisputable. The claim forms were in her name with her handwriting and her signature. The calls logged by insurers documented her inquiries and requests. In a strict financial sense those documents were not evidence of murder. They were evidence of money sought and received. When prosecutors finally grouped the murders and the claim files into a single mosaic, the power of the pattern became their argument.

The third killing in particular showed elements of planning that go beyond the instant when a trigger is pulled. Clarence Goode's premiums had fallen behind because his bank account had been closed. The insurer sent a letter explaining the grace period during which the policy would remain in force. That letter was delivered to Josephine's address. The killing happened before the grace period expired. The beneficiary named in the application was Josephine. The file contains the claim she submitted and legal papers she later filed in the interpleader case. The trunk where his body lay had been closed by someone who knew how to conceal a body long enough to make a call to police less likely before night fell. The garage stain and the vacuum suggested that the body had bled in a familiar space and that the person who cleaned the floor had time to wheel out a machine, plug it in, and apply suction in a methodical way. That kind of cleanup is not the work of a panicked stranger. It is the work of someone who believes she can control the narrative that will follow.

The second killing came freighted with warnings that the victim had spoken aloud. Robert Gray told people he knew he might be murdered. He filed complaints. He showed up in a courthouse, the place where private trouble turns public. He stood there and made his accusation and then walked back to his car. That is not the profile of a man who is inattentive to risk. It is the profile of a man who is doing what he can with the tools the law offers. That he was found shot before the next court date is a fact that moved prosecutors to describe purpose. When a witness is silenced between one court date and the next, the inference that the killing was intended to remove a voice is not speculative. It is the gravitational pull of the timeline.

The first killing retains the most mystery because of the passage of time and the limits of forensic tools available in the 1970's. The single shot to the head, the parked car, the position of the body, and the immediate lack of suspects gave it the feel of a roadside robbery or a personal execution in a remote spot. Through the lens of later cases and later testimony, the early reports about Josephine sounding out acquaintances for help to kill Norman become the bridge between what could not be proved then and what later witnesses would describe. It is the nature of some stories to make sense only after the third time the cycle repeats.

Firearms are part of this story not because they are mysterious but because they do exactly what they are designed to do. A handgun at close range is final. In the two killings in the 90's the choice of a forty five caliber and a 9mm is telling. Those are common calibers. Ammunition for them is widely available. Possession of such a weapon is not in itself a suspicious fact in a region where many people own firearms. What matters is how the weapons turn up in the accounts that surround the deaths. A witness saw a 45 caliber handgun in Josephine's possession. A bullet of that caliber turned up in her purse. Another witness described a 9mm being used by a man close to Josephine to intimidate Robert. When Clarence was killed, a 9mm round to the head ended his life. The kinds of weapons and the times they were mentioned in fear and in violence tighten the weave.

Insurance is the other constant that gives these killings their pattern. Each of the three men had life insurance policies active at the time of death. Each policy named Josephine or designated a beneficiary that would benefit her directly or indirectly. After Norman's death a check for sixteen thousand dollars went to Josephine. After Robert's death, a mortgage protection policy paid the bank and freed equity in a house that was sold, and another policy sparked legal proceedings in which Josephine asserted her right to funds that an insurer did not want to pay because of her suspected role in his death. After Clarence's death, a one hundred thousand dollar policy led to litigation in which the company sought a court's direction and then, through a settlement, paid ninety nine thousand nine hundred ninety dollars to Josephine and the remainder to Clarence's minor son. When federal prosecutors later alleged mail and wire fraud, they did not need to solve every question in the homicides. They needed to show that she had intentionally caused two of those deaths and then used the mail and the telephone to claim policy proceeds despite a legal doctrine that bars killers from profiting from their crimes.

The administrative acts surrounding the deaths made their own imprint. Claim forms were mailed. Calls were placed to ask about double indemnity provisions. Address confirmations were made. In one instance, years after a mortgage had been paid, an insurer followed up to locate a spouse who was owed a balance. That inquiry led Josephine to ask whether an accidental death provision would increase the payout. Her question was specific and practical. It assumed that the death could be treated as accidental. The gulf between that question and the allegations that she arranged the killing is the gulf between paper and blood. The paper sat in files and could be retrieved. The blood washed down a drain in a garage and left a dark stain that investigators would later see and document.

Silence is the last element that ties the murders together. After Norman's killing, those who might have spoken did not. After Robert's killing, those who had accused Josephine and her companion on paper did not carry their accusations to a final verdict. After Clarence's killing, those who knew the most either stayed quiet or were not persuaded to lay their evidence before a jury. In each case the absence of sworn, sustained testimony allowed the years to pass without a murder conviction. Yet in each case the acts after death were loud in their own way. An insurer cannot avoid writing a check while waiting for an arrest forever. A bank cannot hold a loan balance open when a policy calls for a payoff. A claims department cannot suspend a file indefinitely because investigators express doubt. The world of money continues even when the world of prosecution stalls. Those continuing movements left tracks that future investigators could follow.

By the time federal agents and prosecutors assembled these tracks into a single narrative for a jury, the murder scenes themselves were old. The car on River Road was long gone. The Gaithersburg apartment had been turned over to new tenants. The Baltimore trunk had been towed and cleaned. The garage floor had aged and the vacuum had long since been unplugged. What remained were photographs, measurements, autopsy reports, sworn statements, and the ledger of payments that had been made when claims were approved. It is a paradox of violent crime that the physical drama is brief and the paperwork is endless. In Josephine's case the paperwork gave the government tools that the fear and silence of earlier years had denied to county prosecutors. It also gave a documentary spine to a story that had been told in whispers long before anyone put a formal title on a case file.

The murders, viewed together, present a portrait of calculation. That does not erase the human details at their center. Norman was a husband who ended his day with an errand or a drive and did not return. Robert was a man who believed that raising his hand in a courtroom and saying plainly what he feared would save him, and who died with a detective's card in his pocket anyway. Clarence was a partner who thought he could manage complex loyalties and found himself trapped in a trunk in a different city.

Each death left children and siblings who had to bury their confusion beside their grief. Each death left households that had to be packed up and emptied. Each death left a circle of friends who had to decide whether to keep their memories to themselves or speak them aloud.

The documentary record of the killings does not deliver catharsis. It offers a ledger of acts. A bullet here. A claim there. A call logged. A check cut. A stain photographed. A signature notarized. A warning ignored. A court date that was never reached. It is in that ledger that the shape of what happened becomes visible to those who did not live through the fear directly. It is that ledger that allows a jury many years later to look across the span from nineteen seventy four to nineteen ninety six and say that where there were once three separate tragedies there is in fact a repeated method. The method is to end a life, to deny involvement, and to collect.

In the end, this chapter is the record of how three men died and how the aftermath of those deaths was managed by the person who stood to gain from their policies. It is the record of how killings that began as sudden violence became part of a longer plan to turn death into money. It is also the record of a woman who kept her face steady when asked about it and who learned how to make systems designed to provide comfort to the bereaved work for her instead. The details that give weight to that conclusion are not imaginative embroidery. They are the verifiable points left behind by guns, by bodies, and by forms filled out in ink.

ARREST, TRIAL AND SENTENCE

When the federal case opened in Greenbelt in the final months of 2001, it did not begin the way most homicide stories do. There was no murder count at the top of the indictment and no state detective sworn to recount a step by step knock and talk that ended in handcuffs. The paper that described the government's case used another vocabulary altogether. It spoke of schemes, of mailings, of telephone calls, of claim forms and notarized statements, and of a body of state law that disqualifies a killer from taking the benefit of a policy written on the person they have killed. It was a financial case in its shell, but inside that shell were the same grim facts of three violent deaths that local prosecutors had carried for years.

The arrest on the federal charges took place on a December day. By then

Josephine had been a familiar name in Montgomery County case logs since the 1970's. She was in her mid fifties, a mother and a grandmother, long employed as a custodian in the school system. She had seen homicide detectives before and knew where chairs were placed in interview rooms. This time the charging papers came from the United States Attorney's Office. The counts were for mail and wire fraud arising from claims on life policies after the deaths of two men. The jury that would eventually hear that case would not be asked to return a murder verdict. It would be asked whether she filed claims and made representations to insurers while having intentionally caused deaths that created those claims. The government called this the slayer rule frame. It fit the evidence investigators already had and it answered the recurring problem that had stalled state prosecutions. The federal case did not need to produce a unanimous verdict on a charge of first degree murder. It needed to convince jurors that she had a role in the killings and used the mail and the telephone to profit, making her not only ineligible to collect but criminally responsible for the fraudulent scheme.

At the first detention hearing federal prosecutors pressed a theme that had followed the name Josephine Gray through three decades of police work. Witnesses were afraid. Some had recanted in the past. Others had moved or stopped answering calls. Prosecutors told the court that officers who searched the family home years earlier found dolls with pins and other ritual objects that had fueled rumors of voodoo and hexes. They told the judge that a wiretap had captured a ritual in which names of police investigators were spoken and harm was wished upon them. They told the court that a boyfriend had been warned to remain silent. They argued that the fear that had permeated old state cases would resurface if she were released. The judge ordered her held without bond. That decision mattered. Witnesses began returning calls. Some said plainly that their fear had eased because she was in custody.

From the outset the federal strategy was to pull the curtain back on the financial aftermath of two of the deaths. Investigators had spent months combing insurance archives. They obtained claim forms bearing her signature. They secured recordings and logs of calls to insurance offices. They requested files from law firms that had represented her in civil interpleader actions years earlier. They located checks and cover letters that documented the flow of funds. They interviewed a woman who had become close to

Josephine in the year 2000, a woman who would later tell a jury that Josephine had spoken to her in a flat tone and said that she had killed both husbands and a man who had helped her. They compiled testimony from witnesses who had in prior years described solicitations to kill a first husband, who had described seeing a particular caliber handgun in her possession, who had been approached to supply an alibi. Forensic reports from the older files were refreshed and summarized. Each piece of this record had existed for years. Together they made a story that a federal jury could follow even though the courtroom would not hear a count labeled murder.

In January of 2002 Montgomery County prosecutors made their own move. They filed new murder charges for the deaths of the two husbands. They did so with the knowledge that a federal case based on fraud would run on a separate track and that the standard of proof and the rules of evidence would be policed by a different bench. The county state's attorney explained publicly that the calculation had changed because witnesses had found the courage to speak while Josephine remained in custody. The newspapers printed again the nickname that neighbors and former coworkers used in whispers. It had traveled from one tabloid headline to another for years. It was meant to signify calculation dressed in charm. It also carried the uglier undertone of a trope long used to sensationalize the crimes of women who kill. What mattered to the county office was not a nickname. It was that for the first time since the nineteen seventies they believed they could take their cases past arraignment and survive long enough to select a jury.

The fraud case nevertheless moved first. That was not a slight to the state case. It was a recognition that the federal indictment did not rely for its elements on the cooperation of every witness who had wavered in the past. If a witness became unwilling to testify in detail about a night on River Road in the nineteen seventies, the federal theory did not collapse. The files contained the autopsy findings. The insurance company had already printed a check to the named beneficiary decades earlier. If a witness flinched at the thought of describing in open court the brandishing of a handgun three decades ago, the federal case could advance along its financial rails. That calculation led both offices to the same place. Try the fraud counts, establish the deliberate causation of two deaths through the civil disability doctrine, and hold the state case back until after. If the federal jury convicted,

Josephine would be in custody for years. That would further steady the state witnesses. If the federal jury acquitted, the state could reassess what would remain.

The trial in Greenbelt began in late July of 2002. The court imposed a gag order that kept lawyers from speaking broadly to television crews outside the building. Inside the courtroom the rules were as they always are. Openings with no argument. Witnesses under oath. Objections and sidebars. No camera lens was trained on the jurors to capture their reactions, but the transcript records where they heard laughter and where they leaned forward. The prosecution's theme was stark. This was a book of chapters, the lead prosecutor said. Some of those chapters were written in blood. He then set about reading the financial ones into the record.

The government called an array of witnesses whose presence underlined the nature of the case. There were claims managers from insurers who explained how benefits are calculated and paid and how a company decides to seek a court's help when a beneficiary is under suspicion. There were bank representatives who could authenticate records of mortgage payoffs and property sales. There were medical examiners who reviewed older files in clinical language, reading cause and manner of death from reports and photographs. There were police officers who recounted what a man had told them in the weeks before he was shot and what they found in a Gaithersburg apartment and what they saw on a garage floor. There was a former Montgomery County prosecutor who admitted plainly from the witness chair that fear had saturated the earlier state cases to the point that witnesses vanished and charges were dismissed.

The woman who had befriended Josephine in 2000 took the stand and told the jurors about a conversation that had chilled her. She described the matter of fact tone, the lack of remorse, the description of a first husband shot during a ride and a body left in a place where it would look like robbery, the admission that a second husband had been killed with help, the claim that the helper later tried to extort money and had to be removed as well. The defense pressed her on motives. Why come forward now. What had she gained. She held her ground on the central point. She said Josephine had said those words to her. The jurors had to decide whether they believed her.

A legal fight threaded through the trial over the admission of evidence about the older killing and about what the second husband had told others.

The court allowed limited testimony about the first husband's death under the rule that permits proof of other acts when offered to show motive and intent rather than character. The judge kept tight control, admitting what was necessary to understand the alleged scheme and excluding what would draw the jury into a full blown retrial of a 1974 homicide. On the statements of the second husband, the court applied the principle that a defendant who renders a witness unavailable cannot complain that his out of court statements reach the jury. The judge found by a preponderance that the timing and context of the killing supported the inference that one purpose of the crime was to keep that man from walking into a courtroom again. On that foundation the jury was allowed to hear that he had reported attacks and threats and had carried a detective's card for help that never came.

The defense responded with a portrait of Josephine that diverged sharply from the prosecution's image of a manipulator moving lovers and policies like pieces on a game board. They said she was a three time victim who had endured the worst kind of loss and had been the target of tunnel vision by investigators who wanted the easy narrative of a woman profiting from death. They called her a mother and a worker with a long employment history. They said the government's case was built on gossip, rumor, and innuendo. They argued that the insurers had no true property interest in policy proceeds and that at most their claims amounted to a civil dispute dressed as crime. They pressed that every murder count that had been brought in state court had fallen apart. They told the jury to question why, if the proof was so clear, the government was not trying a murder case in the building across the street.

The prosecutors patiently walked the jurors through the legal definitions that made the financial case criminal. A scheme to defraud can be proved by concealment as well as by outright lies. The victims of the fraud were the companies and the courts that had been deprived of control over their funds by her failure to disclose that she had caused the conditions precedent for payment. They supplemented those definitions with illustrations from other cases where arsonists collect fire payouts or drivers stage collisions for hospitalization checks. Fraud, they said, is not only about fabrication. It is also about hiding what matters most while demanding money.

A striking moment came when a former defense attorney took the stand after the court allowed the government to reopen the proof to show mailing.

He testified in simple terms that he had mailed specific pleadings from his office in Rockville to a court clerk in Baltimore. That kind of small brick can be crucial in a mail fraud case because each count rests on a particular use of mail or wire. The defense objected to the reopening, but the judge allowed it after finding no unfair surprise. That ruling would be upheld on appeal.

When the jury retired to deliberate, the binders of exhibits included policy declarations, checks, claim forms, telephone logs, transcripts of prior testimony, photographs of a bloodstain and a vacuum, and the sets of instructions that explain the elements of fraud. They returned with guilty verdicts on all counts. It was a clean sweep for the prosecution. The court set a sentencing date and ordered a presentence report. In interviews after the verdicts, which were limited because of the gag order, team members from federal and local agencies spoke politely about cooperation. The joint effort had been years in the making. It had finally produced a verdict in a courtroom where verdicts stick.

The sentencing hearing became its own legal battleground. The question was how to translate a fraud conviction into years in prison when the conduct in question involved homicide. The guidelines contained a cross reference that permits a judge to use the murder guideline if the offense conduct includes deliberate killing. The court made the finding that the two deaths at the center of the federal counts were premeditated and used the murder guideline as the starting point. As an alternate path to the same range, the court applied enhancements for multiple victims and for the possession of a firearm and then departed upward because the fraud had been bound to homicide. Either way the result was the same. The court set the term at forty years. The judge spoke plainly that the sentence was driven by the deaths, not just by the forms that were mailed and the calls that were placed.

An appeal followed. The defense argued that the evidence was insufficient to show that the insurers had any property interest in the benefits and that the proof did not establish a fraudulent intent toward one of the companies. They challenged the decision to let the government reopen to prove mailings. They attacked the admission of testimony about the first husband's murder and the admission of the second husband's out of court statements. A three judge panel heard argument and issued an opinion that upheld the convictions on every point. The court wrote that the fraud statutes protect a victim's right to control the disposition of assets and that the companies had lost money in fact and had lost the right to decide who should have it under the law. The court also upheld the evidentiary rulings, concluding that the first husband's death was relevant to motive and that the second husband's statements were admissible because the killing had been intended at least in part to prevent his testimony.

The panel vacated the sentence and sent the case back for a new hearing. In the months between the original sentencing and the decision on appeal, the Supreme Court had ruled that the federal guidelines could not be applied as mandatory and that facts that increased a sentence had to be handled within that framework. The appellate court held that the district judge had committed plain error under that new rule by treating the guidelines as binding. The case returned to the trial court. On remand the same judge considered the now advisory guidelines and the broader statutory factors that guide a sentencing court. The judge reached the same place. The forty year term was reimposed. The court explained that whether one used the cross reference to the murder guideline or a series of enhancements and departures, the appropriate range remained unchanged because the fraud rested on premeditated killings. The judge took account of age and health and family ties as the law requires. The answer remained the same. The financial scheme existed because men were dead. The criminal punishment would reflect that.

At the same time, the state murder charges continued to drift in and out of the calendar. Witnesses who had found their voices after the federal detention now faced the prospect of reliving events in a different courtroom with a different standard. In that arena the defense would be entitled to hammer again at inconsistencies and the passage of years. The county office had to weigh the costs of a second full trial in light of a federal sentence that would keep Josephine in custody into old age. The public record shows that the murder counts did not overtake the federal case. The state could still point to the federal judgment and say that at last there had been accountability tied to the acts that shaped three families. It was not a murder verdict. It was a verdict that said the law recognized what had been suspected for so long.

The years after the resentencing saw additional appellate motions and collateral petitions. One significant pleading was drawn from the Supreme Court's decision that had shifted the sentencing law. The argument was that a woman whose sentence had been crafted under a now advisory system should have relief. The trial court had already addressed that point and had made clear that the same term would be imposed under either regime because the facts that mattered most were the deaths that animated the fraud. In those years federal agents and local detectives who had spent careers pushing this case watched from a distance as the legal process settled.

In the federal case file there is a list of allegations that did not become necessary to the verdict. It contains a reference to an attempt to obtain insurance on a man who was dating Josephine in the years after the third killing. It contains notes of calls made to an agent in another state to ask about policy terms. It contains the cut thin edge of a plan that did not fully form. The record shows that when agents interviewed a friend who had heard the inquiry she immediately asked about that man's safety. The prosecutors did not need to take that sliver to a jury. The scheme they charged had enough weight without it. The list of what was not used is a reminder that a courtroom story is never the whole story. It is the story the law can tell.

The most striking aspect of the trial and sentencing may be how ordinary much of it looked. A fraud indictment reads like dozens of others. A claims manager is not a character out of crime fiction. A bank officer is not a dramatic lead. A clerk whose job is to time stamp a pleading is rarely described as a star witness. Yet those voices were enough to carry this case to a place that three decades of fear and silence had never reached. The law sometimes makes its way to a just result by taking a narrow road when the wider one is blocked. Here the narrow road was the law of mail and wire fraud. The wider road, the one with the word murder painted on its surface, had washed out repeatedly. In Greenbelt the narrow road held.

The sentence fixed not only the term of years but also a judgment about what happened to the men whose names formed the backbone of the case. It said that their deaths were not misfortune or coincidence. It said they were the engines that drove a plan to extract money from policies that are supposed to shield families from hardship. It said that the person who stood to benefit from those policies made the deaths happen. That was as close as the law could come to a murder verdict in that courtroom. It was close enough to keep a place for them in the official record as victims of deliberate killing rather than as names in an actuarial ledger.

When the marshals led Josephine from the courtroom after resentencing, the women and men who had worked the file returned to offices where other cases waited. Some of them would retire. Others would be promoted. A few would take their experience from this case and help build training programs that teach how to look at financial paper when bodies lie in old files and witnesses are scattered or afraid. That is the quieter legacy of this prosecution. It shows how the overlap of fraud and homicide can give a community a measure of justice even when the most direct path is obstructed. It also shows why persistence matters. The first murder in this story was committed in 1974. The resentencing that fixed the final term was entered in 2006. Between those dates are the lives of three men that ended and the lives of their families that bent around that loss.

The docket lines that close the federal case do not capture the human cost. They do not record the sound of a mother asking why no one could protect her son when he had done everything right by calling the police. They do not record the weight carried by a child who grew up hearing two versions of how a father died, the one whispered at home and the one told by the street. They do not record the exhaustion in the voice of a detective who read through four boxes of old files in a windowless room because a young prosecutor wanted to know whether any thread had been missed. But the docket lines do mark a finality that had been missing. They mark a point at which the state and the federal government could say that this was not just a run of bad luck in a circle of lovers. It was a deliberate conversion of death into cash. The forty year sentence says that for the law, and for the record, that is what it was.

AFTERMATH WITH FAMILY AND PUBLIC OPINION

The courtrooms went quiet after the resentencing, but the case did not end in the minds of the people who had lived inside it. It lingered in family kitchens where framed photos sat next to small memorial candles. It persisted in police squad rooms where new detectives flipped through training binders and saw this file used as a model for how to bring an old case to ground when direct charges meet the wall of time and fear. It surfaced in conversations among claims managers who were young staffers when the first checks went out and who, years later, retold this matter to teach what due diligence looks like when a beneficiary is accused by rumor and by affidavit. It entered the quiet routines of a prison where one more inmate served a very long term for crimes that were defined on paper as frauds and on the human ledger as deaths.

Families measure aftermaths in the smallest things. In one family it was a tool a man used on weekends to repair a porch. In another it was a suit jacket left on the back of a chair near a front door. In another it was a car that sat in a driveway because the person who drove it would not return. Those objects do not appear in appellate opinions. They are the evidence that never leaves a house, the proof that loss is daily and unspectacular and also impossible to escape. The relatives of the men whose names anchored the federal counts had lived for years with uncertainty and with community narratives that were loose and often cruel. Some neighbors had said a man should have known better. Others had said the police would never take the risk to refile charges. A few had called the deaths a curse. After the federal verdict and sentence, those families could point to a judgment that spelled out a finding that deliberate acts had set the insurance machinery in motion. It was not a murder conviction in a state court. It was something they could hold up when old rumors bubbled. It was an official text that said the deaths were not bad luck.

For the Montgomery County police who had inherited a cold first file and a complicated second one, the aftermath meant a change in posture. Detectives who had surrounded witnesses in the early 1990's, and watched them falter could now tell new recruits what went wrong and what survived. They could explain that a statement taken from a man who later could not testify might still reach a jury if a judge found that he had been silenced to keep him from court. They could describe that delicate distinction between a sloppy resort to other acts evidence and a targeted admission that tells a jury why an intent to hide and profit is not an accident. They could describe the power of small details that the financial case captured as a matter of routine. A clerk who time stamped a pleading. A printout of a customer service call. A photocopy of a check attached to a form letter. In the aftermath, investigators used those illustrations to show that homicide work is not only about canvasses and crime scene tape. It is also about the paper that follows after.

The federal agents who had coaxed the old case into a new strategy saw their judgment validated when the appellate court affirmed the convictions. They took note as well when the sentence was sent back in the wake of a

Supreme Court decision that altered the shape of federal punishment. When the same term was reimposed under the now advisory framework, the agents learned a second lesson. Build your sentencing theory on more than one foundation. The judge had used alternative paths to arrive at the same range, and the resentencing opinion explained both. That approach became a cautionary tale in training programs. It meant that a trial team could absorb a change in sentencing law without losing the essential measure of punishment that the facts warranted.

The case also traveled into the offices of the companies whose checks had once been made out to a woman later convicted of fraud. Claims directors used the file in in house seminars and in industry gatherings. They emphasized careful review when a beneficiary is connected to a death investigation. They examined how old laws that bar killers from collecting can be honored in practice when criminal cases stall. They discussed interpleader as a tool to put disputed money into the hands of a court. They studied how investigative partnerships with local law enforcement can be nurtured in ways that respect privacy and due process and still protect policy funds from wrongful claims. In those sessions the details of this case were not used to sensationalize. They were used to teach the value of documentation and patience.

Within the prison system the case had its own quiet life. Corrections officers knew only what the intake summary said. It listed mail fraud and wire fraud and a term long enough to carry a person into very old age. The dorm culture is built to sort people by the labels on their papers, so in that space this case looked like a financial crime. The reality behind the labels sometimes came into view when a television documentary name checked the nickname that had followed the case in the local press. On those nights arguments flared over what the legal truth was and whether the moral truth should matter inside a place that measures every person by a number and a date. On chapel days and in counseling sessions, some women spoke of contrition and some spoke of victimhood. The staff who run those programs try not to sort souls. They look for behavior and for quiet, for compliance and for earned privileges. They learned that a very long sentence can be served without incident by a person who remains at the center of a case that still disrupts lives outside the fences.

The communities that had watched the case for decades also adjusted their stories in the aftermath. In Germantown and in Gaithersburg and in

Baltimore City there had been a long habit of whispering about this name. It was an index of fear that made some witness statements go dark and then surface and then darken again. After the federal judgment, the unsteady legend of voodoo and hexes and charms lost some of its grip. People who believed back then that curses could stalk a neighborhood were never going to be persuaded by a jurist in a robe. What did change was the conversation among neighbors who had sat on the fence. They heard prosecutors and judges and juries say clearly that this case had been about agency and choice, not about spells. That change mattered because it allowed some witnesses to say aloud why they had been afraid, not because of magic but because of very real threats. That honesty also forced a hard conversation about the power of rumor to intimidate, and about how fear spreads when law enforcement cannot guarantee protection.

Reporters in the region wrote a different kind of story once the resentencing was complete. The early features had depended on the shock value of the nickname. Later pieces treated the case as a study in persistence and in the reach of federal statutes. The best of those articles moved past the trope of the woman who kills husbands for money. They studied how gendered narratives shape public perception and how the same facts would have been presented if the person charged had been a man with a string of partners and a taste for policy proceeds. Scholars in criminal justice programs used the file to show how stereotypes can bend coverage and even seep into argument. They also used the file to demonstrate that careful judicial instructions and rigorous standards can blunt those biases at trial.

Victim advocates took the federal verdict and sentence as a sign that statutes aimed at financial crime can be turned toward healing when other options fail. They built support groups for families who were years into unsolved losses and showed them that other paths to accountability might be open if a loved one's death had been leveraged for money. They cautioned families not to see financial crimes as substitutes for murder prosecutions, but they encouraged them to think creatively with law enforcement about civil disability doctrines and about how concealment can be the heart of a fraud. In roundtables, they explained the emotional complexity that follows such verdicts. Relief sits alongside grief. Vindication walks with a sense that something essential did not happen because the word murder was never spoken by a state jury of peers.

Within local law schools the opinion affirming the convictions became a staple in seminars on evidence and on white collar crime. Students learned how a trial judge can admit statements from a dead witness when the court finds that the death was intended at least in part to keep that witness from testifying. They debated the proper limits of admitting older acts to show intent rather than to smear character. They studied the concept that an insurer has a property interest not only in its money but also in its right to control the disposition of that money. They tested the logic that a company harmed by a wrongful death is a fraud victim when a claim is presented without disclosure of the wrongful act. In those classrooms the case stopped being a headline and became a set of tools to be handled carefully.

For former coworkers in the school system where Josephine had drawn a paycheck for years, the aftermath brought a different kind of reckoning. Some remembered a woman who kept to herself and did her job. Others remembered a charismatic figure who could be funny and fierce. The federal sentence forced them to ask what they had not seen. That is a painful inquiry. In many workplaces the people who clean the rooms and keep the heat on are invisible. They pass through after hours. They keep their own counsel. The lesson those coworkers took was not that evil can hide in the quiet. It was that people carry lives that cannot be read from shifts and time cards, and that judgments formed from small interactions can be very wrong.

A quieter aftermath unfolded in the courts that handle civil disputes. It showed the value of staying payment while cooperating with investigators. It also showed the limits of civil process when witnesses are unwilling to testify. The history of the payouts in this case contains a mix of delayed checks and settlements that reflected the evidentiary posture of the moment. Civil judges who read those files reminded advocates that law is not static and that patient coordination across jurisdictions can keep wrongful claims from being consummated.

There is also the aftermath that belongs to the accused herself. In prison, routines calibrate the days. Education classes, health appointments, count times, phone calls purchased in small units, letters exchanged with family. The legal fights shift from direct appeal to collateral petitions and then to requests that call on the mercy of a system that rarely grants it. A woman serving a long sentence ages into new medical needs. Friendships form and end. People on the outside die. Grandchildren are born and grow tall before the end of a sentence that outlasts them. In visits, family members talk around the case. Some urge confession as a path toward a peace they want for themselves as much as for her. Others remain convinced that the verdict was a product of politics and a hunger for a win. The truth about those conversations sits between the visitor and the woman in a room with loud air ducts and vending machines that dispense cans of soda and packs of crackers.

What, finally, does a community do with a case like this when the person at its center is locked away and the families of the dead have grown older. One answer is that the community builds better habits for the next case. Detectives write more careful reports and preserve more thorough files. Prosecutors keep earlier notes in case a witness becomes unavailable and a court needs to know what was said and why it matters. Insurers maintain alerts that trigger closer review when a beneficiary surfaces in repeated death claims. Journalists learn to restrain the easy lure of a nickname and to do the slower work of describing legal structures to their readers. Clergy and counselors teach their congregations and clients that fears about rituals and curses are themselves tools that can be used to silence and control. None of that brings back the dead. It changes the next case, which is what systems can do.

Another answer is that the community keeps telling the story but tells it differently. The story becomes less about a person tagged with a sensational label and more about the men whose lives left holes that could not be filled. They become more than names in a caption. People begin to remember what they did before they became victims. A hobby. A job well done. A joke told at a cookout. As the years lengthen, that work remains difficult. It must be done by those who knew them, because history always wants to flatten complicated people into one event. The record in this case preserves cause and effect in legal terms. It does not record a laugh or a gesture that made a friend feel known. Only families and friends can do that, and in the aftermath they often try.

The most useful legacy a true crime narrative can leave is not a thrill but a map. This case gives one. It shows investigators that when direct paths are blocked by fear and recantation, another path exists. It shows lawyers how to assemble a trial out of paper and motive and statements that require careful legal gateways. It shows judges how to control a courtroom so that a jury hears enough to see purpose without being overwhelmed by prejudice. It shows companies how to guard their obligations with patience and with cooperation. It shows neighbors how to talk openly about fear and rumor. And it shows all of us that justice sometimes arrives late wearing a suit that looks nothing like the one we expected. The suit may be called fraud. Inside it is a vow that a community will not let deliberate death be made ordinary by check stubs and claim numbers.

At the end of the file, there is a page that lists dispositions and dates. It states simply that the convictions were affirmed and the sentence was reimposed. It contains nothing about grief or relief. Those feelings happen in kitchens and in small offices with fluorescent lights. But those feelings are connected to that final page. The page anchors them in a public decision that says this is what happened. In the years after that decision, the men who died were remembered by people who loved them. They were also remembered by a system that learned from their cases. That is not a fair exchange. It is the only one the law can offer once the doors to the past have closed.

CHAPTER 5
AMBER CUMMINGS
WHEN MURDER IS THE ONLY ANSWER

A story like this does not begin with a single morning or a single room. It begins with the slow arrangements of a life that will later be examined from every angle. Years before a judge addressed a crowded courtroom, before investigators inventoried a house and before headlines reached far beyond Maine, Amber Cummings and James Cummings were simply a couple who had left one coast for another and bought a tired property that needed work. They arrived with a child and plans. They chose a harbor town where the streets tilt toward the water and where old buildings in red brick look out on a working bay. That is the surface of the story. Under that surface are choices about privacy, money, ideology and control that shaped every day that followed.

Belfast is a small city on Penobscot Bay. People know their neighbors. A fixer upper purchased through a foreclosure sale gets noticed, especially when it is bought by newcomers who arrive from far away. The Cummings family made that kind of purchase in two thousand seven. From the outside, the move could have looked like a chapter change that many families make. The paperwork is signed, the keys are passed over, and a house with good bones but a long to do list becomes the focus of the next year. Roofing. Insulation. Painting. Plumbing. In a town where contractors talk to one another and where hardware store clerks see customers come back for the right screws or the better primer, a house under renovation can be a public act. The frame goes up. The windows come in. The lawn is cleared of old lumber. Neighbors walk by and nod.

The Cummings family did not arrive empty handed. James talked about money and had resources to spend. That sort of confidence can make a renovation move more quickly. It can also create a sense of insulation from ordinary limits. Money allows a person to attempt a larger vision and to do so without seeking approval from others. In practical terms it meant that repairs could be paid for and that the family could remain largely self contained while work went on. In social terms it meant that the voice directing those repairs was rarely in doubt. The person with the resources sets the pace and defines the priorities. That basic truth about household power would take on deeper significance as the months passed.

There is a long tradition of people starting over in Maine. Some come for work. Some come for the view. Some come for the promise that a smaller place with a slower rhythm might add balance to a crowded life. In that way the arrival of the Cummings family was unremarkable. They appeared to fit a familiar pattern. The story that followed would be anything but familiar. The renovation became a screen behind which a very different daily life unfolded. Privacy became the norm. Doors closed. The household cultivated routines that did not invite visitors. The child went to school. Errands were run. A winter or two passed. From a distance, it looked like any other family settling in.

Inside the house the domestic order was defined by James. The public record that would later emerge describes a man who prized control and who chose to broadcast a set of beliefs centered on domination and purity. He spoke openly about his admiration for Adolf Hitler. He collected items connected to that period and to that ideology. He presented himself to several people as someone who valued strength as he defined it and who treated empathy as weakness. The choice to bring that identity into a new town was not a private hobby that lived only on a shelf. It was an organizing principle that infused conversation and set the tone for the home. Those who encountered him did not hear the language of careful historical study. They heard the language of praise for brutality, purity and command. That matters because the same script often plays out in intimate spaces, not only in public declarations. The way a person talks about power in politics and history is frequently the way that person constructs power at home.

The move from California to Maine put thousands of miles between the family and the places where they had lived before. A move like that can be a fresh start. It can also be a way to reduce outside scrutiny. Old friends and relatives are no longer near enough to see how a family functions day to day. Doctors and counselors who might notice a pattern of stress or anxiety are not part of the new routine unless the family chooses to involve them. Teachers see a child for a few hours and may never be invited into the home. A renovation project provides a ready made reason for declining social invitations. The work is ongoing. The dust is everywhere. We will have you over when the kitchen is finished. The kitchen is never quite finished.

Amber's daily life in Belfast, as later described in court records and reporting, centered on caretaking and on the thousand small decisions that keep a household moving. She made a point of giving her daughter steady routines. Morning meals together. Checks on homework. Attention to the ordinary tools of childhood like backpacks, boots and lunch bags. That commitment is a visible thread in the narrative of the family's time in Maine. It shows a parent making space for her child to feel normal even when the rest of the house felt precarious. It also shows how the tasks of caregiving can become a shield against stress. Folding laundry, cooking a meal and walking to the car together are not only chores. They are rituals that keep anxiety at bay.

At the same time, the emotional climate in the home was not neutral. It is now part of the public record that James used degrading language and enforced compliance through a mix of ridicule and threat. Partners in such situations adopt survival strategies. They become experts at reading tone. They retreat from confrontation because the cost of a small victory can be measured in days of renewed hostility. They adjust their own wants and habits to the schedule and preferences of the person who controls the mood.

In this way a house can be quiet without ever feeling calm. Amber learned that quiet was the safest default and that her energy belonged to the child who depended on her constancy.

Belfast itself has a way of keeping time that is useful to understand. In summer, the sidewalks fill. In winter, the streets empty and the wind coming off the bay finds every gap in a coat. The town has galleries and coffee shops and a library that looks out over the water. There are free concerts, school events and small parades that mix local pride with the practical magic of keeping people in conversation with one another. When outsiders read about Belfast in connection with this story they are often surprised that a household in such a place could feel so closed. But geography does not guarantee transparency. A beautiful town can shelter an ugly private life. In fact, the beauty can make the contrast more profound. The view from a kitchen window can be stunning while the air inside the kitchen is heavy with dread.

James's habits and pleasures included collecting. The items he prized were not neutral artifacts. They were emblems of a movement that celebrated racial hierarchy and violence. Placing such objects in a home is not like placing a vase on a shelf. The objects declare allegiance. Visitors forced to see them are also being told who holds power in that space. For a partner and for a child, the message is constant and unmistakable. It says that empathy is weakness and that submission is expected. Over months and years, such objects can exert a pressure that is deeper than any speech. They become the scenery of the house and the scenery of a child's memory.

Much of Amber's life in those years can be seen through the lens of management. She managed schedules, budgets, meals and moods. She managed the logistics of a renovation and the demands of school. She managed the constant calculation required when a partner's approval must be won every day anew. That last form of management is particularly exhausting. People who have lived in similar circumstances describe the same kind of mental math. If the jacket is misplaced, what excuse will be safest. If dinner is late, what words will defuse the first reaction. If a friend from school invites the child over, how can the invitation be accepted without inviting attention back to the house. This is not melodrama. It is the texture of life in a home where one person insists on control and where the other adult spends energy keeping the storms from breaking over the child.

Neighbors remember what is visible. A car leaving in the morning. A porch light that never seems to turn off. A new door leaning against a wall, waiting to be hung. In that way, the Cummings house fit into the neighborhood. It was another project among many. Belfast has plenty of houses like that. Some take years to complete. Some never look finished and yet they are lived in fully and happily. The difference in this case is not in the lumber or in the paint. It is in the atmosphere inside the walls. That atmosphere cannot always be seen from the street and that is one reason such stories persist in every region of the country. A door closes and the rules inside are set by the person most willing to enforce them.

The couple's decision to keep their world small is also part of the verifiable record. They did not cultivate a large social circle in town. They kept their own hours and their own counsel. For a child, that kind of seclusion can be explained as privacy. We are busy with the house. We are catching up after a move. We will see people more once the kitchen is done. For the adult in charge of care, seclusion can be a tool for survival. Fewer visitors means fewer chances for a confrontation. Fewer commitments outside the home means fewer moments when tardiness or absence might draw questions from teachers or neighbors. The seclusion also meant that people who might have seen a pattern and offered help never had enough data to reach a conclusion, let alone a plan.

Amber's own words after the case became public did not swing toward self promotion. She spoke in measured terms about her daughter and about the path that led to the decision that would change everything. She thanked people in the community who offered support. She did not seek to make the story more dramatic than it already was. That restraint is itself a clue to the way she had been living. When someone has spent years trying to keep the temperature of a room from rising, the habit persists even when the crisis has passed. A steady voice is not denial. It is evidence that the speaker has had to learn how to live inside a storm without adding wind of her own.

In the background of all of this is the reality that the family's move to Maine coincided with a broader national story about property, foreclosure and migration. Across the country in those years, houses changed hands under financial stress. People with resources could pick up properties at auction or through the bank that would otherwise have been out of reach. Communities like Belfast saw new owners arrive with plans to put their stamp on a place where others had failed or had simply moved on. The narrative of improvement and renewal is powerful. It also provides a convenient frame that can hide other truths. When a house is constantly under construction, disorder can be explained away. When a family is constantly busy, absence from community life can be written off as temporary.

Through all of this, the child at the center of the household remained Amber's focus. Routine became a lifesaving tool. That is a lesson that social workers and counselors repeat for families under stress. Make the morning predictable. Make homework predictable. Find ways to turn ordinary acts into anchors. If the adult environment is volatile, the rhythms of a school day, a library visit or a grocery list can give a child the sense that time moves forward and that tomorrow will be familiar. In that sense, Belfast provided tools even if the house did not. The small scale of the town and the nearness of everything makes it easier to build a schedule that holds.

There is a temptation in the early pages of any true crime account to foreshadow the violent act that later defines the case. The better way to understand what happened in this family is to refuse that temptation here. The purpose of this section is to map the terrain of a life that was not yet a headline. The couple moved to Maine. They bought a house through a foreclosure sale. They kept to themselves. The public face was of a renovation under way and a family with resources to undertake it. Inside the house, there was a hierarchy enforced by one person and endured by another. There was a child whose days were arranged to be as normal as possible. There was a pattern of seclusion that made outside intervention unlikely. Those facts are enough to form the picture needed at this stage.

When people in Belfast later looked back, they did so with the shock that comes when a story you thought you knew acquires new chapters. The house you passed on the way to the grocery store becomes the subject of a national report. The new couple who bought a property at a bargain price becomes a cautionary tale about what privacy can hide. The child you saw at a crosswalk becomes the focus of a community's desire to protect and nurture. The town endures. The bay keeps its rhythms. The lines painted on Main Street fade and are repainted. Belfast has seen fires and storms and the long ups and downs of the fishing economy. It can absorb a single family's tragedy. What it cannot do is rewrite the years inside one particular house. That is the task of the record and of careful narrative. This early life section holds back from the later disclosures intentionally. It asks the reader to stand on the front steps of a house in need of repair and to feel what it is like to carry groceries past the threshold into a private world. The rest of the chapter will cross that threshold, but not yet.

One final observation belongs here. When we read about families in distress, we often look for the moment when things went wrong. In this story, there is no single moment. There is a long settling into a life that was tightly controlled and very private. There is the construction of an identity that glorified power and treated empathy as weakness. There is the steady work of a mother to shield a child from the worst of it. The move to Belfast did not create those conditions from nothing, but it gave them a stage on which to play out with minimal interruption. The address on a quiet street became the fixed point around which fear and routine orbited. By the time outsiders understood what the house contained, the early life that had made later events possible was already complete.

THE MURDER

The morning that would end James Cummings's life began as a winter dawn that came late and gray over Belfast. By the clock on the kitchen stove the day was still young. There was the faint smell of coffee and toast. Outside the yard wore a thin crust of old snow and the street was quiet. It looked like the kind of time when a parent gets a few minutes to gather thoughts before the busy hours begin. The ordinary surface of that morning is important because the decision that followed did not erupt out of visible chaos. It emerged from a long private reckoning that met a single point in time on December 9th 2009.

Amber Cummings moved through those first minutes with deliberate calm. She settled her child with a simple breakfast and the measured conversation that parents use when they want to project safety. The child ate and talked about the minor details of the day ahead. There is no sensation in that scene and that is precisely why it matters. It shows that Amber had chosen to make a space for her daughter that felt normal in the middle of everything else. When the meal ended and the plates were washed or left to dry, Amber walked away from the kitchen into the part of the house where the next actions would take place.

What happened next had been rehearsed in Amber's mind during hours when no one else could see her. She had thought about taking her own life. That thought had visited before like a storm that crosses the bay and darkens the windows without warning. On that morning she reached the point of action. In her bedroom she lifted a firearm and put the barrel to her mouth. It is a stark image and it conveys something essential about her mental state. For a few long seconds she did not imagine a courtroom or a news story. She imagined an end. Then a second thought took hold. If she died, the person she believed to be dangerous would remain alive in the next room. The child who had just eaten breakfast would remain in his orbit. The calculation that followed was terrible and simple. She would live and he would die.

She took the gun from her mouth and set her path. She left her bedroom and crossed the distance to his room. The house was still. There is a particular quiet inside a winter morning with the windows closed and the radiators or the forced air humming low. Every footfall is louder than usual. Every breath can be heard if someone is awake. But James Cummings was not awake. He was asleep in his bed and the door between them was a barrier she had crossed in small ways a thousand times. This time she crossed it with a loaded weapon and a plan that allowed no room for delay. She stepped in, lifted the gun and fired into his head. Then she fired again. The movement and the sound collapsed years of fear and calculation into a few seconds. The room absorbed the blast and the smell of burned powder. The bed absorbed the impact. The man in the bed did not wake or speak. The scene was fixed.

What happens after a shooting is both physical and procedural. The physical part is shock and adrenaline and the push to get away from the place where the gun was fired. The procedural part is the unwinding of every rule that governs a homicide inquiry. Amber turned from the bed and left the room. She did not linger to examine the body. She did not attempt to hide the weapon or to stage the scene. She returned to her daughter and moved with her toward the door. The first priority was distance. She needed another adult and a phone. She needed what people reach for when something terrible has happened. She needed help.

They crossed the yard to a neighbor. In small towns neighbors are a first line of response, and that morning the neighbor was the lifeline. A call was made to authorities. The details the dispatcher would have heard are the measured questions that triage a violent event. Where are you. Is anyone hurt. Are there weapons. Is the suspect on the scene. The answers focused the response. Police and emergency medical personnel were dispatched to the address. The time was still early. The roads were passable. The drive took only minutes.

The first officers arrived with the dual mandate that governs a scene like this one. They had to secure the area to protect responders and the public. They had to preserve evidence for the investigation and any later prosecution or hearing. The house was entered with caution. Commands were issued in clear voices. Rooms were checked. The man in the bed was found with mortal injuries to the head and with no signs of life. The weapon would have been located and made safe. Officers would have noted the position of items in the room and the condition of the bed and the floor. They would have stepped carefully to avoid contaminating patterns in blood or other trace material that might inform the reconstruction of the shooting.

In the neighbor's home or next to a patrol car, Amber would have been separated from her daughter so that the child could be shielded from the procedural steps that were about to begin. An officer or a member of a crisis response team would have stayed with the child. Another officer would have begun the process of taking an initial statement from Amber. In such a statement the goal is to capture the essential facts quickly and clearly. Who is inside. What happened. What weapon was used. Where is the weapon now. Were there any other persons present. Did anyone else hear or see anything. The answers shape what investigators do first inside the house.

The medical team entered and confirmed what the officers already knew. James Cummings had been shot in the head and could not be resuscitated. Paramedics may have monitored the body for a brief period to establish the exact time of death for the record. The coroner or medical examiner's office was notified and arrangements began for the removal of the body once the scene had been processed. A homicide scene is not relinquished easily or quickly. It is mapped and photographed and searched. The presence of a firearm and the short time between shots and response allowed investigators to move with precision.

The weapon itself and any fired cartridges or bullet fragments were collected and placed into evidence containers that prevent contamination. Swabs might have been taken from surfaces for possible DNA or gunshot residue analysis. The bedding and the mattress would have been documented for patterns consistent with close range discharge. Soot deposition around the entrance wounds and stippling of the skin are markers that help estimate the distance from muzzle to target. Trajectory rods may have been used if bullets passed through pillows or mattress and into the wall or floor. Those rods help confirm angles that in turn confirm where the shooter stood. Given that James Cummings was asleep, the pattern was likely simple and direct, but good practice demands verification.

Elsewhere in the house, additional items would have been noted and tagged. The purpose on that morning was limited to the homicide itself. Investigators look first for any signs that contradict the initial account. Forced entry is noted or ruled out. Evidence of a struggle is examined. In this case there was no report of a struggle and the immediate facts aligned with a scenario in which the victim was shot while asleep. The forensics would eventually affirm that picture. The absence of defensive wounds on the victim and the lack of displaced furniture or broken objects supported the conclusion that the shots were delivered without warning.

While the interior of the house was being processed, Amber was likely taken to the police station for a recorded interview. The transition from an initial field statement to a formal interview marks a shift in detail and pace. She would have been advised of her rights. She would have been given the opportunity to request an attorney. If she chose to speak without counsel present at that first stage, the interviewers would have asked her to walk them through the morning minute by minute. They would have asked her to explain where the gun was kept prior to the shooting. They would have asked her to describe the condition of the house when she left and to specify what she did with the child in the moments after the shots. They would have asked about the history of the relationship only as it related to intent and motive. The focus at this phase remained on the immediate facts.

Back at the scene, neighbors gathered at a distance behind the tape that cordoned off the property. In a town the size of Belfast, a cluster of patrol cars and an ambulance outside a house draws attention within minutes. People call one another and word spreads. By midmorning, curious residents would have known that a death had occurred. They would have known that police were treating it as a homicide. They would have known the address. The name of the man on the bed might already have been spoken from porch to porch. The name of the woman who had walked to a neighbor for help would have been on the same circuit, though law enforcement typically holds names until formal notification and verification steps are completed.

Later that day, the medical examiner received the body for autopsy. The procedure documented the entry wounds and recovered bullets or fragments if they were present in soft tissues. The analysis recorded soot and stippling to validate the range of fire. It examined the skull and brain for damage patterns that correlate to caliber and bullet construction. Toxicology samples were taken from the victim as a matter of standard practice. The autopsy report would state the cause of death as gunshot wounds to the head and the manner of death as homicide. That document is a foundation stone for the investigation and any later proceedings.

Alongside the central acts of shooting and autopsy, there was the unfolding timeline that linked each step in a simple chain. The breakfast ended at a particular time. The walk down the hall took seconds. The shots were fired within a minute. The departure from the house took only as long as it takes to collect a child and open a door. The walk to the neighbor took a minute or two. The call to authorities was logged with an exact time stamp. The first patrol car arrived within a specific number of minutes. The ambulance arrived a few minutes after that. The first officer entered the bedroom and saw the condition of the victim at an exact time. These points anchor the narrative in the precise world of clocks and logs that investigators rely on to cut through the fog of memory and emotion.

Once the body was removed and the last evidence bags were sealed, the house was secured. In some cases a residence is released back to occupants quickly. In others access is restricted for a longer period while additional searches are planned. In this case the immediate events were straightforward, but the house itself contained items that drew wider attention later. On the day of the shooting the focus stayed tight. This was the scene where a sleeping man had been shot. The instrument was a handgun. The shooter was the person who had called for help. The motive would be explored in interviews and in evaluations that would come later.

That afternoon and evening, Amber faced the first quiet hours after a violent act. Anyone who has ever been interviewed after a traumatic event knows the peculiar emptiness that follows. The noise and the lights and the constant questions stop. A room is offered. A cup of water is placed on a table. A clock ticks in that room as firmly as the clock ticked on the stove that morning, but now the sound is larger. The mind replays the movement down the hall again and again. It checks the door and the position of the bed and the angle of the arm that extended with the gun. It checks the second shot and the way the air smelled and the way the world failed to change because the person in the bed did not wake. It checks the path to the neighbor and the words that were said and the way the child's hand felt in hers.

The next day and the days after brought the institutional steps that follow a domestic killing. Property had to be inventoried. The child had to be placed in a safe and stable environment. Social services had to be notified as a matter of routine. Counsel had to be retained. In each of those steps the echo of the morning remained. The most important facts were not open to dispute. A man was dead of gunshot wounds to the head. The shots were fired at close range while he slept. The person who fired them was his wife. She did not flee the area. She sought help immediately and made no attempt to disguise what she had done. Those are the elements that separate this case from many other homicides, where investigators must chase a suspect or unravel a chain of deception. Here the act was swift and the acknowledgement was just as swift.

For the community, the first reports were hard to align with the quiet postcard image of the town. The phrase domestic homicide carries a heavy charge because it suggests betrayal of the basic promise of safety in a home. It also provokes questions that citizens ask themselves about warning signs and about the role of a neighbor. Should someone have known. Could anyone have intervened. In this case, the visible part of the event was only the arrival of emergency vehicles and the taped perimeter. The invisible part was years long and private. The morning of December 9th 2009 was not an eruption of new conflict. It was the end of a line drawn by a person who believed that delay was no longer possible.

From the perspective of law enforcement training, the response that morning followed the evolving best practices for scenes involving a family member as shooter and a child as a potential witness. The child was kept at a remove from the most graphic parts of the process. A single officer or counselor stayed with the child to create continuity in a day when every other frame of reference had been torn away. The interviewer tasked with speaking to Amber would have worked to keep the exchange calm and focused, avoiding accusatory tones that often shut down cooperation. The evidence team would have taken more photographs than they thought they needed. The rule of thumb is that the photograph you do not take is the one you will wish you had when an attorney asks a pointed question months later.

There is also the human dimension among the responders. Officers and paramedics carry these mornings with them. They drive back to the station and hang up their jackets. They wipe their boots and fill out forms. They talk to one another in a careful register that acknowledges the gravity of what they have seen without letting those images flood their thoughts. In a small town that shared sense of duty is a kind of shield. It helps that the scene was controlled and that there was no chase or gun battle. It helps that the child was safe. It does not remove the memory of a bedroom where a person died in his sleep because another person decided that there was no other path.

By the time the sun set that day, the immediate narrative was clear. A wife had shot her husband in his bed in the early morning. She had then taken her child to a neighbor and called for help. The police had responded and secured the scene. The medical examiner had taken custody of the body. An interview had been conducted. The case would move forward across weeks and months toward a courtroom where the deeper questions would be asked in public. The murder itself, however, would remain simple in its mechanics. Two shots. Close range. A man asleep and a woman who had made a choice she believed necessary.

It is tempting to conclude this account of the murder with a flourish or a moral. The better approach is to hold to the spare outline that the evidence supports. There was a date, December 9th 2009. There was a place, a bedroom in a house in Belfast. There was a sequence that took less than a minute and changed a family forever. In the long sweep of homicide cases, this one is unusual for its lack of mystery about the act itself. The mystery that remained for the court and for the public was about the why, and that question belongs to another section. Here the story ends the way it began, with a quiet morning that carried a decision to its end and with the immediate steps that follow a death by gunfire. The rest of the narrative moves outward from that room to interviews, evaluations, court filings and arguments about responsibility and mercy.

THE ARREST, TRIAL AND SENTENCE

When a person walks from a neighbor's doorway after reporting a killing, the next steps are shaped by a mix of routine and the unique facts of the case. On December 9th 2009, once officers had secured the Cummings residence and confirmed that James Cummings was dead, Amber Cummings entered the formal machinery of a homicide investigation. The officers on scene treated her as both a source of information and as the principal actor in a fatal shooting. That dual role is not unusual in a domestic case, but it requires careful handling. The interview space must be quiet and orderly. The record must be clear. From the moment she was transported for questioning, the state's responsibility was to document what had happened and to safeguard Amber's rights while deciding whether to seek charges.

At the station Amber was advised in the standard way that she had the right to remain silent and the right to an attorney. The first interview after a killing is rarely the last. Investigators tend to start with a chronological account of the day in question, anchored to clock times whenever possible, and then broaden the frame to capture any immediate history that informs motive or threat. The point is not to litigate the past during a first session. It is to understand intent and to determine whether claims about necessity or fear are specific enough to merit further evaluation by experts. By the end of the day, the state had enough undisputed facts to open a homicide file and to treat Amber as the person responsible for the death. She was taken into custody, booked, and held pending an initial appearance before a judge.

In the first court session after a homicide arrest, the judge ensures that the defendant understands the nature of the allegations and the rights attached to those allegations. The state outlines its probable cause. Defense counsel either appears if already retained or is appointed. Bail or other conditions of release are discussed, though in many domestic killings the initial posture is to hold without bail or to set conditions that are difficult to meet until more facts are known. Amber's case would not be an exception in its first posture. The court treated the matter with the gravity that a fatal shooting demands while acknowledging that the full story could not be told in a single short hearing.

As the days passed, the investigation widened in the customary way. Forensic work continued. Prior contacts between the family and any agencies were checked. Digital and physical records were collected pursuant to warrants. Witnesses and neighbors were interviewed. Each new item either corroborated or complicated the initial frame. In a case that arises within a family, the prosecution team pays close attention to any evidence that supports claims of long term abuse or imminent threat. These claims are not excuses in the casual sense. They are legal facts with potential consequences for charging decisions and for sentencing.

Maine prosecutors have charging discretion within the boundaries set by statute. When a person deliberately shoots another person, the default decision is to charge a form of murder. The defense may later present facts and expert opinions that mitigate culpability or alter how a judge ultimately punishes the conduct, but the initial charging choice reflects the seriousness of a conscious lethal act. In December two thousand nine, the state moved forward along those conventional lines. The case was routed toward Waldo County Superior Court in Belfast where homicide matters are heard, with the expectation that any trial or plea would occur there.

Defense counsel Eric Morse entered the case for Amber and began a parallel process that is essential in any homicide defense. He moved quickly to assemble mental health experts with experience in trauma, abuse, and the psychology of chronic coercion. He gathered records that would aid those experts in forming opinions that could be presented in court. He also organized interviews with people who knew the family and could add specific verifiable details about the relationships inside the home. In difficult domestic homicide cases, the defense never rests on vague claims of a bad marriage. The strongest mitigation cases are built of precise accounts that can be checked. Dates. Times. Statements. Actions. Medical visits. Counseling sessions. Emails. Photographs. The objective is to build a picture that allows a judge to weigh the totality of circumstances rather than the few seconds in which the trigger was pulled.

From the state's perspective, the next milestone is to test the strength of its case before a grand jury or to proceed by information if the parties stipulate. Grand juries in Maine sit regularly and hear evidence on a schedule set by the court. The prosecutor outlines the facts, calls witnesses as needed, and seeks an indictment if the legal elements of the offense are supported. The case against Amber had the unmistakable spine of a confession to the act, a confirmed cause of death, a recovered weapon and an accurate timeline. It was not a whodunit. The legal questions that would matter most were about intent and justification, and those questions often do not carry the same weight at the charging stage as they do before a sentencing judge. In any event, the case moved toward a posture where the defense could begin to negotiate with the state.

The negotiation phase is seldom dramatic in the public sense. It is a steady exchange of offers and information. The defense highlights expert evaluations and the lived context surrounding the killing. The prosecution emphasizes the moral and legal imperative to denounce lethal violence and to protect the public. Where the parties can find common ground, they do so through an agreed cap on prison time, a set of facts to which the defendant will plead, and an understanding about what evidence will be presented at a sentencing hearing. That was the shape of the process here. Assistant Attorney General Leane Zania represented the state. She understood the evidence of abuse yet insisted that the court send a message that private lethal force cannot be normalized as a remedy, even in a hard case. Defense counsel and the state reached a framework that allowed Amber to enter a plea that would avoid a trial while making room for a robust sentencing presentation by both sides.

During the winter of two thousand nine into two thousand ten, the formal pretrial events marched forward on the docket. Evaluations by the defense experts were completed and written. The state reviewed those materials and prepared its own position. The court scheduled a sentencing hearing where the judge would receive testimony from experts and weigh the arguments that each side would present. In that preparation, several core themes emerged. The defense would ask the court to regard Amber as a survivor of long term abuse whose judgment on the morning of the shooting was shaped by years of coercion and by a sharply escalating fear that her child was in danger. The state would ask the court to recognize those factors but to impose some incarceration to make unmistakably clear that taking a life without an immediate threat in progress is a crime that must be punished.

Sentencing hearings in homicide cases are measured affairs. They do not mimic the adversarial show of a trial. There is no jury. The judge receives evidence and addresses the defendant directly. The tone is calm even when the subject matter is brutal. On January 7th 2010, Waldo County Superior

Court convened for the hearing that would decide Amber's fate. The courtroom was full. Observers wore small stickers that read Free Amber. Family members and supporters sat together. Reporters held notebooks open on their knees. There was no dramatic legal question to resolve. The question was about mercy and its limits. It was about how far a judge could go in recognizing the crushing force of abuse without erasing the rule that homicide is the most serious crime in the state's code.

Eric Morse addressed the court with a plain argument grounded in the record he had assembled. He described James Cummings as a man whose conduct over a decade had humiliated and wounded his wife and had, in the last year, provoked an acute terror that focused on their child. He drew a line between Amber's mental state and the single minute on the morning of December 9th 2009. He asked the judge to consider leniency not as a gift, but as a measured acknowledgment of cause and effect in a closed system of abuse. He did not romanticize the killing or suggest that the law should look away. He asked for a sentence that did not require incarceration. He attached those requests to evaluations prepared by three mental health professionals who had examined Amber and who were prepared to tell the court that prison would harm her recovery and serve no clear public purpose.

Assistant Attorney General Leane Zania rose for the state and conceded what could not reasonably be contested. Amber had been abused. The psychological weight of that abuse was real. The danger signals present in the home were not inventions crafted for litigation. Yet, said the state, there must be a line that separates private judgment from lawful authority. If citizens substitute personal lethal force for the intervention of law and social services, even in cases where an abuser seems beyond reach, society invites a breakdown of the norms that protect everyone. The state did not ask for the maximum. It asked for a year of incarceration within a larger sentence that would include a long period of probationary oversight. That year, the prosecutor argued, would mark the gravity of taking a life while leaving room for treatment and for a new start with the child.

The defense called its experts. They spoke without melodrama. They discussed the effects of chronic coercion on perception and decision making. They described the way fear can become the only coin inside a household, how it pays for compliance day after day until the account is depleted. They laid out their diagnosis and their recommendations. Their conclusion was that Amber did not pose a danger to the public and that incarcerating her would set back the work of healing. In the measured cadence of specialists accustomed to courtrooms, they urged the judge to impose a sentence that recognized the harm already done to Amber and to the child and to allow mother and daughter to build a stable life under supervision rather than behind a jail door.

When it was his turn to speak, Justice Jeffrey Hjelm framed the matter as a whole. He did not limit his analysis to the short interval in which the shots were fired. He placed that interval within the entire course of conduct that had led to it. He spoke of the duty to uphold the law and the duty to look honestly at the life that preceded the killing. He acknowledged the state's argument about the danger of endorsing private lethal force as a form of self help. He balanced that with the defense evidence that Amber's actions were born of a prolonged campaign of degradation and fear that had narrowed her options to a desperate choice. The judge's words were restrained but pointed. He conveyed that the law is not blind to human context.

The sentence he announced carried an eight year term, fully suspended, with a lengthy period of probation to follow. Suspension meant that Amber would not serve that prison term so long as she complied with conditions set by the court. The conditions would include standard provisions such as law abiding behavior, cooperation with supervision, and a prohibition on possessing firearms. They would also likely include mental health treatment, counseling focused on trauma and parenting, and any other tailored requirements that probation officers and therapists deemed necessary to ensure stability. The structure placed responsibility on Amber to maintain the progress she had shown since the day of the shooting and to continue building a safe life with her daughter.

The reaction in the courtroom to the sentence was immediate. Those wearing Free Amber stickers applauded when the judge left the bench. In the hallway Amber received embraces from supporters, including clergy who had counseled her. Outside on the Belfast sidewalk in the cold air of January, she thanked community members who had offered rides, meals, and quiet encouragement through the months of waiting. Her tone was controlled. She did not speak in celebration. She said that her husband had been mentally ill and asked that people not direct their anger at him. That remark mattered. It signaled her refusal to turn the day into a public ritual of vengeance. It kept the focus on healing and on the obligations of the future rather than on a recitation of past cruelty.

From a legal perspective, the outcome illuminated how Maine courts can exercise discretion in a hard domestic homicide. The court did not accept a narrative that erased the seriousness of the act. The court did not accede to a call for a purely punitive response that would have ignored the weight of expert testimony and the corroborated record of abuse. Instead, the sentence employed the tools available to balance denunciation, specific deterrence, and rehabilitation. A suspended term held in reserve underscored the gravity of homicide. Probationary supervision ensured accountability over time. The absence of immediate incarceration honored the finding that Amber's conduct grew from a unique and intensely coercive environment that is unlikely to recur now that the environment has ended.

There are procedural ripples that follow any homicide sentencing, even one that resolves without a prison door closing. Probation offices build a plan. Therapists coordinate care. Family court and social service agencies confirm guardianship and schooling arrangements for the child. Victim services units, which often assist families of the deceased in ordinary murder cases, have a different role when the surviving spouse is also the person who fired the shots. In such cases, their work may focus on helping extended family process grief while recognizing that the court's decision reflects a fuller account of the home than an outsider might have known. Managing those ripples requires a community that can hold two truths at once. A man is dead by an act that is a crime. The woman who committed that act is not well served by prison because the evidence shows she acted under the crushing force of long term abuse and imminent fear for a child.

Observers sometimes ask why cases like Amber's do not culminate in a formal verdict after a trial, as if a plea or an agreed sentencing hearing lacks democratic legitimacy. The answer lies in the purpose of the criminal process. Trials test disputed facts before a jury. When the material facts are not disputed and the conflict lies in how to apply judgment to those facts, a focused sentencing hearing before a judge can be the most honest and efficient means of reaching a just outcome. In this case, no one doubted who pulled the trigger or when or where. The debate was about the meaning of those acts in light of a long and well documented history. A trial would have layered months of delay and spectacle over questions that were better answered by expert testimony and judicial discretion.

The sentence also contained an implicit message to the broader public. It affirmed that courts will listen when a defendant presents credible, corroborated evidence of long term abuse. It affirmed that mercy does not have to conflict with public safety when a judge has a full record and a tailored plan of supervision. It also affirmed that the law does not excuse homicide merely because the victim behaved in cruel or alarming ways. The balance struck is delicate. It requires confidence that the court has enough information to make a thoughtful decision. It requires a community willing to accept that justice sometimes looks like treatment and supervision rather than a prison term. The reaction in Belfast suggested that many residents understood that balance and were prepared to support a mother rebuilding her life.

In the days after January 7th 2010, much of the ordinary legal work shifted from the courthouse to offices and living rooms. Paperwork that had loomed for months was filed and archived. The child's daily schedule took precedence over interviews and hearings. Amber met with probation personnel to confirm appointments and expectations. She met with therapists to map a plan that fit the conditions of probation. She reentered the rhythm of a town where a person can walk to the library and the grocery store and feel the slow stitch of a community binding itself back together after a hard season. The legal headlines were over. The quieter work of obeying the sentence began.

Lawyers and judges sometimes talk about cases that leave an imprint on a courthouse. Amber's case is one of those. It sits at the intersection of crime and harm and protection. It demonstrates how a court can acknowledge the full story of a family while applying the rules that define the crime. It reminds professionals in the system that every domestic homicide carries a past that matters as much as the scene of the shooting. And it stands as a public example of a sentence calibrated not to a thirst for retribution but to the needs of a child and the evidence of a long and punishing history. Those are not soft values. They are disciplined conclusions reached in a room where every word is recorded and where every decision is subject to later scrutiny.

The arrest, the pretrial steps, the negotiated path to a hearing, and the sentence announced on January 7th 2010 together form a coherent arc. The state did its job. The defense did its job. The experts did theirs. The judge did his. What remains, once the transcript is closed, is the life that a defendant must build under the conditions set by the court. That life belongs to the aftermath. The public would have its own reactions. Family and friends would speak more freely once the case was resolved. The wider country, which had read headlines about a strange house in Maine and a killing before dawn, would move on to the next story. In Belfast the people closest to the case would keep living with the memory of a winter day and with the knowledge that justice, in this instance, wore the face of mercy bound to supervision.

AFTERMATH WITH FAMILY AND PUBLIC OPINION

In the weeks after the sentencing hearing the center of the story shifted from the courtroom to the community. The noise of legal argument faded and what remained was the daily work of living in a small city where people meet each other on the sidewalk and in the grocery store aisle. A case that had once been a headline became a topic that neighbors approached more carefully, not with the giddy energy of scandal but with the quiet forward lean of people trying to make sense of what it means to keep faith with one another after a calamity inside a family. This section traces that aftermath from several angles. It considers the reactions of friends and relatives who had watched the case unfold, the responses from religious and civic leaders, the reflections of reporters and readers who had followed the narrative, and the practical matters that attend probation, counseling, and the reshaping of a household where a child must grow into adolescence without the shadow that had darkened her early years.

Public conversation took on a tone that was distinctive to a coastal Maine town in winter. The streets were cold and the days were short. People had time to talk in coffee shops and at the library. The dominant sentiment was not triumph and not outrage. It was relief mixed with sober acceptance. Residents had seen a judge apply the law with care and had watched a family come through the courthouse doors into the light of an ordinary afternoon. There were people who would have preferred a more punitive outcome and there were people who would have gone further toward leniency, yet most recognized the complicated balance that had been struck. Relief expressed itself in simple gestures. A hand on the shoulder. An offer of a ride to an appointment. A casserole left on a porch with a note that did not ask for anything in return.

Friends who had known the family best were more candid in private. They spoke of years when they had worried but did not know how to ask the right questions. They spoke of the odd distance that can grow between people who live a few blocks apart when one house begins to shut its doors. One lesson that rippled out through these conversations was that the signs of isolation are not always dramatic and that it is reasonable to check in on a neighbor even when doing so feels awkward. Out of those exchanges came a renewed attention to how schools, churches, and community groups can knit a net that catches families before a crisis becomes irreversible. Librarians who had chatted with the child at the circulation desk remembered her quiet courtesy and found themselves thinking about ways to notice when a child seems tired or distracted. None of this was grand policy. It was the slow work of a town adjusting its posture toward watchfulness.

Religious leaders in Belfast and nearby towns reacted as they often do after a painful case. They preached about mercy and responsibility. They emphasized that mercy does not erase accountability and that accountability is not limited to punishment. Some congregations organized small support circles in which people touched by domestic abuse could speak without fear of gossip. The point was not to litigate the case in miniature. It was to give survivors a place to name their experiences and to hear practical advice from advocates who understood the terrain. In a town where many residents have a long memory and where stories can harden into labels, such circles were a way to keep the focus on healing rather than on the permanent branding of anyone involved.

Reporters who had covered the case turned, as responsible reporters do, to follow up stories that looked beyond the single house on a single street. They spoke with educators and counselors about the prevalence of domestic abuse in rural and coastal counties. They described the role of probation in supervising a person who has been sentenced in a homicide case yet allowed to remain in the community. They explained in plain language how therapy for trauma proceeds and why it can be a long process. They did not sensationalize. Their work helped the public see the difference between a case that is over in court and a life that is not yet settled.

Letters to editors and comments at public meetings reflected a range of views that can be organized around a few common threads. One thread was the insistence that the safety of children must be the supreme guide in difficult decisions. Another thread was a defense of the idea that courts must be permitted to weigh context, especially when people who have endured long term coercion make choices that would otherwise be hard to understand. A third thread was a caution against romanticizing lethal force as a solution. The debate was serious but mostly respectful. The lack of invective was notable in an era when public argument often dissolves into slogans. The tone in Belfast was grounded in the knowledge that many residents had met the people involved face to face.

Family reaction unfolded in the private rooms where such matters are usually processed. Relatives did not all agree about what had happened or why. Some struggled to reconcile love for the dead with anger at the conduct that had poisoned a household. Some felt grief that did not have a simple outlet because public opinion was complicated. Even within families that had not been close to the Cummings home there was a sense of reckoning. People told each other that they would pay more attention to changes in the moods and habits of their kin. They promised to reach out more often and to ask more direct questions. The case served as a mirror in which many families saw hints of their own tensions and secrets, though usually in far less dangerous forms. That mirror did not provoke panic. It prompted seriousness.

One question that arises in any aftermath is how a community welcomes a person who has been at the center of a homicide case. In this instance the obligations were clear and public. Probation requires appointments, check ins, and an openness to supervision that can feel intrusive and yet is meant to be supportive. The work of therapy requires honesty and persistence. Parenting requires the steady attention that allows a child to rebuild confidence after years of fear. Community members who understood those obligations tended to grant space rather than make demands for interviews or appearances. The best sort of support in such a setting is quiet and competent. People offered to help with logistics. They drove to appointments. They kept confidences. They understood that the story did not need to be retold to every new acquaintance. The town did not erase what had happened, but neither did it insist on replaying it.

Another dimension of public reaction involved attention from outside the region. People elsewhere in the country had read early accounts and formed impressions that were not always accurate. Belfast residents saw those impressions and felt the familiar mix of irritation and resignation that comes when a small place is summarized from a distance. The local response was to continue being who they were. They kept doing the practical things that make a town work. They shoveled sidewalks. They attended school concerts. They volunteered at the food pantry. In this way the aftermath was an assertion of normal life not as denial but as an act of commitment to the future. The theory that most people in Belfast seemed to adopt was that a child deserves a childhood shaped by ordinary days and that adults have a duty to manufacture those days through consistent care.

Advocates who work on domestic abuse used the case to educate without exploiting. They held sessions for teachers and health care workers about recognizing patterns of coercion and about the complicated decisions that survivors face. They emphasized that leaving a dangerous household is often the most dangerous moment and that planning must be meticulous. They explained how restraining orders and safety plans function and where their limits lie. They did not present the case as a template. They used it, rather, as a reminder that no system of protection can be effective unless communities understand how abuse actually looks in real homes. The lessons they offered were practical. Check on neighbors. Believe disclosures. Keep resource lists current. Coordinate among schools, clinics, and community centers so a person does not have to tell her story five times to five different strangers.

Law enforcement officers also debriefed in their own way. They reviewed the response to the scene and the investigative steps. They asked whether there were any gaps in training that could be addressed. They looked at protocols for working with children present at traumatic incidents. They discussed the delicate balance between thorough questioning and the need to avoid retraumatizing a survivor who has just made a terrifying decision. The purpose of that internal work was not to relitigate choices made in the moment. It was to improve the craft so that future responses would be as professional and humane as possible. In that sense the aftermath was part of a cycle of learning that every police department undertakes as a matter of routine.

The press attention to the case had earlier been fueled by shocking discoveries and by the starkness of the act itself. In the aftermath the narrative that most residents preferred was quieter. They wanted the country to see Belfast not as a backdrop for something grotesque but as a place where people take care of one another after trouble. That desire influenced the way local sources spoke to reporters. They offered careful quotes that emphasized community support and the seriousness of the court proceedings rather than the lurid details that had once attracted national outlets. Over time this strategy worked. The national gaze moved on. The local attention remained, and it was focused on healing.

The most important part of the aftermath, as many residents said in private, was the well being of the child. Adults organized themselves around that priority. Teachers monitored progress in class with special care and showed flexibility when days were hard. Counselors coordinated with caregivers to build a plan that promoted resilience without forcing disclosures. Friends set up play dates that were gentle and predictable. The goal was to give the child a network of adults and peers that felt safe and ordinary. The evidence from other contexts is clear that such networks can make a decisive difference in a young person's recovery. Belfast did not need a research paper to tell it so, but the knowledge matched the instinct of people who have raised children in a small place for generations.

One sensitive question that floated through conversations involved remembrance. How does a family and a community remember a man whose conduct had become a source of fear and harm. The answer settled into a humane middle ground. People close to the family grieved the death because death itself is an occasion for grief. At the same time they did not insist on a public honoring that would have misrepresented the truth of what the household had endured. Private remembrance in such a case becomes layered and complicated. It does not reduce easily to a speech or a plaque. For those concerned most with the child, the emphasis was on honesty without cruelty. Children do not benefit from false stories, but neither do they benefit from endless rehearsals of pain. The art in such situations is to tell enough of the truth to give a young person a coherent account without loading her with adult judgments that she is not ready to carry.

Another theme of the aftermath was the recalibration of trust. People who had known Amber adjusted to her new role in the town. She was not only the person who had stood before a judge. She was a parent at school events, a neighbor who carried groceries, a citizen in the library line. Trust is built through repeated small interactions. When those interactions go well, the community discovers that it can rest alongside a hard memory without letting that memory govern every encounter. That is not to say the memory disappears. It grows less sharp at the edges. It becomes part of the texture of the town instead of a constant alarm.

Conversations about policy continued for a short time in county and state circles. Professionals asked what could be learned about prevention and intervention. They looked at the alignment of social services in rural counties and at the gaps that appear when a family moves far from its previous connections. They discussed training for judges and probation officers, not because this judge needed it in this case but because the system must maintain a standard for the next hard case. They explored the question of how communities communicate risk without sliding into rumor. The conclusion was not a single new program. It was the ongoing commitment to strengthen the ties between agencies and towns so that information and support can move quickly when needed.

Friends who had stood with Amber during the court process stepped back slightly once the sentence was in place. That change was deliberate. Support is not the same as constant presence. People need room to breathe after a long legal ordeal. They need to develop their own routines and to experience days that are not organized around hearings and interviews. The best friends know when to check in and when to let time do its work. In the months after the hearing that wisdom shaped the social perimeter around Amber and her child. The house was quiet. The calendar was full of simple commitments. Work. School. Therapy. Meals. Sleep. The railing that keeps a person steady after a storm is built of those plain boards.

Civic organizations took note of the community response and tried to preserve the momentum. They updated resource lists and made them visible in places where people might look for help. They trained volunteers to listen well and to avoid promises they could not keep. They clarified how to connect callers to professionals. They encouraged a culture in which asking for help is treated as a sign of strength rather than a source of shame. These were incremental steps, but incremental steps are how towns actually change. Grand declarations have their place. In a place like Belfast, quiet planning and reliable follow through matter more.

There was also the patient work of probation itself. Officers met with

Amber at regular intervals and verified compliance with conditions. They coordinated with therapists. They documented progress and setbacks. They maintained a tone that was firm and fair. Probation in a homicide case is not merely surveillance. It is stewardship. The goal is to help the person under supervision become the stable version of herself that the court believed she could be. When that goal is met the community benefits, not only because risk is reduced but because a family becomes a stronger participant in the life of the town.

In time the story of the case came up less often in conversation. Children grow. Seasons turn. The human mind cannot remain pitched at the high note of crisis. It needs release. For Belfast that release came in the form of the steady continuity of life on the bay. Boats left and returned. Shops opened their doors each morning. Schools held concerts and graduations. The town remembered the case, but the memory sat in the same drawer as other difficult stories from other years. Residents could fetch the memory when the subject of domestic abuse or sentencing arose, and they could set it aside when they wanted to talk about art exhibits or baseball games. This is not indifference. It is survival.

The aftermath also included a refinement of language. People learned to talk about domestic abuse with more precision. They used phrases like coercive control and trauma informed response. They learned that these were not academic terms but practical tools. They learned that asking why did she not leave is the wrong question and that better questions begin with what made it so dangerous to leave and who was available to help. This change in language matters because language shapes what actions seem possible. When towns become more adept at speaking about harm, they become better at preventing harm.

The final measure of an aftermath is whether the people who had the most at stake can live forward. In this case the answer took the shape of an ordinary life reconstructed piece by piece. The public did not need to watch every step. It needed only to keep its promise to remain a place where a mother and a child could walk down Main Street without being stopped by every stranger who wanted to revisit the worst day of their lives. Belfast kept that promise. The town did not pretend the past had not happened. It made space for the present to take root.

In the end, the reactions of public, friends, and family settled into a pattern that is both simple and profound. A crime had been committed and judged. A community had to decide what to do with the knowledge that came from the courtroom and from the lives that had led there. The decision, in practice, was to hold the family in a circle of attentiveness without smothering them, to respect the sentence as an expression of justice tempered by understanding, and to return as quickly as possible to the business of living well together. That is not a dramatic conclusion. It is better than dramatic. It is durable.

CHAPTER 6
SUSAN SMITH
DEATH BY 193 CUTS

True crime stories often leap straight to the terrible moment, but the more honest way to understand them is to begin earlier and move patiently through the choices and pressures that shape ordinary days. Before headlines and trials, there was a life in Houston, a courtship that sped toward marriage, two children, and a modest house in a northwest subdivision. Those facts form the stage on which everything else would later unfold.

Susan Lucille Wright was born in Houston on April 24th 1976 to parents whose lives were rooted in that sprawling city on the Gulf Coast. Houston in the late nineteen seventies and nineteen eighties was a place of rapid growth, with freeways unfurling outward and new neighborhoods arriving almost overnight. The city's middle class widened alongside the oil economy and the service sector, and young people often entered adulthood through restaurant work, retail, and other jobs that paid the bills while they figured out what came next.

As a teenager, Susan tried to earn quickly in the way many young people do when money is tight and options feel narrow. At seventeen she worked briefly as a topless dancer at a club called Gold Cup, a job she held for a short period before moving on. The choice was not a defining career. It was a few weeks of work by a teenager testing the practical edges of independence and income. That brief stint would later be used in a courtroom to frame her image, but at the time it was simply one stop on a young woman's quick path toward steadier employment.

By the late nineteen nineties she was waiting tables in Galveston, a short drive from Houston along the causeway. Restaurant work on the island requires stamina and social skill. A server has to hold orders in mind while reading the room, remembering refills, keeping up with the kitchen, and smoothing frayed tempers when a dish arrives late or a ticket prints wrong. The job also brings a stream of faces through a server's life. One of those faces belonged to Jeff Wright, a customer who would soon become much more than a face.

Susan met Jeff in 1997. Their relationship moved quickly, as many do when chemistry and circumstance align. They married in 1998, a decision made when she was eight and a half months pregnant with their first child. The timing made for a modest wedding. No long engagement, no elaborate reception. The priority was legal and practical, to place a clear frame around a family that would begin within days. Early parenthood and early marriage arrived together, and that double weight would shape the rhythm of their lives.

Newlyweds with a newborn have little room left for leisure. Money must stretch. Sleep is interrupted. A small apartment or starter house fills with baby gear. The little tasks of care take over the day. Bottles, diapers, laundry, lists. Parents tell themselves that the first months are a tunnel and that the light ahead will come into view if they keep walking. In the Wright household, that tunnel opened into the ordinary work of building a life in Houston, one errand and one paycheck at a time.

Houston is a city of neighborhoods that act like small towns. The northwest reaches of Harris County mix working families, retirees, and new arrivals in winding subdivisions set back from busy arterial roads. Driveways fill in the evening. Lawns become weekend projects. Corner stores know the regulars. Schools serve as daily gathering points where parents exchange quick news at pick up and drop off. The Wright family would eventually join that landscape, choosing a house in the White Oak Bend subdivision, a development in an unincorporated area of the county where modest houses line streets with names meant to evoke trees and creeks. This was not a gated enclave or a high profile district. It was a place where many young families try to find stability.

Before that move, the household adjusted to the arrival of a second child. Their daughter was born in 2002, four years after the marriage. A family of four changes the scale of daily life. The grocery list grows. The car fills with child seats. Parents move in a practiced relay, passing duties back and forth. A mother who also works outside the home becomes a timekeeper and a scheduler, keeping the appointments in her head while making dinner and finding missing shoes. A father finds his own groove within that routine, whether in long hours, irregular shifts, or a mix that keeps the income coming.

People who knew Susan in these years often remember her as soft spoken and focused on the children. Friends and relatives recall a young mother who was consistent in the rituals of care that give small children a sense of safety. Breakfast at the same time, bedtime stories, the familiar sweep of a day arranged around naps, baths, and school. That kind of structure is not dramatic, but it is the fabric of early family life, and it tells you something about a person's priorities. Order is not fussy when children are small. It is a shield against chaos.

The world outside the front door was busy and hot and sprawling. Inside, the household settled into the common loop of work, errands, chores, and weekends. There would have been trips to grandparents or cousins, birthday parties in backyards, holidays that brought relatives to a table layered with staples and casseroles. There would have been bills to pay, checks to deposit, and quick decisions about what could wait until next month. Many families in Houston can recognize themselves in that picture. The city's economy rewards hustle and persistence. Most households keep moving forward through effort and habit rather than through windfalls.

The public record that later emerged includes claims by Susan that the marriage became marked by intimidation and abuse in its early years. Such claims belong to the legal and factual debates of later sections, not to this one. The point here is more basic. In any large city, and particularly in a proudly self reliant culture like the one that shapes much of Texas, families often keep troubles private. The reasons are practical and cultural. People fear gossip. They hope the next month will be better. They do not want to be judged by neighbors or even by extended family. Resources exist, from police to hotlines to counseling, but reaching for them can feel like crossing a line. The result is that the life visible from the driveway can look perfectly ordinary even when tension rule the rooms.

Parenthood does not pause for adult conflict. Children bring a steady stream of obligations that are both demanding and joyful. There are pediatric visits, school registrations, field days, and first performances in cafeterias that double as auditoriums. There are new shoes in August and winter jackets that hang unused most years. There are scraped knees to wash and report cards to sign. A mother who keeps these threads in order creates a stability that children carry in their bones. The Wright children had that structure. Whatever the adult dynamics, the calendar of childhood was maintained.

Work remained an anchor for Susan. Restaurant shifts can be unpredictable, but the rhythm of service work teaches a person to anticipate needs and to keep moving even when tired. That habit carries over into home life. A server knows how to juggle competing demands and still set a plate down with a smile. A mother with that training does the same with baths and meals and bedtime, turning chaos into routine by force of will and repetition. The skills are related. They also exact a toll. By the end of a long day, the person who has done the invisible work is often out of words.

The purchase or rental of the house in White Oak Bend brought the family to a community where quiet was the default setting. Neighbors waved as they mowed. Children rode bikes in small packs. Parents compared notes about teachers. Residents drove out to the larger roads for work and returned to the looped streets each evening. The subdivision had the feel of a place meant for growing families. Fences created discreet borders and the yards were neither big nor small. The mail arrived in the middle of the day. Trash trucks rolled through on a set schedule. A home in such a place promises a version of the American middle, not grand and not bleak, a steady middle.

Those who met Jeff in these years often describe him in brief strokes, some friendly, some sharp. Memory of a couple is never uniform because people behave differently with different audiences. A man may be calm and affable at a barbecue and different at home after a long shift. A woman may be open with a friend while guarded with a relative. What can be said with confidence is that the couple built a life that looked like many others in northwest Harris County. They joined the flow of commutes and school events. They kept their business largely their own.

The timeline of the early life is therefore straightforward. Birth in Houston on April 24th 1976. Service work as a teenager and young adult, including a short stint at a club and later, steady restaurant jobs in Galveston. Meeting Jeff Wright in 1997. Marriage in 1998, with a baby due within days. A second child, a daughter, in two thousand two. A move into the house in White Oak Bend before the middle of the next year. Nothing in that bare chronology demands attention from police or courts. It is the scaffold on which millions of American family stories are built.

Culture and setting matter because they influence how people respond to stress. Texas carries a strong ethic of family loyalty and self reliance. Those values shore up families in hard times and can also keep them from seeking help when help might be wise. In a county as large as Harris, agencies and nonprofits provide services, but those services only reach the people who call or walk in. Many do not. Instead they lean on pride, faith, and a belief that the next day will be better. That ethos shaped the world around the Wright family.

To see the full picture of this early chapter, imagine the daily scenes that are not dramatic but are crucial. A grocery cart rolling down an aisle under fluorescent lights. A list written on the back of an envelope. A child in the basket fidgeting with a box of cereal. A second child in the seat kicking her feet. A mother checking prices and moving quickly because the budget and the clock are both tight. The drive back up a busy road into a quiet loop. The unloading of bags and the small cheer that runs through a kitchen when a late afternoon snack appears. Bedtime later with a story and a light clicked off. Those are the acts that mark a home as a home, the acts that keep children feeling held by a steady world.

Friends and relatives saw these ordinary scenes and added their own small impressions to the family album in their minds. A smile across a table at a holiday meal. A weary look that passed quickly. A plan to meet that had to be rescheduled because somebody had to cover a shift. Nothing that would alert an outsider to a future crime, only the familiar tides of a young family holding together.

The early life of Susan Wright is therefore best understood as the creation of a circle. Into that circle came marriage, two children, and a house in a neighborhood meant for families like theirs. The circle held routines, budgets, hopes, and the private negotiations that define any partnership. Some later accounts would place darker elements within that circle. Those elements will be examined in the sections that deal directly with the crime and with the arguments made in court. For now it is enough to see the circle as it looked from the street and as it felt in the small acts of care that filled the rooms.

When a reader asks how a story like this one could unfold, the answer often begins with the quiet persistence of the early years. There is nothing exotic about them. A young mother from Houston worked, fell in love, married, and had children. She and her husband moved into a modest house in a northwest subdivision. They joined a landscape of families doing the same. The larger city moved around them with its roar of traffic and its endless errands. The interior of their life contained the same fragile mix of joy, fatigue, expectation, and pride that governs so many households.

That is the story of the first section in this chapter. It is not an argument and not a verdict. It is a portrait of a family at its most ordinary scale. The next part of the chapter will leave that quiet kitchen and step into a particular night and a room that became the focus of national attention. Before we go there, hold the image of a mother buckling children into car seats in the heat of a Houston afternoon. She closes the doors, starts the engine, and turns the air to full. She looks in the rearview mirror to be sure the children are settled. Then she pulls onto the road that loops through White Oak Bend and heads out to the larger streets that connect every house in Houston to every other house. For a moment, nothing about that scene announces tragedy. It is simply a family moving through an ordinary day.

THE MURDER

The calendar places the event on January 13th 2003. The address was a single family house in the White Oak Bend subdivision in the northwest part of Harris County. The scene that would later be reconstructed in reports and testimony began in a bedroom where a husband and wife had argued many times before. By the end of that night, Jeff Wright was dead of multiple stab wounds, and his body would be buried in a shallow grave in the yard behind the house.

The plain facts are stark. Susan Wright was twenty six. Jeff Wright was thirty four. According to the case presented by the state, Susan tied her husband to the bed and stabbed him a total of 193 times with two different knives. The count was not an estimate. It was the result of a methodical autopsy that cataloged injuries one by one, distinguishing cuts and stabs and mapping their locations. The number entered the public record and became a shorthand for the violence of the act.

The immediate physical setting matters because it frames the possibilities. A standard bedroom in a modest Texas subdivision is not a large space. A bed anchors the room. Nightstands carry small clutter. There is a dresser, a closet, perhaps a television on a shallow cabinet. The state's account, supported by photographs and later expert analysis, described wrists and ankles bound to the bed. Whether the restraints were applied as part of a routine of intimacy or as a trap was a question that would be argued later. Here, in the strict register of the killing itself, the bindings explain how the stabbing could proceed without the victim escaping the bed during the first violent minutes.

Two knives were involved. One was a larger kitchen knife, the other a smaller blade. At some point one knife ceased to be used and the second was taken up. The switches and pauses would later be charted by investigators through wound tracks and through the recovery of the blades. The change of weapon is an important detail only because it confirms that the assault continued across more than a single frenzied instant. It moved through steps and choices inside a narrow window of time.

Violence on this scale produces more than blood. It produces marks on the room that linger even after hurried efforts to clean. The bedroom took the brunt. Spatter patterns followed the geometry of the bed and the walls. Sheets and blankets were stained. A pillow was likely soaked. The floor received the rest. The science that reads these scenes is careful. It attends to arcs and drops and angles. It tells a story of how a person stood and how the blade moved. That science, as applied to this case, reinforced the core truth that the stabbing occurred at the bed, not elsewhere, and that it involved repeated blows delivered at close range.

The night did not end with the last wound. It continued through a series of actions that moved from the bedroom to the yard. Prosecutors would later describe how the body was removed from the bed and transported outside. The distance between the bedroom and the chosen patch of ground is measured in steps that must be taken with effort. A human body is heavy and unwieldy, and moving it requires strength and determination. In the yard there was a space where soil had been recently disturbed. Reporting at the time noted that the hole used for burial had been dug earlier by Jeff for a project in the yard. Whatever the origin, it became a grave. The body was placed inside. Soil was spread to cover it. The yard was raked and patted in an attempt to erase the signs of what lay beneath.

Back inside, the bedroom became the focus of a different kind of effort. There was painting to be done if the walls were to be made presentable. There was bedding to be stripped and hidden or removed. There were bleach and cleaners to be applied to surfaces that could be scrubbed. These are not details meant to add shock value. They are the elements of a domestic crime scene where the killer tries to return a room to the appearance of normal life. In the Wright house, the fresh paint and the smell of cleaner stood out when investigators later walked through the door.

The day after the killing, Susan took a step that would complicate the narrative in a way that cannot be ignored. She went to court and filed a domestic abuse report to seek a restraining order against her husband. The record shows that she claimed fear and asked for protection. In the narrow timeline of mid January, the filing had a practical effect. It created a paper trail that said Jeff had left the home in a storm of anger. It positioned Susan as a person seeking legal protection rather than as a person covering a crime. The restraining order was granted. The order would later be important evidence when the state argued that the filing was part of a plan to delay discovery.

Days passed. During those days the yard was quiet. The house sat on its loop in the subdivision and the routines of the neighborhood continued. Children went to school. Neighbors came and went. Nothing about the front of the house announced what had happened behind it. On January 18th, the legal posture changed when Susan contacted attorney Neal Davis and asked him to come to the house. When he arrived, she told him she had stabbed her husband and that his body was buried in the yard. Davis informed prosecuting authorities that a body was present at the property and that his client had confessed to killing her husband. That call brought law enforcement to the scene and altered the case from a missing person narrative to a recovery and investigation.

The recovery unfolded in a standard way. Investigators secured the property. Photography and video documented the exterior and the interior before any digging began. Technicians marked the area of disturbed soil and then heaved back shovelfuls of earth to reach the body. Fresh Texas soil gives way in layers, and the moment when cloth and skin appear is unmistakable. The body was lifted with care and placed in a body bag for transport to the medical examiner. The hole was examined for items that might have fallen during the burial. The house itself was searched with a warrant. The bedroom became a secondary crime scene to be cataloged in detail. The act of painting the walls counted as a form of tampering. That would not be forgotten when the case moved to court.

The autopsy confirmed what the room and the yard had already suggested. Jeff Wright had been stabbed 193 times. The wounds covered multiple regions of the body. Some were shallow, others deep. Forensic teams diagrammed each wound and noted directionality and clustering. The pathologist distinguished between injuries that were immediately fatal and injuries that compounded the death through blood loss. The report also noted the absence or presence of defensive wounds. In a tied down victim, such wounds are less likely to appear on the hands and forearms. The overall pattern supported the conclusion that the attack occurred while the victim was restrained and that it continued for a sustained period.

A homicide on this scale does not exist in a vacuum. There were two small children connected to the household. The investigative reports and later court records do not place them in the room of the killing. Their exact whereabouts on the night and during the immediate aftermath belong to protected parts of the record and to the care of family services. What can be said is that their welfare became a priority for authorities once the case turned from missing person to murder. Child protection protocols were activated. Relatives were contacted. Arrangements were made to keep the children out of the direct line of the legal process as much as possible while ensuring their safety.

As evidence was collected, the narrative of the days after the killing sharpened. The painting and cleaning were not effective enough to erase the forensic trace. Blood has a way of announcing itself under light sources and reagent sprays. The fresh coat of paint could not obscure what seeped through at the seams and baseboards. Bedding was accounted for or its absence noted. Knives were found or their disappearance was recorded for later argument. The filing of the restraining order the morning after the stabbing became a pivot point in the timeline. The call to the attorney and the attorney's call to the authorities became the hinge that swung the case into full view.

When the first uniformed officers arrived on January 18th, they faced the ordinary decisions that define a well run homicide scene. They established a perimeter. They separated family members and potential witnesses. They placed an officer at the bedroom door to prevent stray footsteps from corrupting the scene. They kept a log of who entered the property and for what purpose. These steps are not theatrical. They are the unseen discipline that keeps a case intact when it moves later into court. In the Wright case, the documentation was thorough enough that the essential facts could be presented to a jury without gaps.

The days between January 13th and January 18th are often described as a period of attempted normalization in which Susan tried to present a face of routine life while living with the knowledge of what lay under the soil. The restraining order added a layer of credibility to the idea that her husband had stormed out. Friends and relatives had to be told a story that could hold for a few days. The house had to be kept in a state that would not invite close inspection. There is a peculiar strain in such an interval. It requires pretending that time is moving forward normally while every hour is heavy with fear of discovery. In this case discovery came quickly because Susan herself set it in motion through her attorney.

The choice to call a lawyer and to confess before the house was searched likely spared the neighborhood a longer period of uncertainty. It also shaped the legal pathway from that day on. The confession meant that the fact of the killing would not be in doubt. The arguments would revolve around reason and motive and the degree of planning. But those are questions for the next section of this book. The purpose here is to hold the lens steady on the night and the immediate steps that followed.

These are the pillars upon which the rest of the case stands. The room, the bed, the blades, the grave, the paint. Around those pillars the legal system would begin to build its arguments. The prosecution would frame the sequence as a planned killing executed to rid the household of a husband and to clear the way for a new life and a life insurance payout. The defense would frame the same steps as the desperate acts of a woman who feared for her life after years of abuse and who sought to protect herself and her children. Those frames belong to the courtroom and to the section that follows. What remains in this chapter is the absolute center of the story, the act that turned a private home into a crime scene and a married couple into a defendant and a deceased.

It is important, even in a documentary account, to resist the pull of sensational language. The number of wounds is shocking enough without adornment. The burial in a backyard is grim enough without metaphor. The painting of a room to cover blood needs no embellishment. The atmosphere of those days is best conveyed by the simple listing of events and the recognition that each step followed from the one before with a terrible logic. If a reader wants to understand how a suburban bedroom could become the site of a killing that would be discussed across the country, the answer is not in mystery. It is in the plain sequence of a night that began in a marriage bed and ended in a yard under disturbed soil.

In the end, January 13th 2003 is a date that fixes the entire case in time. Before that night, the Wright family was one among thousands in a quiet part of a large county. After that night, the address became a point on the map known to reporters and to a jury. The bed became evidence. The yard became a grave and then a pit under police lights. The freshly painted walls became exhibits. The days that followed carried the case from secrecy to disclosure and from the private language of a household to the public language of sworn statements and chain of custody forms. From this point forward, nothing about the house in White Oak Bend would be only a matter of family.

ARREST, TRIAL AND SENTENCE

The legal arc began in the last week of January when the case crossed the threshold from a grim discovery to a formal accusation. After her lawyer notified authorities that a body was present on the property and that his client had admitted to a killing, the question was no longer whether a crime had been committed. It was what charge would be filed and how the state would present the narrative to a grand jury and to the public. On January 24th 2003 Susan Wright went to the courthouse and surrendered. She was booked and brought before a magistrate for the first appearance at which the state read the charge. The words were plain. Murder under Texas law. From that moment she moved within the tight framework that governs a serious felony. Counsel was confirmed, bond and conditions were addressed, and the calendar of pretrial events began to fill.

Booking and intake are administrative steps that carry heavy consequence. A defendant is photographed and fingerprinted. Biographical information is collected. The charge is entered into the system. The jail assigns a housing location appropriate to the level of risk and to the nature of the charge. Contact with family is limited and controlled. For someone who has lived only in homes and workplaces, the sudden confinement is a shock that strips away the familiar. A person moves at the pace set by officers and by automatic doors. Food arrives on a schedule that cannot be adjusted. Lights turn on and off on a fixed pattern. That first weekend after surrender is usually the longest weekend of a life. Time stretches because nothing can be decided until court opens and lawyers can file the first motions.

Within days the Harris County District Attorneys Office began to assemble a package of evidence for presentation to a grand jury. This package would include reports from the scene, the medical examiner's findings, photos, and the statements that formed the spine of the case. The goal before the grand jury is not to present every shred of evidence. It is to establish probable cause that the crime charged was committed by the accused within the county. The standard is not beyond a reasonable doubt. It is a lower threshold meant to test whether the state has a legitimate basis for taking the matter forward. In a case where the body had been recovered from the property and a confession had been relayed by counsel, the presentment was straightforward. An indictment followed and the case was set on the felony docket in a district court authorized to hear homicide matters.

From that point the legal system shifted into its adversarial posture. The state filed discovery. The defense filed requests for additional material and set in motion its own investigation. The court scheduled status conferences to monitor progress and to rule on early motions. The defense ran a parallel track, interviewing friends and relatives, collecting medical records, and engaging experts who could evaluate the claims that would later be central to the defense posture. These claims were familiar to anyone who has seen a domestic homicide case. They spoke of fear and of prior conduct inside the marriage. The challenge for the defense was to move those claims from the realm of assertion to the realm of admissible evidence and expert opinion.

Trial preparation on the state side was led by an experienced prosecutor who understood both the evidentiary burden and the storytelling burden that attend a murder case. The evidence itself would not be difficult to explain. The difficulty would lie in persuading jurors to set aside any sympathy for a young mother and to focus instead on the deliberate nature of the act and the steps taken afterward. The prosecution did not ignore context. It pressed a different context. It framed the bedroom, the cleanup, and the burial as parts of a plan rather than as the panicked efforts of a person acting in fear. It signaled that the state would show the jury how a sequence of calculated decisions produced a death and an attempted cover story.

On the defense side, attorney Neal Davis began to shape a narrative aimed at mitigation and at justification. He prepared to argue that Susan had acted in self defense after years of physical and emotional abuse. He secured mental health professionals who could explain how prolonged trauma can shape perception and decision making. He gathered records and photographs that would support the claim that pain and fear were present long before the fatal night. He prepared to call relatives who could testify to what they said they had seen and to the bruises they said they remembered. He planned to put Susan on the stand, knowing that her testimony would be a pivotal moment.

Thirteen months passed between arraignment and trial, a span that was neither unusually long nor short for a homicide case of this complexity. During that time the defendant remained under the control of the court, either in custody or under conditions set by the judge. The children did not become a spectacle. Family services and relatives saw to their welfare under protective protocols. The court managed publicity with a firm hand. The case drew attention because of the location and because of the details that were leaking into the public conversation, but Judge and counsel kept the proceedings on schedule and focused on law rather than on rumor.

Jury selection began on February 24th 2004. In a high profile case this requires patience. Dozens of potential jurors are questioned in panels and individually about their exposure to news, their views on domestic violence, and their capacity to apply the law without bias. The prosecution wanted jurors who could accept graphic evidence and who were not inclined to rationalize a killing as a private solution. The defense wanted jurors open to the reality of abuse and to a self defense claim even when the facts of the scene seemed hard to reconcile with a struggle. Both sides exercised strikes to remove those they believed would not be fair. The panel that took the oath represented a cross section of the county with a range of ages and backgrounds.

The state opened its case with a methodical presentation designed to build credibility, point by point. First responders traced the timeline of discovery. Crime scene technicians walked the jury through photographs that showed the condition of the room and the yard. The medical examiner explained the injuries in clinical language, careful to avoid drama while still conveying the extent of the assault. The prosecutor maintained a tone that was firm but controlled, letting the images and measurements carry the weight rather than rhetorical flourishes. The jury sat with notebooks and followed the sequence as each witness marked exhibits and identified items for the record.

In a move that would ensure the trial became a subject of national attention, the prosecution brought the couple's bed into the courtroom. The decision was strategic. It allowed the state to anchor its theory of the case in a physical object that jurors could see and touch. Assistant District Attorney Kelly Siegler used the bed to show how bindings could have been applied and to suggest how a restrained person could be held in place while the assault occurred. The demonstration was unusual but not improper. Courts permit exhibits that help jurors visualize the events as long as the probative value outweighs any unfair prejudice. The judge allowed it, and the image of a bed sitting in a courtroom beside a witness stand became an emblem of the case.

The state also pursued a motive theory that turned on money and on control. Prosecutors reminded the jury that life insurance is a common feature of adult life and argued that it served here as a dark incentive for a plan to remove a spouse. The number was two hundred thousand dollars. The state did not argue that the policy alone explains all conduct. It argued that the policy fit within a pattern of decisions that included an effort to disguise a killing as a departure and to forestall discovery through a restraining order filed the next morning. The calendar entries and the paper trail mattered to the state because they transformed what could have been seen as chaos into what the state urged was calculation.

The defense case took a very different course. Susan Wright testified. Defendants are not required to take the stand, and many do not. She did. In a voice that was by turns quiet and intense, she described years of fear. She said the violence in the home had increased and that on the night in question she believed she would die if she did not fight. She said she could not stop once the struggle began because she was sure he would recover control and kill her. She said the cover up that followed was not the work of a planner but the frantic behavior of a terrorized person who did not know what else to do. Her mother testified that she had seen bruises and that she had worried for her daughter but had not been able to force a change in the home. Mental health professionals called by the defense explained concepts like battered spouse syndrome and the way trauma can narrow choices until only fight or flight remain visible.

The prosecution cross examined Susan with the practiced rhythm of a seasoned trial lawyer. The tone was skeptical. The questions returned again and again to choices made before and after the killing. Why tie a person to a bed at all if the goal is safety. Why clean and paint. Why file a restraining order the next morning. Why bury the body in the yard. The questions aimed to erode the link between fear and action, replacing it with a picture of manipulation and guile. The prosecutor also addressed the defendant's emotional presentation, suggesting that tears and pauses were calculated. That line of attack is risky because jurors do not like to feel that a witness is being bullied. In this courtroom the give and take remained within the bounds of acceptable advocacy. The judge sustained objections when phrasing strayed and allowed the jury to hear full answers when the questions were fair.

Closing arguments presented the stark contrast at the heart of the case. The state asked the jury to regard the bedroom, the cleanup, and the legal paperwork as the marks of a plan to rid a household of a husband and to profit through insurance. It asked the jury to reserve sympathy for the children and for the idea that the law must apply equally even when the defendant is a mother who presents a gentle face. The defense asked the jury to believe that the killing happened in a context that makes sense only if one accepts the reality of prolonged abuse. It asked the jury to see the aftermath not as cunning but as panic. It reminded the jury that self defense need not look neat to be real, and that a person who fears for her life is not required to choose perfect steps in perfect sequence.

On March 3rd 2004, after more than five hours of deliberation, the jury returned a verdict of guilty of murder. The courtroom received the verdict in a hush that always attends the reading of a single word that will shape the next decades of a life. Susan showed little visible reaction. Her lawyer placed a hand on her arm. The state remained still. Family members on both sides absorbed the outcome with the practiced dignity that courtrooms compel. The judge thanked the jurors and released them from further duty with words of appreciation for their service. The case moved to the next phase.

In Texas the punishment phase in a murder case can be tried before the same jury that heard the evidence of guilt. The day after the verdict, the courtroom reconvened for sentencing. The state argued for a long term, saying that the level of violence and the steps taken afterward deserved a severe denouncement. Prosecutors asked for at least fifty five years. The defense asked for mercy in the form of a sentence that would allow Susan to return to her children while they were still young. They even asked the jury to consider probation, an option that exists in the code under narrow circumstances but that is rarely granted in a case involving a death. The defense pointed to her lack of prior criminal history and to the testimony about her fear. It reminded the jury that punishment is not only about retribution but also about the possibility of rehabilitation.

The jury chose a middle path compared to the state's request. On March 4th 2004 it set the term at twenty five years in the Texas Department of Criminal Justice. The sentence was within the statutory range and reflected the jury's weighing of the competing narratives presented during punishment. The court pronounced the sentence formally. The clerk entered it. Deputies prepared to transport the defendant to state custody following the completion of local processing. In the gallery, the reality of the number settled on the faces of those who had lived with the case for more than a year. Twenty five years is a long time in any life. It is a childhood and part of an adulthood. It is a measure of separation that cannot be captured by quick reactions.

The transfer to state prison changed Susan's daily world again. County jail is a holding environment. State custody is a long term system with its own geography and rules. She was assigned to a facility for women located in Gatesville, part of a cluster of units on land that has housed prisoners for generations. Intake repeated the routines of identification and medical checks, then settled into classification that would determine housing, work assignments, and access to programs. A person with a high profile case soon learns that notoriety has little currency behind the fence. The daily incentives and pressures are immediate and practical. Follow rules, avoid infractions, seek programming, and maintain contact with family under the restrictions set by policy.

Public reaction to the verdict and sentence was divided in the way that hard cases divide communities. Some saw the outcome as measured justice for a deliberate killing. Others saw it as too harsh for a woman they believed had endured years of pain and who acted in a corner. The court spoke the final legal word. The community spoke many words, some in support and some in criticism, but those words did not alter the judgment entered by the clerk. In the end, the law had done what the law is designed to do. It had received evidence, allowed argument, instructed a jury, and overseen a verdict and a sentence that fell within the statutory framework.

When the courtroom emptied after the punishment decision and the last television camera was wheeled out, the place returned to its usual quiet. Courtrooms are built to witness the extremes of human behavior and to manage them without heat. The judge's bench remained. The flag stood. The witness chair sat empty. The bed that had turned the proceeding into a spectacle was gone, returned to the custody of the sheriff after its function as an exhibit was complete. In that silence one could sense the odd balance that the criminal law tries to strike. It deals in guilt and in numbers, yet under those numbers are lives that do not fit easily into the boxes on a judgment form.

The arrest, the methodical assembly of a case, the sharp contest at trial, and the measured sentence together make a coherent narrative. They trace how a private act in a suburban bedroom moved through the machinery of a great county and a great state, arriving at a conclusion fashioned by sworn citizens under instructions that have been honed over time. The legal story is not the whole story. It does not tell what a child feels when a parent vanishes into custody or what a mother feels when she hears the cell door shut the first night. Those parts belong to the aftermath. The task of this section is more limited. It is to show how the state received the case, how counsel fought it, how a jury decided it, and how a sentence was pronounced and adjusted within the lawful process. From that point, the case left the courtroom and entered a longer season of incarceration, petition, denial, reconsideration, and the passage of years, which together formed the final chapter of the Susan Wright story.

AFTERMATH WITH FAMILY AND PUBLIC OPINION

When a verdict settles and the courtroom empties, the story does not end. It moves into chambers and offices and then out beyond the courthouse doors into the long corridors of prison and parole, into living rooms where families reorganize themselves, and into the public square where journalists, television producers, and neighbors try to make sense of what they have witnessed. The aftermath of the Susan Wright case unfolded across years, and it touched the systems of punishment and supervision in Texas as well as the humbler systems by which ordinary people resume their lives. This section follows that long course without revisiting the facts tried at court. It looks instead at the institutions that received Susan after sentencing, the decisions made by appellate courts and parole panels, the fluctuations of public opinion, and the quieter work of families and communities who had to absorb what the law decided.

After the jury announced the first sentence in early March 2004, the county process gave way to the state system. A person sentenced for a serious offense in Texas is transferred to the custody of the Texas Department of Criminal Justice, an agency with its own geography and rules. Susan entered that geography and was assigned to the unit at Gatesville known for holding women. Intake in state custody begins with identification, health screening, and classification. The agency determines housing and work assignments according to security level, institutional needs, and program availability. The routine is stable and impersonal by design. It is built to move thousands of people through days measured by counts, call outs, and strict schedules. A life that had been public for months became private again in a different way, defined by a number, a dorm or cell, and a roster of obligations that include work details and educational or treatment programs when available.

Outside the fence, appeals lawyers took charge of the record. A direct appeal to the intermediate court examined the conduct of the trial for legal error. In 2005 that court upheld the conviction. Years later a separate issue returned the case to a courtroom, not to revisit guilt but to revisit punishment. The highest criminal court in the state determined that the representation at the first punishment hearing had been deficient in a way that mattered. That ruling did not free Susan. It directed the local court to assemble a new jury and to conduct a new hearing on sentence alone so that a fully developed record could be weighed. In November 2010 the new panel reduced the term to twenty years. The legal meaning of that change is specific. It signifies that punishment is a judgment informed by the quality of the presentation and that the law remains open to correction when standards are not met.

Life in prison runs on a calendar different from the one outside. The year is divided by custody reviews, commissary days, visits, and programs rather than by holidays or school terms. A person learns to manage the narrow field of control available to her. Work assignments can include kitchen duty, laundry, clerical tasks, or maintenance. Educational programs range from basic literacy to vocational offerings when resources permit. Counseling and classes associated with rehabilitation and with preparation for release are part of the institutional menu, though availability varies with funding and demand. Family contact, when it is possible and permitted, occurs through monitored calls, letters, and scheduled visits. Policy dictates the terms. Officers enforce them. In that environment, the steady virtues are patience and discipline. A rule followed each day accumulates into a record of compliance. That record matters when the time comes to speak to a panel about parole.

Parole is not an automatic right in Texas. It is a decision made by appointed board members who review files, consider testimony and letters, and apply statutory criteria that include the nature of the offense, the institutional record, and the likelihood of success under supervision. Susan became eligible for parole in February 2014 by the terms of the new sentence. The panel considered the application and denied it in June of that year. The denial reflected the board's judgment at that time that continued incarceration was warranted. Parole was considered again in July 2017, and the panel again denied release. Those decisions were announcements with immediate practical effect but no dramatic gesture. They arrived in letters and notices, and life in the unit continued.

Media interest did not vanish after sentencing. It changed shape. Television programs devoted to true crime produced episodes that framed the case for audiences who had not followed the trial. Court proceedings had been covered live when possible, and the material invited the sort of retelling that such programs specialize in. One national network aired a dramatization titled Blue Eyed Butcher in 2012. Documentary series produced segments in which prosecutors and defense attorneys revisited their strategies on camera. The tone of these productions varied. Some emphasized the shock of the case. Others attempted to parse the legal and psychological questions. The wider public often encountered the case not through court transcripts but through these interpretations. That fact matters because media versions affect public opinion even when the legal process is complete.

The effect on family is more private. Two children had to grow up with a parent in prison and another parent deceased. Their care and protection became the responsibility of relatives and of the systems that oversee child welfare and visitation in difficult cases. The details of their lives deserve privacy. What can be said is that the institutions involved do not make such arrangements lightly. Courts consider the best interest of the child in the specific circumstances before them. That principle guided decisions about contact and about the slow reintegration that would become relevant years later when parole was granted.

The community in Houston and in Harris County continued to carry the case as a reference point in conversations about domestic violence and about the criminal justice system. Advocates used the story to educate residents and professionals about recognizing signs of harm and about accessing resources. Legal commentators used it to discuss the complexity of self defense claims in intimate settings and the weight that juries place on conduct after a crime. These discussions rarely produced consensus. They did not need to. Their value lay in making a community more fluent in the language of prevention, reporting, and fair process.

In July 2020 the parole board reached a different conclusion. It approved release subject to conditions. In Texas a grant of parole does not erase the sentence. It suspends confinement and replaces it with supervision terms that the parolee must follow. Those terms generally include reporting to a supervising officer, maintaining residence at an approved location, avoiding new offenses, observing travel restrictions, and participating in counseling or programming as directed. Conditions may also address employment, substance use, contact with certain persons, and the payment of fees in accordance with law. The exact conditions in any case are set by the board and communicated to the parolee in writing. In late December 2020, after arrangements were complete, Susan was released at age forty four.

Release from prison into parole is not a return to the previous life. It is the beginning of a structured period in which a person must adjust to the freedoms and burdens of the outside world under close observation. The small tasks of living in free society are not small after years inside. A person must learn or relearn the use of a smartphone, the ways banking now works, the expectations of employers, and the etiquette of offices and public spaces that may have changed while she was gone. Many do not think about these details when they read about parole in a newspaper. For the parolee they are daily realities. The officer assigned to supervision serves as both monitor and guide, offering direction while enforcing rules.

Public opinion at the time of release followed the contours set years earlier. There were people who believed the original sentence had been too severe. There were people who believed the reduced sentence was still appropriate to the severity of the killing. There were others who objected to any release at all. The features of Texas parole law made clear that the board had authority to release under conditions once statutory eligibility was met and that the board had weighed the file carefully. News accounts of the release focused on the date and the basic facts. The broader debate did not achieve new clarity. Such debates seldom do. They exist as part of the social processing of violent crime.

The professionals who appeared at trial also continued to feel echoes of the case. Prosecutors and defense attorneys involved in high profile matters find that those matters are mentioned in later proceedings and in classrooms where new lawyers are trained. The questions Taught in such rooms are pragmatic. How was the evidence presented. What exhibits helped jurors understand the scene. How did the defense choose which witnesses to call. What arguments helped or hurt. In that way the case provides lessons that have nothing to do with television stories and everything to do with the craft of trying serious cases within rules that have been refined across years.

Beyond law and media, the case had cultural afterlives. Producers of radio and podcast series included the story in broader seasons about marriages that end in violence. Writers used it in essays exploring the way certain defendants are portrayed in public. Such portrayals often turn on appearance, gender, and class. They raise questions that are not legal questions but that shape audience reaction. These projects varied in quality and in fidelity to the record. Some consulted the transcripts and the appellate opinions and used them as a spine. Others relied on earlier reports and dramatizations and repeated errors. The public receives a mixture of these versions, which makes it important to return to the court record when forming judgments.

Parole brought new responsibilities for Susan that did not exist in prison. She had to find lawful employment or other approved activity, manage compliance with all conditions, and navigate a world where the case remained public knowledge. Supervision is designed to be both supportive and strict. Officers can connect a parolee to resources for housing, employment, and counseling. They can also respond to violations with sanctions, including the possibility of revocation and return to custody. Success on parole is a string of small decisions and obligations met consistently. Over time those small acts become a record that convinces a board that the person can remain in the community without undue risk.

Families affected by the case continued to rebuild in their own ways. Some chose silence to protect children and to lower the temperature of public interest. Others consented to interviews in which they expressed their grief and their conviction about what the story meant. The variety of reaction is a reminder that there is no single correct way to respond to violent loss. Some find comfort in speaking. Others find comfort in privacy. Communities can honor both preferences by resisting the impulse to press for statements and by respecting limits when they are set.

For the city of Houston the case eventually joined the long list of notorious crimes that have passed through its courts. The city has a deep bench of judges, lawyers, and investigators who work such cases every year. Each one yields a few practical improvements in policy or training. One area where this case contributed to ongoing conversations was the use of physical exhibits to help juries understand domestic settings. Another was the handling of sentencing presentations in cases where context plays an outsized role. The new punishment hearing in 2010 demonstrated that better developed mitigation evidence can affect outcomes. Attorneys on both sides took note. That observation may seem technical, but it has a human consequence. It means that future jurors will have more complete pictures when they decide between a long number and a longer number.

The parole decision in 2020 also landed in the larger story of criminal justice in Texas. That year brought national attention to questions of incarceration and release. Within that context, a case from a previous decade acquired new resonance. Observers debated the purpose of parole in violent cases and the weight that should be given to institutional records, to new evidence presented at later hearings, and to the risk assessments that agencies use. Again, consensus was elusive. The virtue of the system is that it provides a process even when agreement is not possible. The virtue of public conversation is that it keeps the process under scrutiny.

A final element of the aftermath is the passage of time itself. Years turn heavy events into anniversaries and then into references. A name that once filled television screens becomes a footnote in another story. For those closest to the case, the time does not flatten everything. It carries both the relief that comes with routine and the ache that comes with memory. For the wider public, the story returns when a parole decision is announced or when a film or program revisits the case. In between, the city continues its ordinary business. The freeways still hum. Children still run on playgrounds. Courtrooms still open each morning and close each evening.

The aftermath therefore looks like this when drawn to scale. A conviction upheld in 2005. A new punishment hearing in 2010 and a reduced term. Parole denied in 2014 and again in 2017. Parole granted in July 2020 with release on December 30th of that year. Media treatments that ranged from documentaries to a dramatized film. Public opinion that remained divided but also tired of reliving the worst day of a family's life. Families who chose privacy and professionals who carried lessons forward into other cases. A parolee who had to construct a life under supervision, one appointment and one rule at a time.

If a reader asks what remains when the legal dust has settled, the answer is practical and human. The state has made its judgments and recorded them. The institutions of custody and parole have done their work. The people involved have found a way to move through days that are no longer marked by hearings and filings. The story returns occasionally in the media and then recedes. The moral conclusions people draw vary according to their values and experiences. The law is less variable. It sets a sentence, permits a second look under specific standards, and allows for supervised release when a board deems it appropriate.

There is no grand epilogue that can wrap a case like this in an easy lesson. At most, one can say that the process created by law did what it was designed to do. It provided a trial with counsel on both sides. It allowed an appeal and a limited new hearing when counsel did not meet the constitutional mark. It required a person to serve a long term and then to convince a panel that conditions and supervision could manage remaining risk. It did all of this under public observation in a state where courts are accustomed to scrutiny. The rest is the quiet work of living carried out by those who survived the case and by the person who left prison with a parole certificate and a list of rules.

In that quiet work one sees the last measure of the aftermath. Not the number stamped on a judgment, not the scenes retold on television, but the daily acts by which people rebuild. Those acts are not dramatic. They rarely make news. They are the proper conclusion to a story that began in a house and then moved through courtrooms and prisons. The chapter closes where most lives are lived, in ordinary rooms where people try to do the next right thing and to keep faith with the responsibilities that remain.

CHAPTER 7
LARISSA SCHUSTER
THE ACID LADY

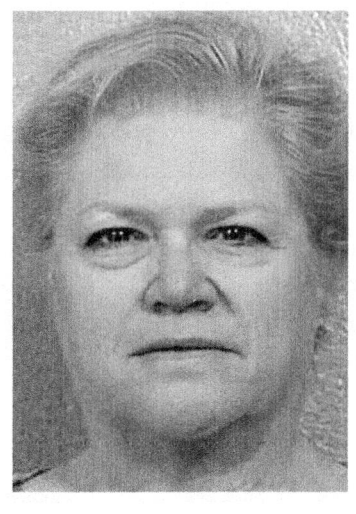

True crime is easiest to follow when you begin before the violence, inside the rooms where ordinary routines try to hold their shape. Years before a judge in Waldo County weighed mercy and law, Amber Cummings was a mother building days around small acts of care while living beside a man whose private world grew darker and more volatile with time. The details that would later spark national attention did not appear out of thin air. They formed slowly in a household that had uprooted itself from far away and settled in a pocket of coastal Maine, where the streets slope toward a quiet harbor and a fixer upper can be both shelter and sealed chamber.

Belfast sits where the river meets Penobscot Bay. It is a small city of brick storefronts and weathered wharves where summer light lingers and winter sharpens every sound. People move there for the promise of slower days, for the idea that a modest house and a short walk to Main Street can add up to a life worth guarding. In that setting Amber and her husband James arrived with a plan that looked ordinary on paper. In the year two thousand seven they bought a house at a foreclosure sale and set out to repair it. Newcomers do that all the time in Maine. They take on the long work of roofs and plaster and old wiring, telling themselves that the inconvenience is the price of a future home. From the street, that is what neighbors saw here as well. Tools came and went. Paint buckets moved from porch to parlor. A family kept to itself and worked.

Privacy is a courtesy in New England towns. People nod and let a closed door be a closed door. That habit often protects dignity. It can also hide harm. The home Amber entered each evening was not a neutral space. James surrounded himself with emblems of cruelty and domination and spoke in a voice that celebrated force. He admired Adolf Hitler. He collected objects that echoed that admiration. These were not curiosities from a history shelf. They were the signposts of a worldview that rejected empathy and elevated control, a worldview that made itself felt in the way he ran his house.

Accounts that would later reach the court describe a marriage narrowed by humiliation and threat. The couple slept in separate rooms. Firearms were kept within reach in those rooms. James set the rules and imposed them with a scorn that wore Amber down. She focused her energy on protecting their daughter and on keeping the daily schedule as steady as she could. A ritual from those years speaks more loudly than any slogan. Amber woke early with her child and shared breakfast before the day accelerated. The pair sat together with bowls and plates in the soft light of morning and tried to begin on a note of safety. For a few minutes the house felt like any other in town. That ordinary scene would later anchor the choices Amber made when fear outran her private defenses.

The renovation that drew Amber and James to Belfast tended toward isolation rather than community. A fixer upper always eats time and attention. Neighbors saw the work and not much else. They had their own chores, their own families, their own winter shoveling and summer mowing. Little about the Cummings house invited guests. A contractor might replace a window and leave. A delivery driver might carry a box to the door and return to the truck without conversation. The home became a closed world that answered to a single will, and within that world the tone grew harsher as the months passed.

Politics bled into the private atmosphere with grim effect. The election of two thousand eight and the inauguration that followed sent James into rants that mixed racism with fantasies of retaliation. The anger that spilled out in talk did not remain only in talk. The home became a place where dangerous materials and instructions were kept along with the symbols of hate. The presence of those items would matter later when investigators entered the house and the country took notice. For Amber and her daughter, they were already part of the furniture. They were reminders that the person who controlled the house prized the idea of power and always kept violence within reach.

A gun under a pillow is a metal object. It is also a message. It says that the person who owns the bed holds the right to decide how any argument ends. The message alters every conversation and every silence. It teaches a spouse to weigh each word. It teaches a child to read a room by the angle of a chin and the set of a mouth. Amber learned the rules and moved within them, not out of submission but out of calculation. She believed that the safest path for her daughter on any given day was to reduce sparks and to preserve the morning ritual of calm. She adjusted her own wants to the pattern that James demanded because she believed the cost of open defiance would be paid by the child she was trying to protect.

Into that claustrophobic rhythm came a fear that was different in kind and not only in degree. Amber later told professionals and the court that James fixated on sexualized images of minors and that he spoke about his attraction to girls. As that fixation grew, a dread that had once focused on guns and temper shifted toward a singular threat. She believed he would turn toward their daughter. The protective strategies that had carried her through long months of insults and intimidation felt suddenly inadequate. The problem was no longer a stormy adult who might lash out at his spouse. The problem was a father who might harm a child. That conclusion is the hinge on which the later story turns. It is the reason Amber began to think in terms of endings rather than endurance.

The ordinary work of a mother did not stop while this fear grew. Belfast is a place of lists and errands like any other town. There were groceries to buy, school forms to sign, mittens to find, boots to dry, and teachers to meet. Routine is the engine that carries children safely from one day to the next. Amber kept that engine running in a house where every adult conversation felt like a calculation. She still turned out the breakfasts. She still kept track of permission slips. She still folded laundry. These acts are easy to overlook in a narrative that later turns on gunshots and sentencing memos, but they are the evidence of a person holding a line for a child in a house that made that duty harder than it should have been.

Relocation from the other side of the country deepened the isolation. A new town means new doctors and new teachers and no old friends or relatives who can press a private conversation to the point of truth. A person intent on control can thrive in such an environment. He can present a face to neighbors and contractors that reveals exactly as much as he wants revealed and no more. He can gather objects and materials that suit his fantasies without fear that a long time friend will walk in unannounced and ask hard questions. For Amber, the new town meant that the burden of protection fell almost entirely on her.

People in Belfast who later tried to reconstruct the years before the shooting spoke of fragments. A story told by a tradesman. A phrase overheard by a neighbor. A display that made someone uneasy. Fragments do not assemble themselves without disclosure. Respect for privacy keeps distance even when a person senses that something is wrong. By the time anyone outside the house knew with certainty what lay inside, the end had already come and the home had been turned into a scene that would be measured and photographed and entered into evidence.

The morning ritual matters again here because it is the thread that runs through the entire cloth. Amber engineered an island of normalcy for her daughter each day. A bowl of cereal. Toast. A brief conversation about school, or a shirt, or a drawing. The smell of coffee or tea. The hush that precedes the first bus of the morning. When a mother is living with fear, that island is not just comfort. It is proof that she still has agency within a narrow range. It is proof that her child can still feel safe at least once a day. It is what she will fight to preserve when she believes the threat is about to cross a line.

The ideology that filled the rooms was not decoration. It set the stage for every other choice. Symbols of Nazism do not drift through a household without changing the air. They declare allegiance to cruelty. They sneer at compassion. They teach a child that the person who rules the home loves domination. When such symbols share space with weapons and with materials that hint at ambitions beyond the household, the pressure on the spouse who sees them is constant. She is never allowed to forget that harm is a possibility that can become a plan. She is never allowed to forget that the rules are written by someone who rejects empathy as weakness.

There is a detail in the way a small coastal town holds stories like this. Belfast is not anonymous the way a city of millions can be anonymous, but it is private in a manner that respects the threshold of a front door. People wave and move on. They do not ask questions unless invited. That custom can be kindness or it can be a blindfold, depending on what happens inside. In this case, it was a blindfold. The house in which Amber tried to protect her child had become a place where hate was practiced as a hobby and where fear shaped every hour. From the outside it looked like any other foreclosure project coming slowly back to life.

When national attention later turned to the discovery of hazardous items in the house, residents of Belfast felt the kind of chill that comes with unexpected danger. The idea that a quiet street might have harbored materials linked to a dirty bomb does not sit easily in the mind. People asked whether they had been at risk. Officials said that they had not. For Amber, those items were not hypothetical. They had been in the rooms where she lived, further proof that the person who set the rules loved the idea of harm. A weapon within reach is a threat to a body. A notebook full of plans is a threat to a town and a nation. Both were present where she woke each day.

What did Amber believe in those last months before the shooting. She believed that the threat to her daughter was moving closer. She believed that the weapons and the ideology amplified that threat. She believed that the small defense she had built out of routine and silence could not protect the child much longer. She believed that waiting could no longer be called love. Those beliefs may be uncomfortable to hear stated so plainly, but they are the map of her decision. A person who thinks she has a year to plan will call a counselor or a lawyer and arrange a new place to live. A person who thinks she has days will hold her child tighter in the morning and listen for the sound of footsteps in the hall.

If you stood in the yard of the Belfast house just before dawn on a winter day and looked toward the windows, you would not have seen any of that. You would have seen the pale light shift behind shades and the brief glow above a stove. You would have seen a mother and a girl at a table and you would have heard a quiet you might have mistaken for peace. The private truth was that Amber was measuring the distance between rooms and replaying in her head the sentences that had convinced her that the threat had crossed a line. She had a plan that was not grand. It was not theatrical. It was plain and terrible. She would use the only tool at hand to make sure that the person she feared would not wake up to harm their child.

This early chapter stops just short of the act that would bring police and reporters to the street and would send a judge into careful analysis of years that had been invisible to the public. Its purpose is to set the stage faithfully without repeating the later arguments about law. The move across the country that deepened isolation. The fixer upper that turned privacy into a sealed world. The symbols and materials that made cruelty a daily presence. The weapons that kept fear within reach. The morning ritual that protected a child for a few precious minutes each day. The dawning conviction that the child had become the target. These are the elements that matter here.

Everything that follows will narrow to a few seconds and then widen again to take in the reactions of officers, attorneys, neighbors, and a community that had to decide what it thought about a mother who said she acted to save her child. For now, hold the image of a harbor town in winter and a house bought out of foreclosure. In one room a woman and a girl finish breakfast in the early light. In another room a man sleeps with a gun nearby and with walls that speak of hate. The mother cleans the dishes and listens to the silence that follows. She has already decided that tomorrow will not be safer than today.

THE MURDER

The calendar fixes the event on December 9th 2009 in a modest house in Belfast, Maine. Dawn came late and quiet. The air outside was brittle with cold. Inside, a mother and her child moved through their routine without drama. There was breakfast, a few soft words, the familiar ritual of dishes and a check of the clock. The room where they sat had been Amber Cummings's small island of calm for months. On that morning it was the place where she mustered her resolve.

When the plates were cleared, Amber walked down the hall toward her own room. What happened next was later described in court in sparse language. She took a pistol into her hands. The weapon was a Colt forty five caliber revolver. She sat with the gun and put the barrel into her mouth. The act says as much about her state of mind as any later evaluation could. A person who places a gun in her own mouth is weighing a final decision. She did not pull the trigger. She removed the gun and decided to live. Then she decided to use the gun for a different purpose. She would end the danger that she believed would reach her child if the day continued on its usual path.

The hallway to James Cummings's bedroom was short. The house, bought at a foreclosure sale two years earlier, was not large and the rooms came one after another. James was asleep. He and Amber had slept in separate rooms. On the bed beside him a pillow hid a gun that he kept there. The house had long been arranged as a place where weapons were close at hand. The door stood between them. Amber crossed that threshold and moved to the side of the bed. She raised the revolver and fired into his head while he slept. She fired a second time. The report of a forty five in a small bedroom cracks wood and cloth and air. Within seconds the room filled with the residue of burnt powder and the sudden quiet that follows two blasts.

She did not linger. There was no attempt to stage a struggle or to rearrange the room. She turned and left. The distance from the bed to the hall took only a handful of steps. She went directly to her daughter. She told the child to come with her and they left the house together. They crossed the small yard to a neighbor. In cold air every breath shows and sound carries. Their arrival at the neighbor's door was the first sign to anyone outside that the private order of the Cummings home had broken.

The call for help brought officers and emergency medical personnel to the address. The first minutes at a violent scene are governed by habit and training. An officer takes in the front of the house and the positions of windows and doors. He listens for voices inside. He calls out in a clear voice, announcing police presence, and enters with caution. The goal is twofold. Ensure safety for those on scene and preserve evidence for a later investigation. As they moved through the rooms, the officers found the bedroom where James lay. He had no signs of life. The wounds were to the head, consistent with close range shots from a heavy caliber revolver. Paramedics confirmed what the officers already knew. The body would not be moved until the room had been documented.

From the neighbor's house or from beside a patrol car, Amber began the formal part of a homicide case. An officer asked basic questions. Who is in the house. What happened. Where is the weapon. Are there other people involved. The answers established the immediate facts. She had shot her husband while he slept. The revolver was no longer in her hand and would soon be recovered and made safe. No one else was present. No one else had been hurt. The child was kept away from the worst of it as procedures require in a domestic scene where a parent has become a suspect.

Inside the bedroom a technician began the quiet work of documentation. Photographs came first. The position of the body on the bed. The angle of the head. The pattern of spatter on walls and bedding. The location of the revolver if it was still in the room. The position of furniture. A scene is photographed as it is found, then examined in layers. Close ups of wounds, the edge of a pillowcase, the stain that runs from a seam into the mattress, the expended cases if any are present, although a revolver retains its casings. Measurements were taken to mark the distances from muzzle to target and from bed to wall. Those numbers later anchor expert testimony. They make the geometry of death traceable.

A weapon recovered from a homicide scene is handled with care to preserve prints and trace. In this case, the revolver was large and heavy, the kind of handgun that announces itself in sound and weight. It was tagged and bagged and entered into the chain of custody. The bedding would be taken later. The bed itself might be left until the medical examiner removed the body. A detective noted the smell and the temperature of the room, the condition of the floor, the presence or absence of signs of a struggle. In a shooting of a sleeping person, the room usually tells a quiet story. There is no overturned lamp or broken chair. There are only two violent marks, both in the same direction, and the pattern of residue that radiates from them.

The timeline on paper began with the time stamp on the emergency call. The arrival times of patrol cars and ambulance were entered in the log. The moment when the first officer saw the body was noted. The time of official pronouncement would come from the medical team. Those marks on a clock seem dry when read later, but they matter because the law likes to know what happened when, and because memory is slippery on hard mornings. The precision of an entry in a logbook keeps the story from blurring under emotional pressure.

Back at the neighbor's house, a second officer focused on the child. When a homicide occurs in a home where a child lives, officers and family services move quickly to shield and to arrange care. The questions put to the child, if any, are limited and careful. The goal is to avoid imprinting fresh trauma. A family member or trusted friend is contacted. A plan is set in motion to keep the child out of the next set of steps while the adults around her begin the formal work that the law requires.

Amber was taken to the station for a recorded interview. Before the formal session, an officer read the rights that control such conversations. The right to remain silent. The right to an attorney. The right to end the interview. She chose to speak. In measured words, she laid out the sequence of the morning. Breakfast with her daughter. A moment moments later when she had sat with the gun and considered her life. The walk down the hall. The two shots fired into a sleeping man. The decision to leave at once with the child and to seek help next door. She explained her fear. She explained why that fear had sharpened in recent months and days. The interview was not a debate. It was a recording of her account to be tested later against what the room and the body could tell.

The medical examiner performed the autopsy that afternoon or the next morning depending on logistics. In any sudden violent death, the cause is established through direct observation and testing. Two gunshot wounds to the head made the cause plain. The bullets were recovered if possible and measured. The tracks were diagrammed and photographed. The presence of stippling and soot around the wound edges helped fix the range of fire. The absence of other injuries conformed to a scene without struggle. Toxicology samples were taken as a matter of routine even when the method of death is obvious. Those samples go into a report that completes the official record. The final summary would read in language stripped of drama. Cause of death gunshot wounds to the head. Manner of death homicide.

Back at the house, the larger team began a thorough search. The warrant, obtained in those first hours, allowed investigators to catalog items in the home relevant to the death and to other potential crimes. The bedroom was the core. The rest of the house yielded objects that would later draw federal attention, but those belonged to a different slice of the story than the morning's shooting. The immediate homicide case stayed focused on the two shots that ended a life and the statements given by the shooter who had not fled.

Neighbors gathered in small clusters at the edge of police tape. Belfast is not a large city and winter mornings are quiet enough that the arrival of several cruisers and an ambulance draws attention within minutes. People called friends. Someone said a man had been shot. Someone else said a wife had done it. Repetition telescoped the morning into a handful of sentences. The official notice would come later through brief statements to the press. For the moment, the visible truth was that a house had been sealed and that the officers inside were moving in the practiced way of people who do this work regularly and with care.

A scene like this one has a second layer of discipline that the public rarely sees. Officers keep a log of who goes in and out. Each person signs with time of entry and exit. The purpose is not merely bureaucratic. It is the membrane that keeps contamination out of the evidentiary heart of the case. If a question arises months later about who moved a pillow or who touched a nightstand, the answer is in the log and in the photographs. That rigor protects the integrity of the case as it travels from a bedroom to a courtroom where every small inconsistency will be pressed.

There is also a ritual of leaving. Once the photographs are complete and the measurements taken and the body removed, a room begins to look abruptly empty. The bed may be stripped. The floor shows chalk and tape. Plastic bags hold items that yesterday were ordinary possessions. An officer takes a last look to be sure no small detail has been left unrecorded. The tape comes down. The door closes. The house is no longer a home for the time being. It is a place under the control of the state, even if for only a short while longer, and the people who lived there must find other beds for at least a night.

The case file grew in that first day and in the days that followed. It contained the initial narrative statements, the crime scene photographs, the autopsy report, the property receipts, the log sheets, and a chronology that stitched these parts into a single timeline. Because Amber did not flee and did not deny the act, the file did not need the kind of spidering investigation that attaches to cases where the identity of the shooter is unknown. The questions would be about motive and state of mind and justification. But that is for a later section. The murder itself stood on those two shots delivered at close range to a sleeping man, followed by an immediate effort to remove a child from the scene and to call for help.

A domestic killing by firearm carries certain common elements that were present here. A familiar weapon in a familiar room. A quiet approach. A short interval between decision and act. A quick exit. The difference in this case was not in those mechanics but in the atmosphere that had settled around the family before the shots and in the materials found afterward that hinted at wider harm. None of those matters affected the reality of the two bullets or the measurements taken by the medical examiner, but they affected the way officers and later prosecutors thought about the house and the people in it.

Some readers might look for a larger mystery in the seconds when the trigger was pulled. There is none. The shots landed where Amber aimed them. The man did not wake. The act was not messy in a cinematic sense. It was grim and efficient and complete. The difficult part of the case was not in reconstructing what happened. It was in assessing why, and in deciding what the law would do with a person who said that the shots had been the last available means to protect a child. That assessment belongs to prosecutors, defense counsel, a judge, and in some respects to the public that watched with unusual intensity when the wider contents of the house became known.

The next days followed a path that is familiar to detectives and new to most people. Items were sent to labs. Reports came back in neat language. An assistant district attorney reviewed the file. A supervisor asked questions about any holes in the timeline. Officers returned to the neighbor to check minor details, to confirm the times of knocks on a door and the exact words that were spoken. The team checked for prior calls to the address and for any reports that might suggest an earlier pattern of violence behind police doors. They wrote summaries and met again to be sure the file was complete before it traveled onward.

The morning on December 9th 2009 acquired a simple outline in those documents. A mother and daughter ate breakfast. The mother went to her room and considered taking her own life with a handgun. She did not. She walked to the room where her husband slept and fired two bullets into his head. She collected her child and went to a neighbor and asked for help. Officers arrived, secured the house, and confirmed the death. The weapon was recovered. The body was removed. The house was searched. An interview was recorded. An autopsy set down the cause with clinical precision. In a legal sense, the story could be told from start to finish without any gaps.

What is left out of that outline is the sound in the hallway once the shots have been fired. There is a silence peculiar to such moments. It is not peace. It is a vacuum in which a person who has acted cannot unact. Amber crossed that vacuum and went for her child. Many defendants in other cases do not do this. They run. They call someone else. They sit with the body for an hour and then try to craft a story. She did not. She did the one thing she had done each day that felt wholly right. She went to her child and led her out of the house. That single gesture is a factual detail like any other in the file. It also reads as a sentence in the larger paragraph of motive.

The presence of a child in a house where a person has been killed alters how officers move and speak. There is more hush. There is more attention to the path a child will travel from this morning into the next few days. The law must manage both case and care. That is why another unit of government exists adjacent to police work to handle protection and placement and the very human business of making sure a small person has a warm bed and a known face to lean on when the day ends. Those steps were taken here, and they are part of the invisible system that activates whenever a domestic scene turns fatal.

As the morning turned to afternoon and the afternoon moved into evening, the tape remained at the property. Lights glowed inside the house as the last searches were completed. Reporters stood at a distance and took notes for the early stories that would introduce the case to the wider state and country. The lines were already forming. A wife had shot a husband who slept. A child had been led to safety. There would be more to say about the contents of the house and about the years that had preceded the act. For the moment, the focus was on two shots, a body, a gun, and a confession.

If one looks for a single physical object that holds the murder in miniature, it is the revolver. Heavy, blunt, uncomplicated, it belonged to a home where weapons were part of the daily furniture. On that morning it became the instrument that ended the private world in which it had been kept. The photographs of it in evidence bags are striking only for their ordinariness. Many homes in Maine contain similar guns. The difference is the hand that lifts it and the reason that hand gives later when asked why.

The last task before officers left that night was to ensure that the house was secured against tampering and that the people with a lawful interest in it knew the conditions under which they could return. Doors were locked.

Notices were posted. A patrol might have rolled by periodically through the night. The neighbor's porch light might have burned later than usual as people continued to talk in low voices about a morning that had refused to be ordinary.

That is the murder in its full factual shape. A date. A place. A mother who made two separate decisions in a span of minutes. First, not to end her own life. Second, to end the life of a man she said would harm their child. Two shots in a small bedroom. A brief walk next door. A call. A methodical response. A body on a table at the medical examiner's office with two clearly described wounds. A file that could be carried by hand from one office to another and that would soon be opened on a prosecutor's desk. The law prefers such clarity about acts. It struggles more with the minds that precede them. That struggle would define everything that came next.

ARREST, TRIAL AND SENTENCE

An act that ends a life in a private home is followed by a swift change of scene. Within hours of the two shots that morning, the house in Belfast had filled with professionals who do not raise their voices and who keep careful lists. The body had been removed. The revolver had been tagged. The rooms had been photographed and measured. The immediate next steps were administrative and then legal. Amber Cummings was transported for formal processing, and the State of Maine began to build the file that would move from an investigative unit to a courtroom where the facts would be measured against the law.

Booking is not dramatic. It is a sequence. A photograph is taken. Fingerprints are collected. Basic identifying information is checked and entered. Property is inventoried and stored. A supervisor confirms the charge to be entered at the first appearance. An officer explains what will happen next in language that has been used so often it might as well be printed on the walls. For any first time defendant, those minutes can feel unbearably long. Everything familiar has been stripped away and replaced by fluorescent light and a clock that seems to run on someone else's power. The law requires that the first appearance before a judge occur without delay. In practice that means the next court day when a docket can be called and counsel can be appointed if counsel is not already present.

The initial appearance in Waldo County Superior Court set the formal frame. A judge reviewed the allegations and confirmed that Amber understood her rights. The State described the case in the spare language used at this stage. A death in a home. A handgun. Close range rounds. A spouse as the actor. There was no dispute about identity. The question that would shape the rest of the process was how the State would charge and how the defense would respond. In many domestic killings, prosecutors choose to begin with a murder charge to preserve the full range of possible outcomes while they test the strength of facts and context. Defense counsel listens, gathers the early reports, and begins to plot a path that will either lead to trial or to a negotiated resolution. In this case, that path ran through an intense period of evaluation and, unusually for a homicide, toward a resolution that would not involve prison time.

From the courthouse the file moved in two directions at once. Investigators completed work on the physical evidence and wrote their summaries. The prosecutor began to assemble the narrative that would justify the charge and later explain any resolution to the court. On the defense side, attorney Eric Morse engaged mental health professionals to examine Amber and to write reports that would help a judge understand the months and years that preceded the shooting. These reports did not rehash the forensic details of the bedroom. They focused on patterns and on psychology. They described a marriage marked by domination and degradation. They recorded a mother's fear sharpening to a fixed point as her husband's behavior and obsessions escalated. They assessed risk, remorse, and capacity for stability outside a prison setting.

Parallel to those evaluations ran the practical tasks of any serious case. The defense secured school calendars and medical appointments to establish the ordinary care Amber provided her daughter. The State compiled phone records, dispatch logs, and the autopsy report. Both sides interviewed neighbors and acquaintances to build timelines and corroborate or challenge details that mattered to questions of motive and state of mind. There was also the federally tinged thread that did not belong to the homicide count itself but that could not be ignored. Search teams had found materials and papers in the house connected to dangerous ideology and to experiments with hazardous substances. Federal authorities reviewed those findings, communicated with local officials, and publicly stated that the wider community was not at risk. That reassurance did not lessen the gravity of the discoveries, but it kept the immediate case focused on the two shots and on the reasons a woman gave when asked why she fired them.

The calendar inched forward. The plea that would ultimately be entered depended on the State's view of intent and on the defense's ability to place a decade of experience in front of a judge in a way that carried more weight than the few seconds during which the trigger had been pulled. The law distinguishes among kinds of homicide. Malice matters. Provocation matters. Justification matters. So does the defendant's history, the presence of a child, the risk perceived, the resources consulted or not consulted, and the plausibility of avoiding the danger without violence. None of these questions can be answered with a single photograph or a single sentence. They require careful argument and a judge willing to listen.

As the parties came closer to a resolution, the courthouse in Belfast began to feel the pressure of public curiosity. The case had already reached beyond the town because of the discovery of extremist paraphernalia and hazardous materials. People had questions that were not strictly legal. Could the items in the home have been used to harm others. What had the family's life really been like before the morning of the shooting. What would happen to the child. The court would answer only the questions the law allowed it to answer. It would handle the rest through the measured pace of motions and scheduling orders and, finally, a sentencing hearing where the judge could say in public what he had considered and why he had decided as he did.

A formal change of plea set the path. When that moment came, Amber did not stand on a story that denied what she had done. She acknowledged it and asked the court to measure her act in the full light of the years that had produced it. The State, represented by an assistant attorney general, agreed to a framework that would permit the judge to hear from experts and from those who could speak to the marriage and to the danger. The agreement did not bind the judge to any particular number. It set the lanes inside which argument would take place and within which a sentence could be imposed.

The sentencing hearing drew an unusual crowd. Supporters filled benches wearing small stickers that carried a simple message of solidarity. The courtroom is designed for quiet. Even on days when emotions run high, wood and stone and the steady presence of court officers keep voices low and reactions contained. Amber sat at counsel table. Her attorney had organized the presentation to proceed from experts to those who could provide specific facts that mapped onto the expert conclusions. The State would argue after those witnesses and then the judge would speak.

The first expert described the effects of long term coercion. He spoke in clinical terms about how fear can become the currency of a household, how the target of control adapts to survive, how judgment can be altered by sustained trauma, and how a specific threat to a child can transform dread into a sense of emergency. He did not excuse the shooting. He explained it. The second expert addressed risk. He assessed Amber's likelihood of future violence and her capacity to function safely under supervision. The third connected the dots for the court between the observed behavior and the diagnosis, focusing on the period leading up to the shooting when the husband's fixation on sexualized images of minors and his rhetoric about domination had, in their view, crossed into a direct threat to the daughter in the home.

The defense presentation then shifted from experts to facts lived and observed. Witnesses spoke to the household's isolation, the separate bedrooms, the constant presence of weapons, the humiliations delivered in private, the controlling rules that changed at a whim, and the impact on Amber's health and judgment. They did not linger over the sensational items found by investigators after the death because the hearing was not about those items. It was about the state of mind in the house and about a mother's calculations in the face of a threat she believed was imminent.

When it was the State's turn, the assistant attorney general took care to acknowledge what the evidence of abuse established. She did not pretend that the marriage had been ordinary. She did not deny that Amber had lived under sustained pressure and fear. She argued a different point. The law cannot become a permission slip for private lethal force. The State carries a duty to denounce the act of taking a life without the immediate necessity recognized by the classic rules of self defense. She urged the court to impose some incarceration as a signal to the public that even a hard case must carry a term. The suggestion was a short period of confinement measured in months, followed by a long period of probation that would keep Amber under supervision. In essence the State sought a middle path that registered the gravity of the act without demanding a punishment that would ignore context.

Amber did not address the court. Defendants are not required to speak at sentencing. Many do. Many do not, especially when counsel has presented a careful record through witnesses and documents and when experts have already given voice to the factors the defense hopes the judge will weigh. Her silence did not leave the room empty. The material before the court had given the judge lines to follow in his remarks. Before imposing the sentence he explained what he had considered.

The judge began with the unadorned truth that a man had died of two shots to the head while he slept. The law does not treat that lightly. He then widened his lens to take in not merely the seconds of violence but the years that preceded them. He acknowledged the persuasive force of the expert testimony and the corroborating facts. He spoke of the obligation to consider the safety of the public, the needs of a child whose future would be shaped by the court's decision, and the utility of incarceration in a case where deterrence seemed less relevant than stabilization and supervision. He noted the State's argument that a signal must be sent. He noted the defense argument that punishment by imprisonment would harm more than help and that a suspended sentence with strict probationary conditions could protect the community and promote healing.

The sentence that followed was precise and unusual for a homicide. The court imposed a term of eight years but suspended it in its entirety and placed Amber on a lengthy period of probation with conditions that included compliance with mental health treatment, a prohibition on firearms, and the standard requirements of law abiding behavior and regular reporting. The immediate effect was that she would leave the courthouse rather than a cell. The longer effect was that she would live under supervision for years, with the suspended term held like a weight that could be dropped if she violated the rules the court had set.

The reaction inside the courtroom was swift but contained by decorum. When the judge left the bench, the room exhaled. Supporters who had sat still through hours of testimony allowed themselves a brief display of relief. In the hallway outside, Amber received embraces from people who had stood with her through the months of waiting. Clergy who had counseled her spoke quietly of redemption and responsibility. On the steps, she thanked the community for its support and said what many were not prepared to hear. She asked that people not hate her husband. She described him as mentally ill and said that anger directed at him would not help anyone heal. Those words mattered. They prevented the morning's legal victory from turning into a rally built on hatred of the dead.

The State's position did not crumble in the face of the sentence. Prosecutors did not argue with the judge in the hallway. They accepted the ruling and returned to their work. That is one of the quiet strengths of the system. The State argues hard in court, then honors the decision even when it would have chosen a different outcome. For the public, the sentence served as a reminder that judges are asked to do more than count years. They are asked to measure human context against legal rules and to choose within the space the law allows. This judge did so with care, explaining that the sentence was not an endorsement of private violence but an acknowledgment of the unique facts of the case and the low risk Amber posed under supervision.

Conditions of probation in a case like this are not window dressing. They are a structure. A probation officer becomes a regular presence. Appointments are scheduled and kept. Reports are filed. Any change in residence or employment is noted. Treatment must be attended and followed, and providers must be permitted to communicate with supervision staff. The prohibition on firearms is absolute. Travel is restricted. A violation can bring the case back into court quickly with the suspended term ready to be imposed. This is the bargain the sentence created. Freedom tied to compliance. Opportunity bound to accountability.

The legal community watched the case not as spectators to sensational elements but as students of process. Defense attorneys saw how a careful record built with credible experts and corroborating facts could alter the shape of punishment even in a homicide. Prosecutors saw how to argue for denunciation and restraint without denying what was plainly established about the life inside the house. Judges saw a colleague balance mercy and law without surrendering either. For the people in Belfast, the hearing confirmed something they had felt since the morning of the shooting. The case did not fit the usual molds. It needed the kind of measured handling that courts promise in their better moments.

There was a final set of housekeeping steps that followed the hearing. Orders were reduced to writing. Copies were delivered to the parties and to probation. The court set review dates for status checks. The clerk entered the sentence into the record. The file moved from the space of criminal trial work to the longer hallway of supervision. What had been public and loud became private and routine again. That shift is as it should be. Courtrooms exist to handle moments of crisis. Once a path forward is set, the system disperses, leaving families to find their footing under the conditions the court has imposed.

What remains from the arrest through the sentencing is a story of procedure that worked the way it should when asked to absorb a hard set of facts. An act occurred. The State investigated and prepared a case. The defense assembled a record that allowed the court to consider more than the seconds during which a weapon was fired. A sentence was imposed that joined denunciation and supervision without incarceration. The community witnessed the process and returned to its daily business with a better understanding of the difference between explanation and excuse.

The next chapter belongs not to the lawyers and the judge but to the people who had to live with the result. A child needed stability. A mother had to meet every condition set by the court while rebuilding a life out of the small routines that had once been all she could control. Friends and neighbors had to decide how to respond to a case that had revealed frightening details about the house on their street. The town had to set an example for itself about how to handle mercy without losing respect for the law. Those are matters for the aftermath, where public reaction, private healing, and the long work of supervision replace the stark geometry of a crime scene and a courtroom.

AFTERMATH WITH FAMILY AND PUBLIC OPINION

When the bench emptied on January 7th 2010 and the judge's words settled into the record, the case stepped out of the language of indictments and affidavits and into the very different language of living with a decision. A courthouse can hold a moment so that everyone can see it. The world outside cannot hold moments. It resumes. People drive home. A town that had been peering through the windows of a single story now returned to the habits that make any community possible. The aftermath of the Amber Cummings case unfolded in that quiet register. It is the story of a suspended sentence tethered to strict supervision, of a small city that chose steadiness over spectacle, of the way national headlines thinned to occasional glances, and of the private work of a mother and child who needed the ordinary more than they needed anyone's commentary.

Inside the courtroom that day, supporters had worn small stickers that said Free Amber. They were careful not to disturb the proceedings. They stood when the judge entered and sat when told. They watched the experts and the lawyers and the measured face of the court. When the judge suspended the eight year term and ordered probation with conditions, those supporters did not erupt. They waited. Only after the judge left did a soft murmur rise and then a burst of clapping that ended as quickly as it began. In the hallway Amber received embraces, including from clergy who had kept company with her through months of uncertainty. On the steps outside she thanked people in the community for what she called a generosity of spirit. She said that her husband had been mentally ill and asked that anger not be poured on his memory. It was not a line crafted for effect. It read as a boundary she set for herself and for anyone who might mistake the day for a victory dance.

The practical meaning of the sentence began to take shape the same afternoon. Suspended time is not leniency without anchor. It is a contract. A probation officer explained the first set of rules and the first set of appointments. Report as directed. Notify of any change of address or employment. Participate in mental health treatment as ordered. Have no firearms and no contact with weapons. Remain law abiding. Obey travel restrictions. These are the bones of supervision in any serious case, and they are as binding as any bars. If the rules are broken, the suspended term can be imposed. Amber did not leave the courthouse free of obligation. She left carrying a list that would rule her days for years.

The officer who took the case had a job that is not well understood by people who only see courtrooms on television. A probation officer is part monitor and part teacher and part translator of what the court meant when it wrote the conditions. The work takes place in offices that do not look like the grand rooms with flags and oak benches. It takes place at tables where calendars are opened and pens click and forms are filled out. There are check ins that are predictable and check ins that are not. There are conversations that are direct. How are you sleeping. Are you attending your sessions. Are there any stresses at home that might cause you to miss appointments. When a person under supervision is living with the aftermath of trauma, those questions are not merely boxes to tick. They are tools for keeping the person steady and therefore keeping the community steady.

Belfast adjusted itself to the new facts with the restraint that had marked the town's bearing since the morning of the shooting. There were no loud arguments on Main Street. There were no posters in shop windows. People knew that a hard case had received a rare sentence and that a mother had left court with conditions instead of a prison number. They also knew that the house on the quiet street had contained items that frightened them when they were first revealed. The discovery of paraphernalia and materials after the killing had sent shivers through a community that takes civic safety for granted. Federal authorities had reviewed the matter and told the public the town was not at risk, but the memory of that inventory lingered. In the aftermath, residents carried both feelings at once. Relief that the danger had been contained and patience for the family left standing. The town's public face was earnest and practical. It kept to its routines.

News travel patterns changed quickly. In the first weeks after the sentence, reporters called for follow up quotes and then moved on to the next place where the lights were brighter. The case remained a reference point in summaries about domestic violence, extremism, and unusual sentencing outcomes, but it no longer consumed broadcast time. That drift is a mercy for families who must now construct a life out of tasks that journalists have no reason to film. Grocery trips. School pick ups. Therapy appointments. Meetings with a probation officer. These are not plot points in a national story. They are the way any story leaves the televisions of a country and reenters the private lives of a few people.

In that quieter season after January 7th 2010, the most important audience was small and local. Teachers and counselors worked with deliberate gentleness. They did not make the child the subject of whispered curiosity. They made sure that the schedule of a school day remained predictable. In a town like Belfast, the adults know that the rituals of morning homeroom and evening homework are a scaffold. They help a young person rebuild trust in the future by giving the future a shape. Librarians and coaches did their part by treating the child as a child, not as a character from a headline. This is a kind of civic competence that never makes news. It is how towns avoid turning a private wound into a permanent identity.

The church community also adapted in a way that deserves notice.

Sermons did not become court recaps. They did not trade the vocabulary of mercy for the vocabulary of gossip. Pastors and lay leaders offered words that acknowledged both harm and hope. In private they helped fill gaps that supervision does not address. A ride to an appointment. An errand when snow was heavy. A check in at the end of a long day. Acts of care are most useful when they are so plain they can be done without fanfare. The clergy who had stood in the hallway on the day of sentencing knew the difference between ministry and spectacle. They behaved accordingly.

Law enforcement officers involved in the case debriefed as they do after any high stakes matter. They assessed the initial response to the scene, the evidence handling, the interview protocols, and the way the department communicated with the public when rumors began to jump ahead of facts. They discussed the delicate balance required in domestic cases where a child is present. They reviewed the moment when federal partners stepped in to examine items unrelated to the homicide count but critical to community reassurance. That internal self critique helps the next team in the next case even when the next case looks nothing like this one. The habits of careful work are general. They travel from scene to scene.

Victim services personnel reached out to extended family in the way they always do after a violent death. The complexity here was unusual. The surviving spouse was also the person who had fired the weapon. The family was therefore both the source of loss and the household that needed compassion and practical help. The unit kept the lines open, recognizing that grief is not a simple shape when a house has held both a threat and the person who ended it. Some relatives wanted to speak. Others wanted to say nothing. The professionals encouraged both choices. A good aftermath makes room for the full range of human responses to a knotted story.

Public debate did not disappear. It cooled. In coffee shops and at kitchen tables, people asked one another what they thought about the judge's approach. Some believed that a suspended sentence matched the facts after the court heard the full account of long term coercion and the specific danger to the child. Others believed a short term of confinement would have sent a better signal while still recognizing the context. The differences were not shouted. They were explored in the kind of moral conversations that small towns still have when the noise from elsewhere fades. In those conversations, something useful happened. People learned to speak with more precision about domestic abuse. Phrases like coercive control and trauma informed response moved from professional training rooms into the mouths of ordinary citizens. Language shapes thought. Thought shapes action. A town that can name patterns more clearly is a town better able to intervene the next time a house grows quiet for the wrong reasons.

Attention from elsewhere returned occasionally when magazines or television programs revisited the case as part of broader features about mothers who kill or about extremist paraphernalia found in unexpected places. The aftermath in Belfast did not hinge on those returns. The people most affected had other clocks to watch. A probation appointment tomorrow. A therapy session on Thursday afternoon. A parent teacher conference next week. A birthday in the spring. Ordinary events have a way of restoring the measure of a life after a long season in which every day was measured by court calendars and filing deadlines.

The mechanics of probation deserve a closer look because they are easy to misunderstand. Supervision is not a simple set of monthly check ins. A person under a suspended sentence lives with constant awareness that any violation can summon the court's power. The relationship with the officer is built on two connected truths. First, the officer is there to help the person succeed by connecting her to services and by responding early when stress rises. Second, the officer is there to protect the community by drawing firm lines and by documenting any failure to keep to the conditions. In practice this means more contact when life is complicated and a little less when the person finds a steady rhythm. It also means unannounced visits, drug testing if ordered, verification of employment, and direct communication with therapists when the court has ordered treatment. The work is as human as it is bureaucratic. It requires judgment.

Over time, Belfast developed a shared understanding of what mercy had looked like in this case. It had not been a public absolution. It had been a decision to put the hard work where it could do the most good, with a probation office and with mental health professionals rather than inside a cell. People who had been uneasy about the presence of hazardous materials in the house recognized that those items had been removed from the equation on the morning of the shooting and that federal and state agencies had said the town had not been at risk. That recognition did not lessen the alarm that had been felt. It simply relocated the alarm to the past where it belonged. The present required a different kind of attention, the kind that helps a family put one foot in front of the other.

The media image of the case softened in a way that often happens when a defendant refuses to perform for cameras after a verdict. Amber did not grant interviews that rehashed the worst days. She kept her public remarks sparse and functional. Thank you to those who helped. Please do not direct anger at the dead. Those sentences held, and because they held, there was less to pick apart or amplify. The appetite for sensational detail starves when the person at the center declines to feed it. That restraint became another way the aftermath protected a child who needed life to be defined by school projects and not by strangers asking questions in grocery aisles.

The child's well being, in fact, became the practical measure by which many locals judged the entire episode. If the student looked steadier at school, if the smile returned more often, if the weight of the eyes lifted, then the town felt that the sentence had done what it could do. Teachers are important witnesses to such changes because they see children in patterns that relatives cannot. They notice when a child once too quiet finds a voice in class. They notice when a student who once avoided eye contact begins to raise a hand. In the seasons after the hearing, those small signs were watched with hope.

Across the bay and along the coast, advocates who work with survivors of domestic abuse used the case as a teaching instrument. They did not exploit. They taught. They reminded audiences that the most dangerous moment for many victims is when they try to leave. They explained why a person might not call the police even when fear is daily. They offered practical advice to neighbors. Check in. Offer specific help. Believe disclosures. Keep resource numbers handy. Avoid forcing a survivor to repeat a story to five different offices. Coordinate. That last word became a watchword among agencies that pledged to sharpen their protocols. A town that can coordinate can interrupt a spiral before it reaches a decision no one would wish on any family.

For law students and young attorneys in Maine, the case entered the catalog of examples used when professors teach about sentencing discretion and the weight of context. The lesson was not that homicide should be excused when households are hard. The lesson was that justice sometimes requires a judge to read the whole book and not only the page on which the worst act is written. When newer prosecutors discussed the matter with mentors, they asked how to present hard facts without hardening a jury or a judge against the person. When younger defense attorneys studied the record, they learned how crucial it is to bring credible experts who can translate years of private erosion into terms a court can recognize. The legacy of the case in those circles is a commitment to do the careful work that allows a judge to see clearly.

The broader public in Belfast also came away with a few conclusions. One was that a quiet street can hold a house in which fear is the air. That does not mean neighbors should knock down doors. It means they should know what to do if they are invited in and asked for help. Another conclusion was that a person can carry an ideology so toxic that it leaches into every room and every conversation. That sort of ideology is not a private hobby. It is a template for harm. A final conclusion was that mercy is not the opposite of accountability. The court's sentence demanded more than good intentions. It demanded compliance. It demanded daily work. People can accept a merciful sentence when they see that it is constructed out of obligations.

Years have their own pace in places like Belfast. Winters taught the town patience long before this case ever appeared. Snow falls. The bay locks in and releases again. The brick on Main Street warms in May and bakes in August. The story of the Cummings household settled into that rhythm. The memory of a morning in December remained, but it did not dominate conversations forever. The house lost its status as a landmark of worry and became once more a building with an address. Children walking to school paid it no special notice. Their parents remembered and moved on. The court file that had traveled from desk to desk and hand to hand was boxed and shelved, available for any later look but no longer an active instrument.

In such a quieting, the people who had been most exposed to the story finally claimed the privacy that had been taken from them for so long. Privacy for a child means being able to make mistakes at school without the weight of a last name. Privacy for a mother means being able to stand in a grocery aisle comparing prices without someone telling her what the judge should have done. They gained that privacy not because the town forgot, but because the town chose not to rehearse the worst day indefinitely.

There is a temptation with any notorious case to end with a thesis about what it means. The aftermath of the Amber Cummings case resists neat closure. It shows a court willing to use the full range of tools the law permits. It shows a small city capable of holding two ideas at once. First, that a person died foolishly and needlessly and that the killing of a sleeping spouse is not a thing to celebrate. Second, that a mother can act from a terror sharpened by years of coercion and by a very specific threat to a child, and that punishment in such a case can be constructed to protect without destroying what remains of a family. Between those two ideas, Belfast chose to behave with caution, quiet help, and the patience of people who know winter.

What remains today is not the sound of two gunshots or the glare of television lights. What remains are the unremarkable notes of a life under supervision that became less supervised over time as the person met each condition and then the next. What remains are teachers who noticed a child steadying and neighbors who minded their business in the right way rather than the wrong way. What remains is a compact memory of a hard morning and a longer memory of a town that chose to handle it without cruelty. For true crime readers, that may not be dramatic. For the people who had to live it, it was exactly what they needed.

CHAPTER 8
SHANA PARKINSON
DOUBLE ELIMINATION

True crime work begins best before the crisis. To understand how a killing took place in a quiet Idaho town on a winter night, it helps to start years earlier, with the people who would one day be central to the case and with the community that framed their choices. This chapter does not recount blood or evidence. It stays with the ordinary patterns that preceded the violence. It looks closely at the relationship that linked Shana Parkinson to her former husband Gregg Whitmore, at the fault lines that opened as their lives diverged, and at the setting of Rigby in Jefferson County where neighbors know one another by name and where a porch light makes a circle of warmth against the long cold months.

Rigby sits between Idaho Falls and Rexburg on a stretch of valley where fields run to the horizon and the sky seems to take up half the map. Winters arrive early and leave late. The town center is compact. There is a courthouse of modest size, a handful of churches, a few cafes, a library, and the sort of parks where children learn the feel of grass under their shoes each spring. Families choose Rigby for its steadiness. Many have stayed for generations.

Others come back after service or school to be near parents and cousins. In such places the measure of a person's character is not what is said but what is seen over time. You watch who shows up for a neighbor in a storm. You watch who sits in the bleachers even when the team is losing by a lot. It is a place where reputation has weight.

Into that setting came the household that would later become the center of a murder file. Gregg Bradley Whitmore, born in the middle of the nineteen sixties, had served in the United States Army as a younger man. Friends remembered a straightforward manner and a willingness to lend a hand. He carried himself with the economy of motion that military service teaches. He also carried the desire for a firm routine, the simple compass that points a person toward home, work, friends, and family responsibilities. Jefferson County was a natural fit for that temperament. The town gave him work, friends who stayed, and a home that others described as tidy and unpretentious, the kind of place where boots sat on a mat by the door and a jacket hung on a hook within easy reach.

In the years before the murder, Gregg and Shana had been married and then divorced. The marriage, like many marriages, saw stretches of calm and periods of strain. They had shared an address, bills, and the ordinary list of repairs and chores that fill any week. They had also learned how much damage words can do when love is cooling and suspicion is rising. People close to them later spoke of arguments that grew hotter over time and of separations that were followed by attempts to start again. The path finally resolved into a divorce that moved through the Jefferson County system with all the formalities that follow a split. Papers were filed and dates were set. Property and responsibilities were split by a judge after hearings that are usually quiet and pragmatic, the way county cases often are when there is not much money to divide and emotions are already bruised.

Divorce in a small place is never truly private. You can protect the details, but you cannot hide the fact. People saw that Gregg and Shana were no longer together. They saw that future plans were being made separately. Relatives adjusted holiday arrangements. Mutual friends chose sides or else chose a careful neutrality that would let them offer support without adding to the current of rumor that runs beneath every breakup. That is how small towns handle such matters when everyone attends the same school plays and little league games and when everyone wants to keep the temperature down for the sake of children and for the sake of their own peace.

It became clear in the months that followed that Gregg was moving on. He met Karen Cummings, who was not from far away. Karen was younger than Gregg and worked hard in the roles that make a life, a job that pays the bills, a network of friends that makes weekends worth having, and a hope that the next few years would be better than the last few had been. Their connection grew quickly in the way such connections sometimes do when two people find room for one another after years of rough water. People who saw them together spoke later of a comfortable ease. She made him laugh. He steadied her. They spent time in the Rigby house where he lived and began the familiar project of making two lives fit inside four rooms.

From the outside, Shana's path in those months carried its own mix of determination and agitation. Neighbors and acquaintances remembered a person whose feelings ran close to the surface and who could cut a conversation to its essentials with a glance. It is not a crime to be intense. It is a way of moving through the world that leaves strong impressions. In the context of a recent divorce, it fueled conflicts that did not always stay inside the house. The distance between former spouses in a small town is narrow. You see each other at the market and at the post office. Court decisions about property or custody create a schedule that has to be worked every week. Every exchange carries the risk of lighting old fuses. In this sense, Rigby's closeness was both comfort and pressure. It kept everyone in view. It also gave everyone a chance to misread or escalate.

The house on the quiet street where Gregg lived became the fixed point around which many of these tensions orbited. It was not grand. It was not shabby. It was a place in which coats were hung near the door and where a table held mail that came in a regular stack. The details are ordinary because lives are ordinary until they are suddenly not. Neighbors saw vehicles come and go at the hours that make sense. They saw lights on at reasonable times. They saw no signs that the house would become a crime scene. The kindness of towns like Rigby lies in the way people do not peer through curtains to invent trouble. Their weakness lies in the way trouble can grow inside a home without anyone noticing until it is too late.

Looking back with the cold lens of hindsight, people tried to map the months before the killings for omens. They remembered words spoken in anger and later regretted. They remembered the posture of a person at a gas pump or the pace of a car leaving a driveway. Those memories are often as much about the guilt people feel for not seeing more as they are about what actually happened. The truth is that even when a split is rancorous, most people do not expect violence. They expect time to do its work. They expect lawyers and judges to return a sort of order. They expect new relationships to absorb energy that had once gone into fighting. They expect the body to relax the way it does when a fever breaks. In this case, those expectations were wrong.

To understand the fault lines between Gregg and Shana without inventing dialogue or speculating beyond the record, one can observe the simple things that mark the end of a marriage. Possessions are gathered up. Keys are returned. Friends become two groups that overlap a little. Phone calls that once lasted an hour shrink to a list of practicalities. The word mine returns to sentences where the word ours once lived. You stop finishing the other person's jokes. You stop ordering for two. When children are involved, calendars become very important. When children are not involved, schedules still matter because they keep people out of each other's way. In an ideal world, those schedules and that new language create a buffer that lets both parties find a new equilibrium. In the world that led to a locked front door and police tape in Rigby, that buffer did not hold.

One of the unavoidable features of small towns is the way news moves. Sometimes it travels in a straight line through formal channels. More often it flows around corners. A friend tells a cousin. A cousin tells a coworker. By the time the story returns to the person who first told it, the details have changed. With Shana's divorce and Gregg's new relationship, the moving pieces lent themselves to this sort of retelling. It did not help anyone. Stories designed to make a cousin lean forward in a booth in a cafe do not prepare anyone for sober decisions. They build a heat that often has little to do with truth. They turn current emotions into folklore. If you ask people later what helped in the months before the crime, they will rarely list gossip.

Karen entered this story without the armor that comes from years of living in the same place. She had friends who looked out for her and a family who worried in the way families always do when a person they love is building a new life. She did not arrive in Rigby as a symbol. She arrived as a person. In later accounts it became easy to describe her solely as Gregg's girlfriend. That is how homicide files label people. They freeze a role. In the months before the violence, she was also a person making a home. She unpacked boxes. She took stock of the kitchen. She learned the way the afternoon light fell across the living room floor. She placed a favorite picture where it would catch her eye in the morning. She began to feel that the place was safe.

Shana's days bore the signs of someone navigating the aftermath of a marriage with more intensity than calm. She had a sharp profile in memory because she made an impact when she entered a room. Some saw her as wronged and admired her for speaking directly. Others saw in her a tendency to carry a fight past the point when most would step back and cool down. Both portraits can be true at once. A person can be fierce in the defense of her view of the world and also capable of small mercies when no one is watching. The combination is not unusual. It becomes dangerous when combined with a belief that another person's happiness is an insult.

Life in Rigby continued around all of this with its own rhythm. The school held concerts. The grocery store ran specials. The Jefferson County fair came and went with animals and pie contests and kids still awake at the end of long days. An early snow could still surprise in October, and a late snow could still insist on its stubborn presence in April. The cadence of church bells shaped Sundays. The courthouse did what it always does, and files were opened and closed, some in the space of a week and some after years of study. The case that would later define the town in headlines in other states did not define it at the time. It was one of many human stories running quietly behind closed doors.

Friends who tried to support Gregg during this transition did what friends in small places do. They offered to help move furniture. They invited him out when they sensed a long evening ahead if he stayed home alone. They took their time when drinking coffee over a counter because a person who has been through a divorce often needs a place to sit without talking for a while. They listened. They did not always advise. When a person is finding his way toward a new life with someone new, advice is not as useful as presence. The presence of friends is what tells a person he can take the next step without the floor vanishing under his feet.

On the other side of the split, friends who looked after Shana did their own version of that work. They fielded late calls. They sat across from her at noon and listened to words pour out faster than sentences could be shaped. They tried to lower the temperature because that is what friends do when they see a person they care about riding an emotional storm surge. Anyone who has ever lived in a small town knows that this work is done in grocery store aisles and parking lots and on porches with a view of a quiet street. It is not therapy. It is not the state. It is what it looks like when a community tries to route public pain through private kindness.

Rigby's police department at the time carried a caseload typical for a town its size. Traffic, petty theft, disputes that could usually be calmed. Officers knew the families. They understood who needed a firm line and who needed a word at the right moment. In that environment, any calls related to the household that would later become a crime scene were folded into the ordinary flow of service. Officers would later look back and ask if a different choice on some earlier day might have changed the outcome months later. That is the heavy work of hindsight that law enforcement officers carry after every tragedy. It is necessary. It is not always fair to men and women who did their best within the rules and facts they had at the time.

By the last weeks of January in the year the murders took place, the pieces that would matter to investigators were in motion. Gregg and Karen were planning a future that felt solid enough to name. The house had settled into the pattern of two people building something together. Shana's world was not at peace. The routines of relocated items and changed schedules continued to feed a sense of loss that had hardened into grievance. In a larger city those emotions can spread into distance. In Rigby the distance is measured in minutes. A person can drive the length of the town in the time it takes a coffee to cool.

The purpose of this section is not to predict what happened next. It cannot. It does not focus on motive as a piece of doctrine or turn the end of a marriage into a brief for the defense or the prosecution. It lays out the setting so that the reader understands that what followed did not occur in a vacuum. It came out of a small city where people make homes and raise children and take care with their words because the same faces recur at church and at school. It came out of a pair of lives that had stopped fitting together and that did not separate cleanly. It came out of a town where a house can look ordinary and be filled with tension that nobody outside can measure.

This matters because one of the central illusions of true crime is that the violent moment explains itself. It does not. The violent moment is an endpoint. The explanation is in the patient accumulation of days, in the choices made and unmade, in the ways people respond to feeling slighted or feeling replaced, and in the way a place like Rigby wraps its arms around almost everyone but cannot, in the end, make their decisions for them. Before a knife ever touched a sheet, the tragedy was busy being written in glances across parking lots and in words spoken in kitchens and in moments of decision in which anger beat patience by a second.

As the last January turned toward February, Rigby carried on. If someone had stood at the corner near Gregg's place in the late afternoon, they would have seen sun on snowbanks and the soft exhaust of cars turning slowly into driveways. They would have heard the ordinary sounds that make a town feel like home, the call of a neighbor across a street, the scrape of a shovel on a path, the brief bark of a dog at dusk. They would not have known that a set of choices would soon turn that house into a point on a map that strangers would mention for years. From the inside, that is how most murder scenes look on the last day before everything changes. They look like homework spread on a table and a late supper and a life that might have been left to find its way toward calm if different choices had been made.

THE MURDER

By the time most porches on West Second South had gone dark and the last late movie wrapped up on living room televisions, the house everyone knew as Gregg's settled into that deep quiet only small towns know. The furnace cycled. The clock in the kitchen ticked as if it had nowhere else to be. If you had stood on the sidewalk you would have heard almost nothing at all. It was the kind of winter night Rigby keeps tucked away like a familiar blanket, numbing and peaceful at once, with stars sitting hard and cold above the rooftops.

Inside, sleep had the place in its keeping. A bedroom held two people who had spent the evening with the unrushed ease that comes after a run of difficult years. The door had been locked more out of habit than fear. A chair still angled toward the television remembered a laugh from an hour earlier. A glass on the coffee table caught the faint reflection of the hallway light.

These were the plain artifacts of a life, the punctuation marks that tell you a story is moving along as expected.

What happened next moved faster than memory and yet felt inevitable the moment it began. A door opened that should not have opened. A figure who knew where everything would be even in the dark crossed the threshold. Carpet absorbed footfalls. Hall air carried a whisper of cold from outside. The person who had no business being there did not pause at the entrance to weigh options or to rehearse lines. The way to the bedroom was muscle memory.

We human beings are so used to sleep finishing our sentences that an attack in the first seconds of waking can feel more tragic than any other kind of violence. The body is simply not ready to file new information. There is no warm up. The blade was already moving when the room understood there was someone else in it. Bedding became a tangle. Breath hitched into a ragged rhythm that could not organize itself into words. A pillow skidded to the floor. And then the room was full of sound.

Knives make almost no noise when they enter flesh. The noisy part of a stabbing is the human part. It is the sharp shock of the first cry, the urgent scrape of hands, the thud of bodies hitting the side of a bed frame, the desperate music of anyone who has ever tried to stop something that will not stop. The blade rose and fell with short hard motions. It was not a single wild swing aimed at terror. It was work. Focused and unrelenting and workmanlike in its way, the kind of ugly work that has only one possible conclusion if not interrupted by a miracle or a gunshot or a neighbor at the door. There was no miracle. There was no gunshot. There was no knock.

Gregg moved. Of course he did. That is the thing about love in a hard moment. It does not ask for permission. It simply acts. He dragged himself out of the torn geography of the bed and made for the one part of the house that felt like a destination you could hold in your head when the world is spinning, the kitchen. People do not run for a kitchen out of sentiment. They run for the layout. Counters and drawers mean corners and handles and potential weapons, anything to break the rhythm of the blade. His path drew a line a detective would later measure with a tape and a camera, dashes and smears that led through the doorway to the linoleum. There the body gave out. That is not cowardice. That is simply the physics of blood loss.

Back in the bedroom, the first target lay in a silence that had fallen too fast. If you have never seen the aftermath of a stabbing you might imagine chaos writ large, a scene out of fiction with overturned furniture and dramatic arcing patterns on the walls. The reality is smaller, tighter, almost domestic in its horror. Sheets bunched in fists and then released. A nightstand shifted half an inch and came to rest. A lamp shade leaned. The violence gathered itself into particular places, a spread the size of a person, a pool that stopped at the baseboard, edges defined by the way the floor was built and the way cloth drinks. Photographs would later frame those facts in the flat language of exhibits. They cannot hold the feeling in the air after the last motion stops.

A child woke in the other room. Children are radar. They read the home's weather through sound and weight. A loud voice can be disentangled from a laugh in a second. The child did not leave the room. She listened. The furnace came on and then off again, adding a meaningless rhythm to a night that had already shattered. Whether she saw anything that could help or hinder the case is not a question a decent person asks a child to answer in detail. Her role in this part of the story is a single act of courage that a dispatcher would later note in a report. She called.

The phone ringing at dispatch is the moment when private catastrophe becomes public work. Words entered a headset worn by someone who has heard everything a county can throw at a person in a year. The voice on the call was young, focused like only a child trying to do a serious thing can be. Officers were sent. The sound of tires in snow is its own siren in a small town. Patrol rolled down West Second South under the dim wash of streetlights, turned in, and stopped at a front walk crusted over by repeated freeze and thaw.

They announced and entered. A door like that one remembers every hand that ever pushed it open after a long day. On this night it remembered a uniform. The house smelled like houses smell, a blend of detergent, coffee, and something new that announced itself immediately to trained noses. The first officer moved along the path anyone would take in a familiar house at night and arrived where the body of a man lay on the kitchen floor. The second stood at the bedroom doorway and knew the second truth of the night. These things go still quickly, and the stillness is not ambiguous once you have seen it a few times. The radio told the others what their eyes already knew. Two down. Scene secure. Send the coroner. Send detectives. Send a blanket for a child.

Work began. Crime scenes are patient puzzles. You do not rush them. You photograph the big frame and then you take smaller pieces until the camera has seen everything your eyes have seen and a few things they missed. You put little numbers on little tented cards near prints and fabric and places where edges matter. You measure distances as if someone will stand in a court months from now and need to hear how far it was from the corner of the bed to the door. Because in fact someone will. You note the marks on the kitchen floor where a shoe slipped and skidded. You follow a line of dark half moons toward the garage, each one a reminder that anger does not float above the ground. It walks.

The weapon was not waiting on a counter for a neat photograph. That absence became a presence of its own. It told detectives what had happened after the last wound. The killer had left with the blade or hidden it on the way. People who act in rage often leave the tool of the act where it fell. People who think while they are still panting throw things into rivers and ditches. The path out of the house told officers where to begin looking. A car had backed out in a hurry and gone the direction that people go when they want to leave town without taking the main roads. A gas station in the next city over already under the eye of inexpensive cameras caught a figure who made the clerk look twice. Hands wrapped. Clothes streaked. The expression of someone studying the smallest details of other people to gauge whether anyone else can hear her thoughts.

By midmorning, a separate crew picked through snow along a river access familiar to anyone who had ever skipped school to fish. Twin Bridges sits unassuming in winter. The water runs black and cold under grey. You can park and walk twenty paces and be out of sight. That is the country definition of privacy. Along the bank where rushed hands would fling objects with the panicked logic of get rid of everything fast, they found what they expected. Torn gloves. A single boot whose mate sat untouched back at a closet. A long thin blade in a sheath designed for filleting a fish, the kind of knife that takes very little energy to do very ugly work. There would be tests later that match micro facts to micro facts and turn a riverbank into a chapter of a proof. But even without them the story ran straight.

Back at the station, officers spoke gently with a child and then sent her to a safer place for the rest of the day. Detectives turned to the other room where a woman sat under pale light. The conversation did not spin magic. People who have crossed a terrible line rarely narrate their journey in a way that satisfies anyone hearing it. She was read the rights that stand between the state and a person. Questions were asked in the calm, almost boring tone good interviewers adopt when they are fishing for holes rather than confessions. Where were you. Who did you see. Why are you hurt. Why are those gloves torn. Boredom is a tool in an interrogation because nerves hate it. They want either anger or comfort. They do not know what to do with paperwork and pauses and a pencil scratching the same question in different words.

Outside, Rigby woke fully into the day and into the first real tremor of collective knowledge. A neighbor stepped onto a porch in boots and peered down the street. A plow passed, throwing a low ridge against the curb. A curious car idled and then moved on slowly. The tape across the yard altered the usual geometry. You cannot walk your dog along the same route once a house has tape. You cannot carry a bag of groceries past a yard where officers wear gloves and call each other by last names as if first names have been retired out of respect.

Nothing about the work inside glorified the violence. That is the quiet dignity of a good scene team. They deal in details because details restore order. The medical examiner came and took careful notes that do not need to be repeated here to be honored. The doctor named the wounds and the reasons for death. He did not speculate. He did not narrate. He drew lines and wrote numbers and chose words that have been used in morgues for a hundred years because new words are not required to describe old tragedies. Sometime in those hours that feel both fast and endless, he moved the bodies with the gentleness that professionals bring to tasks that nonprofessionals cannot imagine doing. The house let them go.

If you have ever watched a detective step through a house after the bodies have been removed you have seen a particular kind of thinking made visible. They take in the negative spaces. The places where something should be and is not. The places where a pattern breaks. In this kitchen that meant a clear stretch of counter where a knife block might have lived but did not. In this bedroom that meant a square of carpet that was newer or older than the rest, a place repaired once and now broken again. The negative spaces in this case pointed outward. The necessary object was not here. It would be somewhere else. When that somewhere else began to produce things to put in bags, the case acquired the momentum all investigators pray for.

Notice what no one did. No one declared the case solved in the first hour. No one called a press conference well before the words could be honest. The department put out a measured sentence that said what needed saying and did not feed the rumor engine. Two people are dead. The suspect is in custody. There is no threat to the public. That is all a town needs at noon on a day like this. It lets children come home from school without hearing their parents break the news in the driveway. It lets shopkeepers wrap up the lunch rush without apologizing for their hands shaking. It lets a city breathe and wait.

By afternoon the riverbank had given up enough that even a defense attorney would have trouble arguing away the logic of it. The fillet knife with its fine edge slid into a paper envelope. The torn gloves followed. The single boot went into a bag that looked almost comic in its disproportion. Small items fall to the bottom of big bags and rattle around accusingly as if they know what they are. In a different room a photograph of a scabbard came out of a printer and went into a folder marked with a name and a case number and a date. The folder, despite how fragile it looked, had the weight of a future inside it.

Once the light went down again, the street fell back under the kind of quiet that makes you wonder whether everything that happened was an invention. The tape was gone. A deputy had come by with a new lock set and a screwdriver and the practical knowledge that there are always small physical repairs after big emotional damage. He finished the job without comment and left a note with contact information for access and questions. Winter reclaimed the yard. The plow came by one more time and pushed gray snow into a tidy ridge. You could stand there in the cold and hear nothing more than tires on the highway and the neighbor's porch swing creak as it shifted against its chain.

A short summary can be cruel because it removes all the breathing. But it belongs here because the readers who love this work know that precision is not the enemy of narrative. A person entered a locked home in the early morning. She attacked two sleeping people with a knife. One died where the attack began. The other fled and fell in the kitchen. A child called. Officers answered. Evidence led away from the house to a river where a knife and other items were found. The person connected to the house was found with blood on clothing and wounds that knives leave when even a killer pays a price in flesh. The scene became a file. The file became the nucleus around which everything else would gather.

None of this tries to say what the victims said in their last minutes. Those words belong to them and to the people who loved them and not to a book. What a book can do, what this chapter can do, is place you inside the rooms where a routine ended and a rare kind of quiet fell. It can remind you that evil inside a home is usually simple and close, carried out with ordinary tools at arm's length by someone who knows where the light switches are. It can tell you that the next place this story goes is a small interview room and then a courtroom, where the same town that stayed calm at its worst hour will sit still and watch as the state and a defense unravel the morning in front of twelve people asked to carry the weight of decision.

Rigby would not sleep the same way for a while. People would double check deadbolts without talking about it. They would look a beat longer than usual at the window across the street when turning out a light. In the house at the center of it all the air went stale with paused life. Mail stacked up because mail always stacks up when death interrupts. Plants drooped. Batteries in an unwatched wall clock ran down and the second hand stopped between numbers. That is how houses register a crime. They stop counting time until someone resets the hands.

The hands will be reset by the living. The dead are beyond clocks. For now, this is where we leave the rooms that saw the last minutes of two people who had plans for the following week. The next turn in the road leads us to a name on a charging document, to the long fluorescent corridor of a county jail, and to a judge who will eventually lean forward on a bench and ask both sides to speak plainly. That is where the story goes when a small town night breaks and a blade writes its brutal sentence.

ARREST, TRIAL AND SENTENCE

The town woke into the second day of February with more questions than anyone could answer over a diner counter. People could point to the lane, to the house, to the tape that had briefly turned their street into a boundary.

They could not point to a reason that made sense. That part belonged to the long work of officers and lawyers and a jury. It began not with a theory but with a person in custody and a chain of choices the law requires as soon as a life is taken.

The woman officers stopped before sunrise did not come to the station by way of the front lobby. She arrived in stages, just as the case itself would arrive in stages to the courthouse. A deputy who had learned to trust routine asked the same questions he asked on any predawn contact that smelled like trouble. Are you hurt. Whose blood is that. Where have you been. The answers were thin and strangely distant. The hands that moved were wrapped and clumsy. A patrol car ride in rural Idaho is not a grand procession. It is a few miles of dark road and a new light at the end. The suspect went to the hospital first because that is where protocol sends anyone whose blood tells a story of fresh harm. Doctors treated cuts across the palms and fingers that looked like the price a person pays when a blade slips or when a hand tries for the impossible in a struggle. Staff made notes that would later matter to a prosecutor, small sentences that joined other small sentences into a clear line of sense. Then the patient became a prisoner and the long walk through the system began.

Booking is a ceremony of control disguised as paperwork. A camera took its small unsympathetic portrait. Ink took fingerprints that would not fade. Belongings were listed in a ledger that clacks as if it were older than everyone in the room. A cell door closed with a sound that many people remember more clearly than anything an officer said that first day. The calm of the process has its own effect. It quiets the dramatic impulses that suspects sometimes bring with them and replaces them with a schedule. Breakfast. Attorney. Arraignment. Lunch that tastes like nothing. The world shrinks to the length of a bench and a rule sheet posted on a wall.

The first appearance in court came quickly because judges do not wait when two people are dead. The room was not crowded. Early hearings rarely are. The judge read out the names of the dead, the name of the defendant, the address where the bodies had been found, and the charges. Two counts of first degree murder. Two enhancements for using a deadly weapon in the killings. The words landed without ceremony, each one a brick added to a wall the State would have to build straight and square if the case was to hold. The judge explained rights in language designed to be unmistakable. Counsel was appointed. Bail was not offered. In a matter of minutes the case that had begun as an emergency became a file on a clerk's desk and a set of dates on a calendar that would decide when and how the public would hear what happened in the house on West Second South.

In the days after that first hearing, detectives did what detectives always do when the outlines are solid and the details still matter. They stitched the night together with time stamps and images. A convenience store camera in Madison County gave them a sequence that fixed the suspect at a precise moment, clothes marked in a way that matched what officers had seen with their own eyes. The gas pump, the bright box of a store at two in the morning, the slide of a car door, the awkward angle of wrapped hands at a counter, and the set of a face trying hard to appear normal were all captured in the washed out palette of late night surveillance. When deputies asked why the clothes were stained the answer drifted and thinned. The machine, spare and indifferent, did not care about tone. It cared about time and place. Those it gave freely.

Evidence recovery at the riverbank built the physical spine the prosecutor would later rely on. January and February in Jefferson County do not make for easy searches, yet the river gave up what it had been handed in the dark. Torn gloves. A lone boot whose mate waited in a closet across town. A long slim knife meant for filleting fish, fitted to a sheath that married cleanly to a scabbard found under a car seat. These were not dramatic discoveries in the sense popular entertainment prefers. They were small, stubborn facts that defeated wishful thinking. They said a person had left a house in a hurry after doing terrible things and had tried to erase the link between the crime and the car she drove. In law, as in carpentry, sound construction requires dependable joins. Here the joins were prints and fibers and a fit that could be felt and seen.

The child who had dialed for help that night did not become a tool for either side to use in a courtroom performance. The system made room for childhood even inside a murder case. Specially trained interviewers took statements once and took them carefully. Prosecutors did not put her on the stand to make jurors cry. Defense lawyers did not attempt to tear a child's memory to pieces in search of advantage. The record held her words, and the court respected the limits that mercy demands when the truth can already be told by other means. That choice would matter to the tone of the trial later. It announced that the State intended to win on proof rather than on pain.

Pretrial weeks are never quiet even when they look quiet. In offices above Main Street and in rooms with bad coffee at the courthouse annex, lawyers worked through motions that would define the borders of the story a jury would be allowed to hear. The State filed to admit photographs that documented the rooms as officers found them. The defense filed to limit any image it believed would inflame rather than inform. The judge studied each exhibit and sorted them into stacks labeled permitted, excluded, and permitted with limits. The State moved to introduce the knife and the clothing from the hospital, all properly tagged and tested. The defense challenged chain of custody in places where the path from riverbank to evidence locker ran through more hands than counsel liked. The judge counted signatures and times and initialed entries on a chain sheet, then ruled. The items would come in. The jury would see them just as twelve strangers have seen such items in countless courtrooms before and since. That is how a system honors the dead and the living at once. It insists on procedure and it keeps its promises to the truth.

There were other motions. One asked to keep out certain statements about the storm of phone calls and the obsession with a former partner's new life. The court allowed some and disallowed some, drawing lines that refused to let motive swallow the elements of the crime while still allowing jurors to understand why a person came to a house at that hour with a blade. One asked to keep the child's account within the transcripts that investigators had prepared and out of the live theater of testimony. Granted. One asked to sequester the jury if the case drew more attention than usual for a county case. Denied, with an admonition that both sides keep their voices out of the halls and their witnesses off the air.

Jury selection in Jefferson County is intimate compared to larger venues. Lawyers looked at a pool made up of people who might share a pew or a grocery aisle with one another and asked them to talk plainly about violence and divorce and whether a person who has been left can be understood without being excused. The voir dire was patient. It had to be. Everyone knew everyone by one or two degrees. The question was not Do you know about this case. The question was Can you hear evidence without letting what you think you know decide the outcome before we begin. People who live in small towns can be very good at that kind of discipline. They talk with each other across differences for a living. Twelve were chosen and two alternates with them, and the judge reminded them twice a day that their job was to listen and then to speak with one voice only when they had finished listening.

Opening statements gave the first clear view of the strategies that would guide the next two weeks. The State spoke in a straightforward line. A marriage ends. A new relationship begins. Rage hardens into a plan. A door opens. A knife moves. The killer leaves a trail out of the house, out of the garage, into a car, and toward a river that fails to hide what it is given. A child calls. A camera at a gas station shows a woman with blood on her clothing. Doctors note that the amount cannot be explained by a single cut. Officers recover a sheath that matches a scabbard, gloves that match wounds, and a boot that matches a gap. The State promised to put each piece on a table and ask the jury to pick them up one by one until the weight of them was unmistakable.

The defense took a different tack. In a voice more sorrowful than angry, counsel suggested that grief can stew memory into something it was not, that the rush of a deadly night can blur faces and voices, that someone else could have been there, that perhaps there is a world in which the person the State has named is not the only person who could have done what was done. Counsel reminded the jury that no one had produced a complete video of the killing. Counsel noted that police did not lock the world at the house the instant the knife stopped moving, that of course they did not because no officer can move that fast, and that every second not controlled by the State was a second during which the possibility of misinterpretation existed. It was a defense built not on an alternative suspect but on doubt cast in careful handfuls.

The State's case unfolded in a steady rhythm of witnesses whose jobs are to notice and to measure. A dispatcher described a call that should never have to be made by someone so young. A patrol officer who was first through the door described the layout of the rooms and the positions of the bodies without performing. His voice stayed at the low register that tells a jury he has bent to this work before and will bend to it again, because the world will always have people in it who do not stop themselves in time. A crime scene technician showed enlarged prints and explained why they were not footprints from boots belonging to the house. A detective traced the line from the kitchen to the garage and from the garage to the car, then to the stretch of county road that falls away toward Twin Bridges where the water runs black in winter. Jurors stared at the exhibits as if hoping for a door in the paper that would lead somewhere else. There was no door.

The doctor spoke without flourish. The cause of death for both victims was blood loss from multiple stab wounds. The pattern of injuries matched the story the rooms told. One person had tried to move, had made it to the linoleum, and had fallen. The other had died where the attack began, with defensive cuts across the hands that are as old as violence itself. The doctor used terms that flatten horror into vocabulary because that is what medicine must do to work. Even so, the jurors' faces gave away their internal rebellion against what their ears were required to accept. It is difficult to hear how fast a person can be ended by a blade wielded by someone who refuses to stop.

A nurse from the hospital took the stand to describe the state of the defendant's hands and clothing when she arrived that morning. The cuts were deep enough to require attention, messy enough to suggest a struggle, and fresh. The clothing bore blood in volumes that did not square with the story of a single small injury. The nurse did not contradict anyone. She merely added her piece. The prosecution did not need her to do more. The goal was not to crown a hero or unmask a plot. The goal was to show that from house to road to river to hospital, the facts met each other like the teeth of a zipper, closing the open mouth of doubt.

A forensic analyst described the blade recovered at the river and its sheath, the matching scabbard in the car, and the way steel and leather form pairs that are not easily confused with other pairs. The analyst explained how trace evidence sticks where it should and does not stick where it should not, and how the glue of reality makes it difficult to slide out from under material truth when the truth has had time to settle. Jurors watched the analyst handle each item with the same combination of care and detachment used in operating rooms when the patient is already beyond help but the lesson for the living still matters.

The defense cross examined everyone. It is their job. They asked whether the camera at the gas station showed a face clearly or merely a figure in motion. They asked whether the chain of custody ever ran through a rookie's hands. They asked whether the child might have been mistaken in describing what she saw in the first seconds of fright, whether she might have heard a name and transformed it without knowing into a different name because that is how language slides around when air is leaving the body. The defense did not have to prevail on all of these questions. Doubt is cumulative. It gathers like water under a door. But jurors, even as they listened carefully, could not avoid glancing back at the table where a knife and a sheath and a scabbard waited like characters who do not leave the stage between scenes.

When the State rested, the defense called a few witnesses who helped sketch a second map that led outward rather than inward. An old friend spoke of a tormented split and of emotions that spun too fast to steer. Another friend said she could not believe the person in the dock would be capable of this even as she admitted that the cuts and stains and hours of the night were a bad fit for any other explanation. The defendant herself did not take the stand. It is a common choice in a case where the evidence is strong and where cross examination would open doors the defense would rather keep shut. The jury would judge without hearing the voice of the person at the center of the storm except in recordings from that first long morning when officers asked and asked again. Those recordings were enough. They captured a mind that either could not or would not give the simple answers the facts demanded.

Closing arguments brought the familiar contrast that marks the end of a well tried case. The prosecutor spoke in short sentences that added up to a plain conclusion. The fingerprints of time and place aligned. The collection from the riverbank aligned. The medical facts aligned. The presence at the gas station aligned. The injuries on the defendant aligned. The child's call and simple description aligned. The words were not angry. They were direct. The State did not demand vengeance. It asked for law. The defense spoke to the narrow isthmuses where doubt still might stand. An identification made in fear. A chain of custody with many links. The absence, for a while, of the weapon itself before it was found where it could be found. Counsel asked the jurors to remember that not every ugly story is proven even when it seems to match the way the world too often goes. The twelve filed out with their notebooks and their solemn oaths and left the room to a silence that deepened by the minute.

The verdict arrived without theatrics. Guilty on both counts of first degree murder. Guilty on both deadly weapon enhancements. In the gallery there was a dull wave of breath as if everyone had been leaning forward for hours and finally remembered that lungs require air. The judge thanked the jurors the way a seasoned judge does, with gratitude and with the reminder that service in such a case changes a person but need not define the rest of their days. Then the court set a date for sentencing and the room emptied into the corridor where emotions returned to faces like color after a faint.

Sentencing was not an afternoon of fireworks. It was a deliberate inventory of harm and of the tools the law allows in return. Family members spoke. Their words were spare and shaking. They tried to condense entire human beings into minutes because that is all a criminal court can offer the dead by way of ceremony. A sister spoke of the way a laugh could straighten a bad day. A relative described what it means to meet police at a taped off doorway and be held back by the practiced kindness of someone who has to say no at a threshold. The State asked for a punishment that would say to every person in every county that this kind of night carries a price that will be paid until the end of a natural life unless a parole board far in the future decides otherwise. The defense asked for a number that allowed for the possibility that a person can change and that decades in a cell can carve room inside a human being for remorse that does not need an audience to be real.

Idaho's sentencing structure for first degree murder sits on the edge between certainty and discretion. The judge had a range defined by statute and informed by the jury's verdict and by the weapon enhancements the jury had found. He spoke at length before saying the number. He acknowledged the bitterness that had fermented into violence and refused to let bitterness explain what the law calls premeditation. He spoke of the child and of the shock that will ring that life like a bell for years. He spoke of the care with which the officers did their work and of how the community had kept its balance in the days between act and verdict. Then he pronounced the sentence. The defendant would serve twenty seven years to life in the custody of the state. Anything short of that number would be a betrayal of the dead. Anything longer was unnecessary to the truth he had heard.

There was a long stillness after those words. Judges know how to end a moment like that. He spoke the procedural language that unfreezes a room. Credit for time served. Orders regarding contact with the families. Conditions that would apply if a parole board ever let the defendant see the city from the other side of a fence again. Transport. Custody. The bailiff took position. The cuffs went on with the practiced gentleness of a man who has learned to do his work without adding more pain to rooms already full of it. The door to the short corridor toward the holding cells closed behind the defendant, and the afterwards began.

A case like this does not end with the bang of a gavel. It slopes away through appeals that do not remake the facts but test the law that was applied to those facts. Counsel filed a challenge that questioned evidentiary rulings and the way certain testimony had been presented. The Court of Appeals reviewed the record with the cold focus that is the appellate craft and affirmed the convictions in an opinion that emphasized the strength of the proof and the care the trial judge had taken to balance the competing concerns of fairness and completeness. The weapon enhancements stood. The structure of the sentence remained intact. This was not a case twisted by a flamboyant error or an experiment in legal theory. It was a straightforward application of statute to a blunt night. (anylaw.com)

Meanwhile the Department of Correction found a place within its network for a prisoner who had become a proper noun in Jefferson County. Intake is a series of indignities wrapped in procedures. Health assessments. Classifications. A new number that does not forget. Eventually the file sent her to the women's facility where inmates count time in sets defined by work assignments and lines and visits and the kind of education that can be had from a small library stacked mostly with paperbacks. From the outside people said the name occasionally in news stories that revisited the case on anniversaries or in documentaries that distilled years into forty minutes with reenactments and voice overs. Inside the wire, a name is a way to call a person to a door when mail arrives. The drama fades into routine. That is what institutions do. They grind the edges down and leave a smoother stone behind.

The parole board exists to hear the future argued in the presence of the past. It is not a guarantee. It is a gate on a hinge that may never swing. Twenty seven years is a number with a long shadow, and 2031 looked far away when it was first spoken. Families marked it anyway because that is what families do for self protection. They pin a date to the future and promise themselves they will be ready to speak then. In interviews many years later, a daughter of one of the dead said plainly that freedom for the person who took her mother would feel like an insult built into the very air.

The system is designed to let her say that in a letter or in a hearing room when the time comes. It is designed to let others say something different if they must. A decent system makes room for those contradictions and lets a board decide what weight to give them.

As the legal process settled into its long tail, closer to home the officer who had first stepped through the door on West Second South reached retirement and spoke about the case in the calm of his later years. He did not turn it into a legend. He told it as a caution, a reminder that divorces can ferment into something worse when a person decides the story of a life that has moved on without them is an insult that must be paid for. He said the motive was simple anger, and he said the community had behaved well in the face of something ugly. For people in Rigby, that mattered as much as any number on a sentencing order. They had done what they were supposed to do. They had let the law work. They had absorbed noise from outside without letting it dictate their days. The victims were remembered as people with plans and not merely as names in a heading on a brief.

In a true crime book, it can be tempting to draw a lesson so sharp it cuts a page as you turn it. The arrest, the trial, and the sentence in this case resist that impulse. They show what it looks like when a small department does careful work and presents it to a county jury with confidence that the facts will carry the day. They show a defense that did what it could with the lines available and a court that kept the center of the story clear. They show a number that walked the line between denunciation and the ritual possibility of parole that the law reserves even for those who bring knives to bedsides. They show the quiet competence of a system that does not need spotlight speech to convince a community that justice, however complicated its textures, has been done.

The house on West Second South sat through all of this without comment. Eventually it learned a new family and new routines. Law moves on. So do homes. Court files are boxed and archived. Opinions are indexed in places where lawyers can find them when they need to argue about a rule in a different case years later. People still pass the address and feel something twist at the memory, but the twist is duller now. That is the mercy of time on a community, though not always on the closest circle of the dead. The sentence ensured that no one would call the defendant neighbor again for a very long time. The words on the judgment guaranteed that the next chapter for the town would be written by people who had no reason to care about that night except as caution and memory.

In the end, the arrest was not a mystery, the trial was not a circus, and the sentence was not a gesture. They were the institutions of a place as ordinary as any place, doing the sober work that follows when somebody decides that love is a possession and not a gift. The jury returned, the judge spoke, the doors closed, and the rest of the town got up the next morning, shoveled snow, brewed coffee, and kept watch over one another in the quiet way that has always been the real defense against nights like the one that started this chapter.

AFTERMATH WITH FAMILY AND PUBLIC OPINION

By the time the courtroom emptied and the last television camera rolled out into the winter light, Rigby began doing what small towns do after a loud event. It lowered its voice. It took care of chores. It made room for grief without turning that grief into permanent theater. Houses returned to their familiar rhythms, yet every day carried a new awareness that the old normal had been replaced. At the cafe a few blocks from the courthouse, regulars switched back to talk about weather and cattle and high school games, but a pause sometimes hung in conversations when someone looked toward the lane that led to West Second South. People carried on, because that is what people do after a verdict. They carry on and they make their respect practical.

Families on both sides had to learn a new calendar. Court dates were no longer the anchors of their weeks. Instead the days filled with quieter tasks that do not make the evening news. There were estate matters to settle for the dead, bills to close, accounts to reconcile, and the strange business of sorting through belongings. Those who stepped into the rooms where loved ones had lived did so with the sort of care that looks like ceremony. A sweater folded and placed in a box. A book left open on a table until someone could bear to move it. Photographs gathered, held, and then set aside for a later afternoon when they could be faced without feeling ambushed.

The child who made the call that night moved through the first months of the aftermath wrapped in the kind of attention that professionals learn to make invisible. Teachers began to keep a closer but gentler eye. Counselors chose corners with good light to have quick talks about feelings that were too big for any single sentence. The school understood that routine is not a luxury. It is medicine. Bell times stayed steady. Classwork offered a shape to days that might otherwise have felt like a series of sudden drops. Friends on the playground did what children often do better than adults. They played. They kept the conversation shallow where depth would have hurt. They brought the weather back into focus. Is it going to snow again. When is field day. Can I borrow that pencil. These small questions are the bar chords of recovery. You play them over and over until your fingers stop hurting.

The immediate circle of Karen's family learned to answer the same question in a dozen ways depending on who asked it. People wanted to know how they were doing. No one who is grieving can answer that straight. The answer moves even during a single sentence. Some days were full of useful activity with friends rotating in to cook, clean, and keep company. Other days were lined with a silence that made ordinary tasks feel like a climb. They found that talking about her laugh helped more than talking about her death. They traded stories that had nothing to do with court or evidence and everything to do with the person they missed. A Thanksgiving dish she always burned and served anyway. The way she tilted her head when listening to music. The phrase she used when a day went sideways. These stories landed softly and stayed where pain could not always reach them.

On the other side, relatives of the woman now in prison had to walk their own complicated corridor. Love does not evaporate when a verdict is read. Families were forced to learn two languages at once. The language that acknowledges the enormity of the harm. And the language that lets a mother or a brother write letters, accept collect calls, and visit a person behind glass without lying to themselves about what happened. The town often saw only the first language. It did not always see the second, spoken softly in kitchens when the house had quieted and the day could be faced without an audience. Even in private, these were not excuses. They were efforts to keep a thread of care intact in a world that had broken apart.

Law enforcement entered their own season of reflection. Officers who walked through those rooms on that winter morning met in a back office a few weeks later with coffee that had sat too long and went cold in paper cups. They reviewed the call, the entry, the first aid they had tried even while their instincts told them the effort was ceremonial. They noted what worked.

They admitted what could be done better. Did the first unit arrive with the right equipment staged where it would save seconds. Did the perimeter hold without gaps. Were the photos complete. Did evidence move from hand to hand without confusion. These questions were not an indictment of their past work. They were an investment in the next time the county would need them to be composed in chaos.

The house on West Second South passed from a place of headlines to a place of practical decisions. After the forensic holds were lifted, relatives faced a choice that families in similar cases always face. Keep the property inside the family or let it go and allow new life to move through the rooms. There is no single correct answer. Some find comfort in repainting, repairing, and staying. Others need the relief of new walls and a new view from a new window. In time a different family turned a key in that lock and began to fill the kitchen with the smell of supper. Neighbors watched with a nervous hope that is easy to understand. A house that has seen a terrible night will never be nothing, but it can learn a different story if people let it.

Faith communities did the work that churches and wards and fellowships have always done in rural places. They gathered people for services that honored the dead without giving the case back its old power. They organized food trains and rides for relatives who needed to be in two places at once. They sat with elderly parents and listened in the way listening is meant to happen, attention without fixing. Sermons did not become court transcripts. They looked outward toward the habits that prevent private storms from becoming public disasters. Not every conflict needs a pulpit, but a pulpit can remind a town that keeping watch over one another is not only about crime. It is about kindness at scale.

Victim services remained in the wings as the first year went by. Help arrived in forms that look unremarkable until you do not have them. Someone filled out paperwork that unlocked assistance for funeral costs. Someone found a counselor who did not treat grief like a project with a finish line. Someone walked a relative through the next legal steps when a separate matter came up because life continues to produce ordinary problems even when families are busy surviving a very large one. In a few cases, services were offered and declined, then requested months later. People often decline when they are still in shock and ask when the fog begins to thin. Good programs know how to stay available without hovering.

The quiet work of the press never fully leaves a town after a crime like this, but the shape of that attention changes. The first weeks attracted quick stories that cut toward the broad facts and moved on. Later attention belonged to slower projects that tried to step through the evidence without exploiting it. Some producers called and asked for new interviews. Most were answered politely and declined. Families learned to say no in sentences that carried no apology. It is a kindness to learn how to ask, and it is a kindness to learn how to refuse. The best programs understood that the story was now held by court records. The living were allowed to have their lives back.

Friends created small memorials in ways that avoided the trap of making a corner of town into a shrine of perpetual sadness. A bench in a park where Karen used to walk. A donation to a local shelter in Gregg's name. A scholarship for a student who planned to study nursing or criminal justice depending on which friends organized the fund. These gestures were as much about the present as the past. They invited the town to attach the names to acts of care. A bench with a bronze plaque that catches the afternoon sun tells children that memory has a place and also that the place is somewhere you can sit and listen to birds when summer finally returns.

The prison system receded into silence as the first year gave way to the second. The woman at the center of the case entered the routines that every long term inmate learns. A schedule of wake up, count, work if assigned, meals, call outs to medical or classes, and lights that insist on their own timing. Communications with the outside world were limited, supervised, and predictable. Time lengthened and then shortened again, as time does when it is charted by clocks and by decisions she could no longer shape. People on the outside adjusted as well. Letters went out either regularly or not at all. Visits were made or not made, and each family's choice found its own level and stayed there.

The subject of parole lived in a future so far away that it rarely surfaced in the early years. Families nevertheless learned how those boards function, because knowledge is an anchor even when the ship is moored for a long time. They learned that victim statements can be placed in the file long before the date approaches. They learned that every board values steady work, rule compliance, and credible remorse more than declarations made for effect. They learned that the law allows letters from the community weighing against release, and that these letters do not need to be angry to be persuasive. A sentence has a public safety purpose. The board measures that purpose with care years later. Until then the community had only to keep living well and let the paperwork sleep in a folder in Boise where no one had to read it yet.

Around the town, people who had never spoken publicly about domestic rupture found a little more courage to ask for help before anger could harden into resolve. Clerks at the courthouse noticed that someone would pause at the window a moment longer and ask which form was needed for a protection order. Officers reported that when they arrived at a home where voices had been raised, one or both parties seemed more willing to accept a cooling off period and a clear plan for the next day. None of this can be measured easily. It lives in the space between people when they decide to accept help that last year they might have turned away.

A few new units inside the county agencies took the case as a quiet spur to update their interagency protocols. Dispatch added a checklist for callers whose age made them vulnerable to panic. The police department gave a refresher on evidence collection using photographs from this investigation as examples of getting it right. The prosecutor's office created a small training for young attorneys about presenting a domestic homicide without turning a court into a stage for vengeance. The hospital reviewed how it documented injuries on people who might become defendants and how those notes become important later without overstepping medical roles. None of these changes made headlines. Each made the next case slightly better prepared.

Years passed as they always do in places where seasons govern moods. The first anniversary brought a few stories that struck the right tone. The fifth brought fewer. The tenth brought a balance that felt healthy. People remembered without reopening wounds. A few gatherings marked the date with gestures rather than speeches. Flowers left on a grave. A quiet meal where chairs were deliberately set for the exact number who could come and no more. Not every loss needs a crowd to be honored. Sometimes the best memorial is a day without disaster, made in part possible by the lessons learned from the disaster that already happened.

The justice system does not pause for anniversaries. It moves with its own machinery. Appeals that once seemed like urgent storms turned into brief weather, clouds that threatened and passed without dropping rain. The verdict and the sentence held. They had been built to hold. The town took comfort in the steadiness of those outcomes. Not a loud triumph, just a sense that the state had done its job competently in front of everyone.

In quieter moments people allowed themselves to wonder about the human being sealed behind the number that the prison assigned. Had understanding grown where fury once lived. Did the weight of years carve new rooms inside a mind once crowded only by grievance. Those are proper questions for a private imagination, not for a book to answer. The relevant public truth was that the sentence placed the future in the hands of a board whose task is to weigh public safety and the reality of change. That truth was enough to let most residents set the matter aside and return to lives that needed their full attention.

As for the officers and lawyers whose names might appear in footnotes, their paths diverged in the usual ways. A detective retired and took up fishing more seriously, telling young officers over coffee about the importance of walk through discipline and humility on a scene. A prosecutor moved to a different office and carried forward a habit of explaining charges to families in plain language rather than in jargon. A defense lawyer began teaching a class at a nearby college about trial practice from both sides, using this case as a careful study in how to maintain professionalism when emotion wants to run the show. Each kept a copy of the file in a box that probably looks like a hundred other boxes, yet weighs a little more for reasons they do not need to explain.

There is a moment in the life of any town when the story that used to stop conversations becomes a chapter that people can refer to without losing their thread. Rigby reached that moment slowly and then all at once. A new family moved into the house on West Second South and planted perennials along the walk. The plants came back in spring on their own schedule, without consulting headlines. The neighbors left for work in the mornings and returned in the evenings and waved in the old manner. Children rode bikes along the curb and marked the pavement with sidewalk chalk the color of sherbet. The name of the street lost its sting for those who did not need it to sting anymore.

The families most affected did not cross any finish line. They reached new plateaus. Birthdays arrived with a steadier mix of tears and laughter. Holidays reassembled themselves around new centerpieces and new traditions. They made an art of carrying memory without letting it pull them under.

This is the private victory most people never see when they think of famous cases. It is the way grief evolves from a roaring wave into a tide that can be anticipated and respected. It does not go away. It becomes easier to navigate, and on some days it releases its hold long enough to let joy walk back into the room and stay.

True crime readers often ask what is left when the last gavel falls, when the last appeal is denied, when the last camera leaves. In Rigby what was left was not a cautionary slogan or a moral hammered to a nail. What was left were the ordinary acts by which communities keep their balance. People baked. People shoveled. People called one another by name. People made sure a child had what she needed for school and that her days had clear edges. People watched the lane on winter nights with the same care they give to their own driveways. They did not turn into detectives. They remained neighbors. That choice may have been the town's best answer to the kind of violence that tries to make itself the only story in a place.

The chapter closes not with a new revelation but with a long look at a town that chose steadiness. There is drama in that decision if you pay attention to how difficult it can be after the kind of shock Rigby absorbed. Steadiness requires discipline. It requires that people reject both the cruelty of gossip and the glee of constant retelling. It requires that officials tell the truth once and then let the truth stand on its own legs. It requires that families be allowed to own their memories and their plans without unscheduled visitors knocking on the door of a wound. Those requirements were met here. That is the proper definition of aftermath. Not ashes, but the work of shaping days into something livable again, with the names of the dead spoken softly and with gratitude for what they brought to the town before one winter morning took them away.

CHAPTER 9
MELINDA HARMON-RAISCH
TWO DECADE WAIT FOR JUSTICE

A true crime story does not begin with the moment of violence. It begins where decisions are shaped and loyalties are tested, in the homes and hallways that come long before a body is carried down a stairwell. To understand the murder of David Harmon in Olathe, Kansas, and the decades of silence that followed, you have to start with a community that prized piety and reputation, with a campus where friendships and courtships bloomed under the watchful eye of the Church of the Nazarene, and with three young adults who seemed, at first, to be living an ordinary Midwestern script.

Olathe in the early nineteen eighties was a smaller city than the sprawling suburb it would later become. The interstate carved a path along its edge, and beyond the exits the land opened into neighborhoods dotted with modest duplexes, starter homes, churches, and schools. The center of gravity for many families was faith. Sunday mornings were not just a habit. They were the lattice that held weeks together. Among the institutions that signaled the town's character, MidAmerica Nazarene College stood out.

Students crossed the grounds with textbooks under their arms and an expectation that the campus was both a place to study and a place to learn how to live inside the rules their elders valued.

Into that world came David Harmon and Melinda Lambert, a pair whose names would later be bound together in a police file and a court record but who first belonged to a simple story about youth and a future held close. David was twenty five in the winter of nineteen eighty two, steady at work and affable enough that friends describe him as the sort of man you could count on for a ride, a favor, or a hand with a heavy piece of furniture. There was nothing theatrical about him. He radiated a plain competence that can make a young man seem older than his years and reliable beyond his experience. He worked at a local bank, a job that suited his temperament. Banks ask their workers to be orderly and patient and to notice the small things that add up. David did all of that naturally.

Melinda, born Melinda Harmon later known as Melinda Raisch, moved in a circle that overlapped with David's church and campus community. She was part of the Nazarene world not only as a congregant but as a daughter. Her father, J. Wilmer Lambert, was a prominent official within the Church of the Nazarene. In a town where church roles carry weight far beyond the sanctuary, that lineage mattered. It created expectations and it offered cover. People assumed that a family highly placed in the church not only would honor its teachings but would seek to protect its name. Those assumptions, powerful and often useful in small religious communities, would later shape crucial choices.

Young marriages rise naturally out of such settings. People meet at services, at campus events, at socials organized by friends and pastors. David and Melinda married as many of their peers did, with families watching from pews and with a reception that included punch, cake, and the usual speeches about faithful homes and patient love. The marriage moved into a small apartment, one of the many rental spaces that housed junior bank employees, student couples, and newlyweds just starting to understand the bills that arrive like clockwork whether romance is thriving or not. They arranged furniture bought with help or borrowed for as long as someone would allow. They made lists of groceries. They settled into the rhythm of two people learning each other's morning habits and evening silences.

Hovering near that domestic routine was the culture of the campus and its network of friendships. Among those friends was a young man named Mark Mangelsdorf. He was bright and energetic, the sort of student who knows how to navigate classes and people with equal skill. He and Melinda found an easy rapport. In communities where everyone seems to know everyone else, friendships wind around each other like roots, growing close without anyone outside quite noticing how deep the connections have become. A dinner here, a cup of coffee there, a joke that lands better with one person than with another. Such benign beginnings are easy to miss. The distance between that kind of harmless familiarity and a choice that will break a life can seem enormous to outsiders. In real time, it is a series of micro decisions that feel defensible until they are not.

The Church of the Nazarene, as taught and practiced in Olathe, discouraged divorce with a seriousness that shaped courtships and marriages alike. Students learned not only what was in the Scriptures but what was expected of them by their elders and their peers. The message was not subtle. Marriage was a covenant to be guarded, not a seasonal arrangement to be traded in when things became difficult. Such teaching can steady a life, and often does. It can also channel a person's fear of shame into strange directions. When ending a marriage feels like a moral collapse rather than a hard decision, a person already in trouble may begin to imagine that confession is more dangerous than concealment.

In that moral climate, the bond between Melinda and Mark deepened. The line between friendship and something else is not a bright stripe on a floor that people step over with commotion. It is a seam in the air you only notice when you have already crossed it. They were young. They were close. They were part of a set that moved in and out of each other's apartments to talk, study, and pass unstructured hours. What they told themselves in the beginning is lost to the private rooms where people say the words they never plan to repeat. What remains is the pattern that emerged. Their connection was not casual. It was not purely social. It had the intensity of a bond that thrives on secrecy and shared risk.

That secrecy grew under a roof where David assumed that the world around him was essentially trustworthy. He worked, he came home, he slept. He attended church with his wife and expected that any strain between them could be addressed within the framework they had chosen together. In church cultures, especially those built on admonitions to fidelity and temperance, the presumption that a spouse will honor vows is not naïve. It is the default. David lived inside that default. He did not know that the plot line running parallel to his marriage would soon eclipse it.

Melinda navigated the two worlds with a practiced smile. People around her later remembered that smile, the way it seemed to be always at the ready, performing composure even when circumstances should have made composure difficult. When you grow up in a house charged with religious authority, you learn the choreography of restraint. You come to understand that a steady face is its own kind of armor. In the months leading up to the crime that would set Olathe talking for a generation, that armor held through church gatherings, campus walkways, and dinners where she played her role as David's wife with outward grace while turning elsewhere for the attention she wanted.

Mark built a life that looked successful from the outside. He dated, he later married, and he kept up with the people who would form his professional and personal network. In the universe of promising graduates from a religious college, he was well placed. Ambition is not a sin, but it often asks people to become good at compartmentalizing. He compartmentalized so well that the line between what he owed his conscience and what he owed his desires became elastic. In that elasticity, plans formed. Whether those plans took shape in whispers over coffee, on drives that wandered back roads, or in stolen minutes in campus spaces is less important than the fact that a plan moved from daydream into action.

The apartment on South Cooper in Olathe where David and Melinda lived was unremarkable in any way a neighbor would notice. A bed that fit the room, a dresser, a closet with the usual mix of work clothes and casual shirts, a kitchen that did its job and a living room that could host a couple of friends on a Friday night. The texture of that place matters because the brutality that would unfold there depended on familiarity. A stranger does not navigate a home in darkness with the confidence shown that night. A stranger does not know the weight of the front door or the creak of the hallway or the way moonlight cuts across a bedroom after midnight. An intimate knows these things. An intimate trusts the cover offered by the predictability of a sleeping spouse and by the stage set that assures them they can play their scene as written.

The young couple's ties to the college and the church meant that, when tensions rose, they rose inside a network that prized deference. That dynamic was personified in Melinda's father. J. Wilmer Lambert's presence in the Nazarene hierarchy lent his family a tone of authority and entitlement that would later shape the earliest hours of the police investigation. Before it warped the case, it shaped the household. A daughter raised in such a home understands that rules are something to be managed, not simply obeyed. She knows that people who carry titles tend to be obeyed even when they bluster. She learns that if she keeps her head down and her smile in place, most adults around her will credit her with sincerity long after she has abandoned it.

When Melinda told herself the marriage could not continue, she was not alone in that judgment. Mark shared it. The question that divided the next few months into before and after was not whether the marriage would endure, but how it would end and who would control the story of that ending. In a secular setting, the answer might have been obvious. Divorce would be discussed, papers filed, names changed, property divided, and friends asked to pick sides. In this setting, divorce carried a heavier penalty. It was not illegal. But it felt, to some, like a public humiliation that would attach not just to Melinda but to her father and to the church culture that had praised her as a daughter of the house. If divorce was, in their minds, unthinkable, the possibilities remaining shifted into darker territory.

The rumor mill in towns like Olathe spins as dependably as any gear in a clock. It churns out small talk about students and teachers, about who sat with whom at chapel, about who left a party early with whose jacket. Most rumors dry up quickly under daylight. They cannot hold their shape once examined. The rumor that Melinda and Mark were closer than they ought to be did not dry up. It persisted because people saw what they saw. They saw looks that lingered too long. They saw the easy way they leaned across a table to speak in a voice that excluded others. They heard the cadence of language that had grown intimate in a way that no longer fit the public roles each of them performed.

David's days moved forward without dramatic scenes that anyone outside the apartment remembered. He was not a man given to outbursts. He handled conflict with the patience of someone who believes in fair dealing. Those traits serve many men well. They did not serve him here. He was not the kind of person to draw lines and issue ultimatums. He trusted the institutions that had shaped him. He trusted the vows he had made. He assumed the woman who wore a ring next to his would also keep faith. The full measure of tragedy lies in that trust. It placed him in the role of the one person in the triangle who could not imagine himself as a character in a crime story.

The days before the murder held another important element that would echo for years. The bank where David worked was small enough that coworkers noticed if he seemed distracted or tired. He did not. He kept his hours and his standards. When a young man in a small town with a job in a bank is killed, there is often a lazy reflex that reaches for a robbery narrative or a misplaced grudge born of money. That would become convenient later for someone who needed a story to offer police. But in the months before the attack there was no pattern of jeopardy, no talk of threats, no money missing, no clients angry enough to stalk a teller or a clerk to an apartment in the middle of the night. The only danger lived inside the marriage.

Young couples in church communities host friends for dinner because that is the currency of fellowship. Melinda and David did their share of such evenings. In those rooms, the line between hosts and guests blurs into family. Shared faith does that. It encourages people to call one another brother and sister and to paper over awkwardness with prayer and dessert. That very courtesy made it possible for the triangle to assume it could keep secrets. When everyone is trained to think the best of everyone else, warning signs look like anomalies rather than like signals to be read and acted upon. The picture on the wall is crooked because someone bumped it, not because the entire house is built out of square.

On paper, the months leading to February of nineteen eighty two were ordinary. In memory, they were freighted with energy that had nowhere honest to go. Everything that would later make the case so absorbing for Olathe was already present in miniature. A couple bound by faith and community expectations. A third figure woven into their social fabric under a banner of campus kinship. A father whose prominence created pressure and provided shelter. A town that assumed its young people were better than they were because that is what towns do for themselves in order to believe their own story.

When storytellers return to this period after the crime, they sometimes apply a heavy brush, painting Melinda as already lost, Mark as already plotting, and David as already doomed. That is comforting because it suggests fate rather than choice. The more precise and more unsettling truth is that fate did not walk these streets. Choice did. Choices made in small rooms with low voices. Choices made on drives that circled the same blocks. Choices made while studying a sleeping man and deciding that a covenant was less important than a wish. Those choices do not announce themselves as evil while you are making them. They present as opportunities to get what you think you deserve without having to tell the truth about what you want.

The last days before the killing felt to outsiders like any other days. Grocery lists were written. A church bulletin was folded in half and left on a table. A pair of shoes waited near the door. The weather, as winter weather does, alternated between damp cold and the sort of bright brittle days that make the air feel sharpened. Within the apartment, tensions tightened. Within the circle of friends, glances lengthened and words softened to conceal more than they revealed. Only the people at the center had any sense of the turn they were about to take. Even they may not have admitted it aloud.

If you were to draw a map of the community at that moment, you would mark the Nazarene campus, the Harmon apartment, the bank, the Lambert home, and the coffee shops and kitchens where talk flowed. You would see how close everything sits. You would see how proximity breeds both concern and complacency. You would also see how a town that defines itself by its values can be unprepared for the degree to which those values can be used as screens. The same network that shelters young couples from the world can also shelter them from consequences until consequences arrive in a surge far beyond what anyone intended.

This is where the early chapter ends, on the eve of an act that would splinter trust and summon investigators into a case that should have been straightforward and instead sprawled across nearly a quarter of a century. The threads are all laid out. A marriage under the weight of expectation. A lover whose easy confidence masked resolve. A father whose authority would later bend the first hours of a police inquiry. A campus and a church that taught their children that promises once made must never be broken, even when the marriage that holds those promises has already failed in private. The next hours would be quick. The next years would be long.

THE MURDER

The calendar fixed the night as February twenty eighth nineteen eighty two. Winter still held Olathe in its narrow light and long cold. The apartment on South Cooper Road was quiet in the hours after midnight. Radiators clicked and settled. A single street lamp outside painted a pale shape against the bedroom wall. In that bed lay a young bank employee in deep sleep. Beside him lay his wife, awake within a few moments of what would become the most violent event in the recent memory of the town.

There was no fight at the door. No shouted demand from a hallway. No warning a neighbor would later recall. Whoever stepped into the apartment knew exactly where to go and exactly what to bring. In his hands was a heavy tool common in garages and construction sites, a crowbar with enough weight and reach to turn a bedroom into a killing ground in seconds. The first blow landed on a sleeping face. Then another. Then another. The tool did what it was designed to do. It transferred force. Wood and steel do not hesitate. By the time the body in the bed understood anything at all, the world had already narrowed to pain and confusion and the instinct to cover his head with his arms. He did not make it out of the sheets.

Detectives later counted at least a dozen strikes. The medical examiner would record a range of twelve to fourteen brutal impacts. The language of that report was clinical. The scene was not. The bed became a spray of shredded bedding and tissue. One eye was torn from its socket and flung several feet across the room. The skull fractured in more than one place. The jaw shattered. There were defensive wounds on the hands that showed a final reflex to ward off the instrument that kept falling. Every mark followed the arc of the tool wielded with two hands and absolute resolve. The apartment's drywall absorbed some of the energy. The rest landed where the killer intended.

The man in the bed was not alone. His wife was there, upright enough to register what was happening, later still enough to walk out of the room with a body on the bed and a story ready to be told. She would say that two men had broken in. She would say one of them demanded bank keys. She would say that she had been struck and that was why her cheek held a faint bruise. Her version was a script that explained why a bank worker might be targeted. It was also a script that steered the officers who would arrive into thinking first of robbery and threats from strangers rather than looking with sharper suspicion at the person who had shared the bed.

The first minutes after any murder are filled with reflex. People call the number they know. An operator answers and asks the questions that impose order. What happened. Where are you. Is the person breathing. Do not touch anything. Help is on the way. The officers who took the call moved through the sleeping town toward the apartment. In small cities like Olathe, these cars carry not only uniforms and gear. They carry knowledge of streets that have been driven a thousand times, of houses that look much the same, of people who wave from porches in daylight. That familiarity made what they found inside feel like a violation of more than one life.

The entry was calm and methodical. Officers announced themselves, stepped around the wife, and followed her gestures to the bedroom. The first beam of a flashlight swept the bed. The second beam held steady on the floor to trace an arc of blood and bone. Protocol took over. Secure the apartment. Confirm death. Call for a supervisor. Call for the medical examiner. Call for the photographer. Set a perimeter. Do not let neighbors into the hall. Do not let the wife out of your sight until detectives arrive to control the interview.

Crime scene work is a ritual that protects fragile truth. A camera made a record of the room before any hand could change anything. Wide shots fixed the context. Closer frames froze the position of the body, the state of the pillows, the tangle of sheets, the spatter that marked walls and the headboard. Markers were placed beside the most significant stains. Measurements were taken from corners, from bedposts, from a dresser whose edge collected droplets that told a story of motion. The instrument that had made that story was not in sight. No crowbar lay on the floor. No blunt tool rested where a panicked stranger might have dropped it. The absence mattered. It argued planning. It argued a familiarity with the space and a confidence that there was time to leave and to carry the tool away without fear of interruption.

The wife played her part from the first moment an officer spoke to her. She did not present as a person who had been soaked in blood. She had a small contusion on her cheek, easily explained by a slap or a self inflicted strike. She said two black men had entered the apartment. She said they wanted the keys to the bank where her husband worked. She said they had knocked her down and then killed him. The specifics were stark and easy to remember. They were also very convenient. The story pushed attention toward a pair of faceless men and toward a motive that was simple to understand in a place where bank workers are trusted and robberies make tidy headlines.

Police did what police are trained to do. They listened. They wrote down the account. They looked for signs that the story matched the room. Two intruders would likely have left prints, scuffs on the door, marks of forced entry. There were none. Two intruders would have ransacked the apartment for cash or documents while their partner applied pressure to the target. Drawers were not upturned. Cabinets were not open. The only uncontrolled motion in the apartment had been in the bedroom where the man died. Everything else was neat or undisturbed. The wife did not appear to have moved in a panic or scrambled to call for help while two intruders roamed the place. If the men had come for a key, as she claimed, they would leave with it. The key ring was still on the dresser where David kept it.

Neighbors woke to the sirens and to the hallway lights that turned their building into a stage. Officers knocked on doors to ask whether anyone had seen strangers in the stairwell or heard an argument. Most said no. One thought she had heard a single heavy thump and then nothing. Another thought she heard a woman's voice but could not make out words. The most striking absence in those interviews was any claim by a neighbor that they saw two men hurry away. If the exit had been that dramatic, someone would have noticed.

The medical examiner's arrival shifted the focus from the living to the dead. In a space no larger than a small bedroom, the doctor worked with the quiet economy of someone who had seen what one human being can do to another in a few seconds. The measurements he took would later become part of the chain linking the murder weapon to the strikes and the strikes to the person who took possession of the tool. The pattern of wounds suggested a right handed attacker standing near the head of the bed. Many blows were delivered from a high angle, as if the killer stood over the pillow and swung down again and again. Wounds on the forearms confirmed that the victim had raised his hands instinctively. One eyebrow was crushed. The eye itself had been displaced with such violence that it landed several feet from the bed. Blood pooled and then spread outward around the shoulders and neck. The bedding matted against the wounds told the story of motion followed by stillness.

Detectives stepped back out into the living room to consider how the killer had entered. The lock was intact. There were no pry marks on the jamb. The windows were shut from the inside and untouched by any scratch that would suggest an attempt to force them. Either the attacker had a key or he was let in. That sentence hung in the mind of every officer in the apartment. It returned again when the wife repeated her statement that two men had appeared without warning, demanded keys, and then fled. There was no explanation for how they had secured entry in the first place.

Evidence technicians gathered what they could. Fingernail scrapings from the victim. Swabs from areas where flesh and blood mixed in patterns that might yield trace material from the tool or from the hands that held it. Fibers pulled from sheets and from the wife's clothing. A small drop on a baseboard that would later match the rest of the blood in the room and offer nothing new but completeness. A married pair in their twenties does not keep a home that easily yields to forensic work. Few strangers come and go. Hairs and fibers tell a narrow story. This scene did the same. The apartment looked as if a single couple lived there and had lived there for some time. There was almost nothing that suggested an intrusion by an outsider.

While the technicians worked in the back of the apartment, the other half of the process began in the front. The wife was escorted to headquarters for a formal interview. The transport was not a matter of custody. It was a matter of control. The kitchen table in a crime scene is a bad place to gather a coherent account. It carries too many associations and too much distraction. A room with a tape recorder and a table strips a story down to its spine. An officer explained her rights. She agreed to speak. She gave her story again. Two men. A demand for keys. A sudden attack. A blow to her face. She gestured to the cheek. The bruise was there but faint.

The first round of questions lasted just long enough to establish the basic shape of the narrative and to begin testing its edges. What were you doing in the minutes before they entered. Sitting up reading. What were you reading. A magazine. What kind of magazine. The witness hesitated, then named a title that did not appear anywhere in the apartment. How did they come in. The door. Was it locked. She thought it had been. The way she spoke allowed space for the idea that she had forgotten the lock. That grace would later become an important gap in which other truths could be fit. Did you see their faces. No. Did you see a car. No. Did you hear voices before they entered. No.

The thread that tied the wife's account to the life her husband actually lived in town was thin. The work at a bank creates an obvious motive for a robber but a strange motive for a murderer. If someone wanted a key, they could threaten and leave. Killing a teller in his own bed does nothing to gain a robber access to the vault. It only brings an entire department and a county prosecutor to the door. The most basic logic of crime did not favor the story she offered. But logic does not close a case on its own. Officers needed evidence or a confession. In those earliest hours the most likely source of both sat with her father at a kitchen table several miles away.

The father arrived at headquarters with an air of command that comes naturally to men who spend their lives at lecterns and behind long tables. He stepped between officers and his daughter as if it were his right to draw a line around her and to tell the state to stay outside that line. The detective in charge explained that the interview would be recorded. The father demanded a different arrangement. A supervisor stepped in to cool the room. The compromise acknowledged the father's insistence while preserving the basic structure of the interview. The daughter would answer. The police would ask. The father would be present but not conduct the session. The stage was set for a conversation that might have cracked the story open and moved the case toward an arrest within days. What happened instead was a retreat. The father pulled his daughter out of the room and took her home. The answers that might have been given that week were postponed for nearly two decades.

Back at the apartment, the coroner concluded the work and removed the body. The space looked suddenly smaller without the weight of a life anchored in it. The bed was stripped, the mattress covered, the floor cleaned in the places where technicians had finished their work. A seal went up on the door and a long pause settled over the home. Friends would later enter to collect clothing and personal items. They would step behind the tape and feel how differently air hangs in a room where a person died on a bed rather than in a place where a bed simply waits for sleep.

The next days brought the formalities of death. Family were notified. Arrangements were made for a funeral in a church where the mourners knew each other and knew the forms. The casket that held the body showed only the chest and folded hands. The face could not be shown. The manner of death had left a mark too deep to disguise. People rose to speak that day who had no training in public address but who knew how to say the few sentences that matter at a funeral. They spoke of trustworthiness and of faith. They spoke of a young man whose life ended before there was time to become the older man they assumed he would be.

The investigation tried to move forward without the one thing it needed most in those first days, a full account from the person in the bed and the person who shared it. Officers canvassed the campus where friends could describe who saw whom and when. They asked which cars were parked outside the apartment building with any regularity. They pulled the time cards from the bank to confirm when David last worked and who had reason to interact with him in the days before his death. They found nothing to support the idea of a targeted robbery. The bank had not received threats. No branch manager reported that someone had demanded key access from any clerk or teller. The only person speaking about a demand for keys was the wife who had introduced that claim to the record within minutes of the first patrol car's arrival.

An investigator returned to the apartment with a more private task. He followed an idea more than a lead. He stood in the bedroom doorway and mimed the action of moving from the door to the side of the bed with a crowbar in both hands. The angles on the wall spatter aligned with his right handed swing. He stepped forward again and looked down at the floor near the foot of the bed. A tiny flake of paint had stuck there, not the paint of the wall but the paint of a tool. The lab would later confirm what his eye already knew. The flake matched the kind of coating used on common crowbars sold in hardware stores within a few miles of the apartment.

Outside the apartment, the air went back to its ordinary winter taste. Inside the investigation, the absence of cooperation hardened into a wall. Without a weapon in hand and without a confession, the case would hinge on the ability to enter the private life of the marriage and of the circle around it. That entrance was narrow. The wife's father had made sure of it. People close to the couple had their suspicions, but suspicion without access to a suspect and without a tool to match to a strike is only talk. The detectives who had come up in a department where personal relationships matter more than in a city where anonymity governs every movement were stunned by the refusal to speak. They had counted on the combination of community ties and the pressure of a murder to push the truth to the surface. Instead, they watched a family put a lid on a boiling pot and hold it down with both hands.

The murder itself, stripped of what would later be argued in court, had a simplicity that only made the aftermath more galling. A man in his bed was struck repeatedly with overwhelming force. The person or persons responsible left the scene without stealing a thing. The story offered by the one living witness did not match the room or the logic of the act. The likely weapon was something a neighbor might keep in a trunk for emergencies or in a garage for weekend repairs. The attacker knew the house, knew the routine, and knew the way to a bed in the dark. The attack ended in a matter of moments. The wife survived with a faint bruise on her cheek that did not line up with the level of violence inflicted on the person beside her. There were no strangers seen. There was no sign of a forced entry. There was no reason to believe that anyone in the city would come to that apartment to demand a bank key at that hour of night.

By the end of the first week, the detectives had written their reports in a language that held their frustration in check. They entered facts in boxes. They logged evidence. They summarized interviews. They wrote down the narrow set of possibilities left by the scene itself. It was an intimate killing committed with intimacy's confidence. They could not say that on paper. They could only place the room before the reader of their reports and trust that those who came later would see what they saw. On that count history would prove them right, but history would take most of a working lifetime to catch up.

There is one more detail from those first days that belongs here because it encodes the crime in an image that stayed with every person who worked the case. The coroner had flagged a specific distance from the bed to the small white arc where the eye landed. In court that distance would become evidence about force and intent. In the memory of the detectives it became something else. It captured how thorough the violence was and how deeply it had changed the shape of an ordinary bedroom. When a single organ can be torn from the face and thrown across the room by the arc of a tool, you do not need to ask whether the attacker meant to kill. You need only to ask who would choose such certainty and why.

The why did not live in the room. It lived in the days before the attack and in choices made by people who had the keys to the apartment and the keys to the story. The room had done its work. It gave up what it could. The state carried the rest forward into interviews, cross checks, and attempts to break through a wall of protection erected around the only person whose version might have offered a straight road to an arrest. For the family of the dead, the pace of the case became slow enough to feel like a second injury. For the wife and for the person she saw most often in the days when she smiled easily for friends, the pace was slow enough to give them hope that sleep would hold their secrets. For the city, the scene became a point on a map that people would pass and think of when a late night drive took them along South Cooper Road. For the detectives, the bed and the arc of a tool became a promise they made to themselves to keep the file open until time or chance loosened the tongue that had been protected by a father whose voice could still fill a pew.

That is the murder as the apartment told it before any confession, before any plea, before any courtroom saw the photographs. Quick. Merciless. Focused. Not the mess of thieves who panic and run, but the certainty of someone who came for a single purpose and accomplished it. No theft. No random cruelty. A targeted killing wrapped in a story written badly and performed with a bruise that did not convince. The next section will move forward into the years when the case went cold in public view and hot in the minds of the investigators who refused to let the file gather dust, and then into the morning when two detectives from Kansas stood on a porch in Ohio and asked the one question that had not been answered in nineteen years.

ARREST, TRIAL AND SENTENCE

The file never slept. It sat in a drawer that detectives opened whenever the hum of daily calls eased and the long case called them back. The first investigation had stalled in a fog of deference and bad luck. Years passed. People moved. Evidence waited. Then a new pair of eyes took the folder into a conference room and read until the pages felt warm. They reached the same quiet conclusions the first team had reached in the weeks after the murder. No forced entry. No theft. A brutal attack carried out with calm focus. A story from the surviving spouse that did not fit the room. What the new team added was patience measured in decades rather than weeks, and a willingness to walk the slow road that cold cases demand.

They started with time, not pressure. By the early two thousands the widow had built a different life in Ohio with a new last name and a household that looked like any other on a quiet street. The detectives knocked one winter afternoon. The sound was not theatrical. It was the clear knock that says we are here for serious work. She opened the door and saw two men from Kansas bringing the past inside with them. Would she talk. She could refuse. She allowed them in.

They began with the night. She gave the same outline she had offered long ago. Two men. A demand for bank keys. A slap that left a small bruise. She used short strokes and no color, as if detail would betray her. They asked how the intruders entered a locked apartment. She said perhaps the door had been left open. They asked for sensory memory that sticks in the mind even when you wish it would not. A voice. A smell. A piece of clothing. A left hand rather than a right hand. She offered nothing that could be tested against the room. People remember tone and texture in shock. The absence of both told its own story.

Then the detectives changed the lens. They asked about her life since. A move. A marriage. Children. A church that welcomed her smile. They made room for her to step toward a truth she had avoided for twenty years. She did not. So they turned the focus to a name that had hovered around the case from the start. A friend from the Nazarene circle, bright and social, who had known the apartment and the marriage well. Her answers wobbled. They did not push her off balance. They noted where the old tale bent and left.

They went home to Kansas with notes that did not amount to a confession but were more than what the file had held before. Silence, after long practice, had begun to crack. Investigators compared the Ohio interview to the original tale. The contradictions were not small. They made a chart of details the room had given them on the night of the murder and details the widow had repeated. Every time the room and the words collided, the room won.

Prosecutors were invited in early. They prefer to watch the build from the foundation rather than arrive when only the roof remains. Reviewing the record, they were struck by how little the central features had changed. The lock had not been forced. The windows were shut from the inside. The keys sat where they always sat. Nothing was taken. The weapon was gone because someone had time and the presence of mind to take it. Those are the facts of an intimate killing, not a robbery gone wild.

Arrest warrants followed, signed without theatrical speeches by a judge who weighed the sworn statements and found enough to bring both figures into court at last. Arrests in long cases seldom look like scenes from television. They are coordinated, quiet, and polite unless there is reason to expect trouble. The widow with the different last name in Ohio met two officers at her door and went without fuss. A booking camera took the portrait that every jurisdiction keeps, the mechanical record that neither accuses nor forgives. The friend who had built a corporate life far away entered custody on a different day and began to learn how small any holding room can feel.

The first appearances in Johnson County were spare and formal. Charges were read. For the wife, first degree murder. For the friend, an open path that could lead to first degree at trial or to a plea on second degree if that was where evidence and negotiation took them. Counsel was appointed or confirmed. There were no speeches. Dates were set. The case stepped onto the careful timetable a court keeps.

Pretrial work in an old homicide is a craft that mixes archaeology and restraint. The lawyers needed to explain to a future jury why a case so obvious in its physical facts could have taken so long to reach a courtroom, and they needed to do it without turning the trial into a referendum on a church or on a prominent father whose presence in the early days had stopped a crucial interview cold. The prosecution prepared to use only what the proof could carry. The defense prepared to ask jurors whether the state could cross the final small distance between suspicion and certainty after so many years.

Jury selection was candid. Prospective jurors were asked whether they could judge a murder from the early nineteen eighties with minds shaped by later decades. Could they accept the weight of circumstantial evidence when the pieces interlocked cleanly. Could they listen to the careful story of a cold case without demanding a single moment of drama. Those who wanted confessions and dramatic revelations were thanked and excused. Those who said they could evaluate methodical proof remained.

Opening statements set the lines. The state told a simple story built on time and place. A young bank worker was beaten to death as he slept. There was no forced entry. There was no robbery. A spouse in the bed offered a tale that did not match the room or the logic of crime. The missing tool, a common crowbar, argued planning. The likely partner had motive rooted in secrecy and in fear of the disgrace divorce would carry in a narrow community. The defense urged restraint. Outrage is not proof, counsel said. Memory can blur. Delay can harm a fair trial. You must hold the state to its burden.

Witnesses came one by one. The first responding officers described the apartment in calm language and located the body in the bed where everyone knew it had been found. The medical examiner explained the injuries without flourish. The number and placement of blows made intent clear. The death had taken minutes, not seconds, but the outcome was certain from the first strikes. The investigation's early derailment was put into evidence not to shame anyone but to explain the long gap. The detectives who had gone to Ohio told how they had approached the widow with patience and how her words had failed to supply the details genuine victims remember.

Photographs were shown briefly and removed. Jurors do not need gore to do their work well. They need continuity. The state provided it. From the lock that showed no pry marks, to the keys left where they always lay, to the undisturbed drawers and cabinets, to the absence of any reason for strangers to linger long enough to beat a sleeping man to death. The theme never shifted. This was not robbery. This was an inside job.

The defense cross examined steadily. Could a door have been left open. Is it possible an unknown third person entered with her and did the killing while she was stunned. Can the state prove beyond doubt that a particular man was present in the room. The questions were not frivolous. Jurors wrote notes and waited for the answers. What mattered most was how often those lines of doubt ended in the same cul de sac. No forced entry. No theft. No one saw strangers. The only person who claimed to have seen strangers was the one person whose presence is known and whose story fell apart in the first hour if anyone had been allowed to ask the questions properly.

The verdict for the wife came first. Guilty of first degree murder. The foreperson spoke softly. The panel was thanked and released. There was no outburst. The defendant sat with the same posture she had carried into every room for years, a careful composure that had once served as armor and now served as nothing at all. For the man, the path bent. With the proof strong and the first verdict entered, he accepted a plea to second degree murder.

The court took the plea after ensuring he understood the rights he was giving up and the punishment that could follow.

Sentencing brought the family forward. A father spoke about the quiet competence of his son and the wound that had never closed. He accepted the workings of the law and still struggled with its math. Others described ordinary things lost. Laughter over a sink after supper. The way one person's optimism steadies a household when money is thin. They did not ask the court to hate. They asked the court to mean what it said.

Kansas law required the judge to sentence under the rules that existed when the crime was committed. That is an anchor against retroactive vengeance. It is also a hard pill for families who have spent twenty years waiting. The judge imposed ten to twenty years on the wife for first degree murder. He imposed a similar range on the man for second degree, acknowledging both his role and his plea. Parole eligibility would arrive sooner than many expected, because that is how the statute measured time for crimes of that period. The court explained as much, making clear that within those limits he had chosen firm terms.

The hallway after sentencing was quiet. Reporters gathered quotes and then left. The family went home to a house that felt both lighter and lonelier. The defendants went to the county jail and then to state custody, where intake clerks turned names into numbers and schedules and the bus carried them toward long routines. Appeals were filed, as duty requires. Panels read the record and affirmed, noting the care with which the trial judge had managed the presentation of evidence and the fairness of the process as a whole.

Parole became the subject of letters more than of headlines. Boards received statements from the family and from community members who wanted the state to remember the brutality of the night and the patience it had required to reach this point. Years later, release came for one and later for the other, under supervision and with the ordinary restrictions that define life after custody. The family spoke again, not to forgive or to condemn with fresh words, but to place on the record the truth that time changes forms of pain without erasing them.

What remains from the arrest through the sentence is less a story of revelation than a story of endurance. Detectives kept faith with a room that had told the truth from the beginning. Prosecutors walked the narrow path between outrage and proof. A jury accepted the task of judging a case almost as old as some of its members and did that work without drama. A judge respected the limits of the law and still spoke clearly about the harm done. In a community once shaped by deference to titles, the courtroom became the one place where titles did not matter and where a father's bluster could not silence a question.

The record now includes everything the first team wished for in nineteen eighty two. A clear account of who decided that a marriage could not be ended honestly. A recognition that a creed meant to sustain fidelity had been twisted into a rationalization for killing. A set of sentences that, while governed by the law of the time, declared that a bed is not a battleground and that anyone who makes it so will answer to the state. The story does not glow. It does not claim that justice arrived at the speed anyone wanted. It says only that justice arrived, and that the people charged with carrying it did so without cruel spectacle, which is its own kind of victory.

THE AFTERMATH

The courtroom emptied, the doors swung shut, and Olathe began the long work of living with a verdict that solved a mystery and left a wound. In the years that followed, the case stopped being an unfinished argument and became something subtler in the life of the town. It was a caution spoken in kitchens. It was an example offered in classrooms. It was a study in how a community shaped by faith and habit copes when the people it trusted most have used that trust as cover. The official story had ended with numbers read aloud by a judge. The human story had no such clean ending. It worked forward through families and congregations and the dull machinery of time.

For the Harmons, the completion of the case did not lighten the house so much as steady it. After a quarter century of rumor and hope, the guilty plea and the guilty verdict gave the family a framework. They could look back without second guessing whether they had misread a sign or failed a duty. They had not. The man they loved had been ambushed as he slept. The people responsible had finally been held to account. That conclusion did not soften grief but it removed a set of corrosive questions. The father who had spoken in court returned to a quieter routine marked by anniversaries and practical tasks that follow a sentence more than a death. There were letters to write each time a board convened to consider release. There were visits with officials who needed an address for future notices and a phone number that would still be in service when the next decision came due. He learned the cadence of parole the way families learn the cadence of oncology. Appointments are set. You prepare your remarks. You say what must be said and you go home to wait.

Those letters set out truths simple and unadorned. A young man who never sought attention became famous for the worst reason a person can. The photographs displayed in living rooms at holidays were the same ones used in court because no new ones could be made. Chairs at family events did not get moved to make extra space. They stayed arranged around an absence. The habits that bind a family together took on extra meaning because they were now acts of remembrance as well as routine. Sunday dinner became not only a meal but a way of carrying forward the manner and humor of someone who would have carved the roast and passed the bread and always found a way to make the younger cousins laugh.

On the other side of the ledger, the families of the people sent to prison had to reconcile two facts that do not sit easily together. They loved their own. Their own had done something terrible. The first visits after sentencing were exercises in translation. Words like yard and count and classification came home on the phone. Those words are not part of an ordinary family's vocabulary until they have to be. Parents who had once offered advice about studies and paychecks learned instead how to advise their children on rules that promised consequences for even small disobedience. Spouses navigated the new identity of long distance partner to a number in a system that accepted their phone calls and their money orders but did not recognize their place at a table. Children were told shortened versions of the truth that made sense at different ages. One day they would read a fuller account and decide how to hold it. Families who never wanted to be known became known. They learned to keep their heads down at school events and to count their allies by the ones who looked them in the eye.

The congregation that had been the social core for so much of the story followed the case with a mixture of sorrow and unease. A faith that discourages divorce and celebrates reconciliation had been turned into a landscape where secrecy could flourish. Pastors spoke gently about the difference between a creed that offers a path for repairing a marriage and a set of expectations that keeps people trapped until they choose a worse sin to escape shame. The sermons did not name names. They did not need to. Everyone knew the reference. The teaching that took hold afterward was less about the rights and wrongs of divorce and more about the necessity of confession. If a marriage is dying, say so. If you have broken a vow, say so. Say it before imagination becomes plan. Compassion was not removed from the vocabulary of the church. It was sharpened.

MidAmerica Nazarene College had to face its own reflection. The campus life that had wrapped the three central figures in fellowship had also provided convenient alibis. Students and faculty who had lived through the early years went back over how they had missed what was in front of them and what they could do in future to avoid the temptations of deference. A school cannot police hearts. It can instruct minds. It can create healthier norms. Workshops became less about lists of rules and more about the costs of pretending that reputation outranks truth. Counselors were given more space to intervene when a student came in with a problem that did not fit neatly into the old categories. Deans made it better known that the school would help someone end an unsafe marriage rather than pressure them to perform happiness. These are small changes in policy and tone. They matter because they influence private decisions long before they become matters for a detective with a tape recorder.

The police department used the case like a textbook in how not to be intimidated and how to recover when the first steps go wrong. No agency wants to admit that any investigation has been swayed by a person's title. This one had, briefly and decisively. In the years that followed, supervisors emphasized what the second team had done right. They wrote down procedures that codified what had been learned. When a witness belongs to a powerful family, two supervisors must be present at critical stages and the interview must be conducted on the department's terms. When a suspect tries to replace counsel with a relative who acts like counsel, the interview stops until an attorney licensed to practice law appears. The idea was not to punish institutions for having prominent members. The idea was to make sure that every person, prominent or not, met the same process.

The cold case unit found a new level of standing in the department. The detectives who traveled to Ohio and asked calm questions on a winter afternoon proved a proposition that officers have preached for years. Patience is not passivity. It is a tactic. The unit received better access to overtime and to technical support. Cases that once sat in a drawer were reopened with a standard script. Reinterview witnesses. Revisit the scene with fresh assumptions. Run physical items through new testing. Call out institutional dynamics that might have warped the first attempt. The culture shifted from embarrassed apology for delays to pride in persistence. The names of two detectives became shorthand around the station for thorough work without theatrics.

The wider public absorbed the case unevenly but absorbed it all the same. People who had lived in Olathe long enough to remember the morning after the murder folded new facts into old recollections. They let go of the bank key story without much ceremony. It had never fit the room and now it had been formally replaced with the simpler truth. For new arrivals to the city, the case became a local legend that carried a moral rather than only a thrill. In neighborhood gatherings you could hear the softer conclusions people reached. Do not assume. Ask. Do not be cowed by titles. Call things by their right names even when it embarrasses a neighbor.

Media attention came in two waves after the sentences. The first wave was retrospective, collecting the story in long arcs and assigning it a place among the larger region's notable crimes. The second wave came with parole eligibility. Cameras and microphones arrived just long enough to record reactions to the possibility that one of the two might step into ordinary daylight again. The coverage fixed on two images that spoke nearly without narration. A black and white portrait of a young bank worker whose face was open and unguarded in the way people are when they have not learned to plan for the worst. And the custodial images of the woman whose smile persisted even in photographs taken under fluorescent light. People debated that smile the way people always debate the tics of public figures caught in private moments. Habit. Nerves. Control. Self regard. The answer did not matter. It was a single frame to which people attached their own explanations, not a lever for changing a board's mind.

Parole hearings themselves instructed the public in how memory can be both disciplined and merciful. The board allowed the family to speak. Their statements were not performances. They were variations on a theme. The pain of losing a son never resolved into any other feeling, though other feelings had turned up around it. Hope for peace in their own lives. Hope that the board would weigh the brutality of the crime alongside whatever evidence the inmate offered about change. The board considered the numbers written into the judgment. Ten to twenty years. It considered the statute that required those numbers. It considered letters from the community. It considered the institutional record of conduct in custody. A decision is a decision, not an argument. It was made. The public reacted with a blend of acceptance and anger familiar to anyone who has watched the parole process for long. The acceptance lives in the reality that sentences in older cases are governed by older rules. The anger lives in a sense that no amount of time can equal the permanence of a death.

Melinda left the state under supervision after the board granted release. She returned to Ohio, where the day to day discipline of parole replaced the rigid clocks of custody. This change did not mean freedom in any heroic sense. It meant living by a set of rules that would have felt suffocating to a person fresh from the outside and yet felt oddly generous to someone used to count times and lights that never go dark. Employment had to be approved. Addresses had to be reported. Travel had to be cleared. Contact with the family of the victim was forbidden. Small missteps would prompt a quick return to a cell. The people who discussed her release in Shawnee and in Olathe measured it against their own lives and settled into a watchful quiet. The law had done what the law allowed. The rest belonged to time and to the choices she would make out of sight.

Mark, still in custody when Melinda was paroled, moved toward his own hearing date with the same mix of routine and paperwork that defines the last years of a long sentence. For some, his eventual release would signal the end of the official life of the case. For others nothing finished anything. They carried the story the way people carry scars that no one else sees. They paid attention to their schools and their parks and their courts with a raised awareness that institutions function best when people watch them.

There were smaller circles of aftermath that the newspapers did not bother with. Old friends met and compared what they remembered of youth on campus and whether they should have said something different at this or that moment. Teachers thought about all the conversations they had had with students over the years about marriage and duty and conflict and concluded that clarity is better than bland counsel. Librarians noted a steady interest in books about famous crimes the year the case came back into court and then watched the number drop off. There are seasons when a town reads about violence to make sense of its own. There are seasons when it reads almost anything else to escape the feeling that bad stories are endless.

The legacy for the city government was pragmatic. It built better connections among the agencies that share responsibility when a major crime occurs. Protocols for early victim assistance were tightened so that families received fewer duplicate calls and had a single point of contact for information. The police adopted a practice of writing public updates that say little but say it well. When they can reassure the town that there is no wider threat, they do that. When they cannot, they say so. The credibility earned in crises carries into quieter days when trust is needed for other work.

The effects on the people who had worked the case were complicated. Detectives aged out and retired. On fishing trips, they told abbreviated versions of the story for younger officers who were preparing to take on their own cold files. They did not make themselves the heroes. They made the facts the heroes. A room that spoke clearly. A record kept tidy enough to be useful two decades later. A willingness to go knock politely on a door in another state and wait through a silence that other people might have tried to fill with speeches. Prosecutors moved on to other homicides and other hearings and carried forward the habit of staying stern without cruelty. Defense lawyers reminded their students that they had represented people the community hated without once forgetting the law's requirement that every person be defended. That is healthy in the long run. A local bar that nurtures such professionalism resists the lure of easy moralizing and shows the next generation how to disagree without intoxication.

As for the town's memory, it settled into form the way concrete does. At landmarks around Olathe, nothing bears a plaque about this case. Yet the people most affected can tell you the block and the window and the way the bedroom faced the street. They do not need bronze to keep the story. They carry it in the angle of their shoulder when they walk past. Rituals have a way of absorbing grief and distributing it so that it does not overload any single person or day. The memorial that mattered most was private. A family gathered. The same prayers were said. The same food was cooked. The same stories were told. The stories that would get told again became obvious over time. A laugh that came quick and unforced. A stubbornness about doing a job right. A patience that made others want to be patient.

True crime readers sometimes ask whether justice felt done. The answer offered by Olathe was quiet. Yes, in law. The case was solved, charged, argued, and punished within the boundaries the statutes allowed. No, in life. A person is missing from a table. A bed was once turned into a place of killing. A church had to admit that its culture could be misused by people intent on preserving appearances. Those two answers do not cancel each other. They live together. That is what most aftermaths look like when the cameras leave. They are a braid of satisfaction and sorrow.

There was one further effect that sits at the edge of news and enters the shape of a community. After this case, the city told its own stories differently. It did not rush to attribute crimes to strangers or to defend insiders instinctively. It learned to hold two ideas in mind. Outsiders sometimes do bad things. Insiders sometimes do worse. Adults who had known the central figures as youths began to say this out loud to younger people. Choose friends for their honesty rather than their brightness. Tell the truth before the lie hardens into a plan. Trust the law rather than extorting it with force of personality. That is a hard sentence for a town to speak about itself. Olathe spoke it.

Years later, when the anniversary of the killing came round to the day of the month again, people who knew made small acknowledgments. A flower placed without a word. A phone call that said I was thinking about him. A walk past the old apartment on a quiet morning with no goal but to mark time. The rest of the city went about its business in the way healthy places do. It did not become obsessed with its worst day. It did not pretend the day had not happened. It built its schools and tended its parks and coached its teams and gathered at tables to eat and laugh and, when necessary, to grieve. That is the mark of a town that understands aftermath. It is not a posture. It is a practice.

ABOUT THE AUTHOR

Matthew Kell Taylor is a seasoned true crime writer with a passion for uncovering the darkest corners of human nature. Taylor's first book "50 CRIMES THAT ROCKED THE WORLD" was met with critical acclaim, earning him recognition for his meticulous attention to detail and his ability to humanize the victims and perpetrators alike. His second book "40 DEADLY WOMEN" followed the same path.

In his highly anticipated third book, "30 KILLER KIDS" Taylor continues to take readers on a gripping journey into the minds of those who commit the unthinkable—children who kill. Drawing from real-life cases, he expertly navigates the delicate and disturbing topic, exploring the psychological, social, and environmental factors that lead to such horrifying acts. Taylor's unparalleled dedication to understanding the intricacies of criminal behavior shines through, offering both insight and empathy as he explores the disturbing nature of juvenile violence.

Next Taylor turned his attention to the unthinkable. In 20 KIDS WHO KILL KIDS as he took his readers on another disturbing journey to the very depths of incredible cruelty and depravity, committed by the least likely perpetrators…our own children!

A skilled storyteller, Matthew Kell Taylor then continued his journey, exposing crimes that captivate audiences with 21 DEADLY INMATES featuring prison inmates who served up lethal justice against their cellmates.

Another offering lists the WORLDS MOST PROLIFIC SERIAL KILLERS. A haunting account of killers with the largest body count…Not for the faint hearted!

His next book offers the first of four books featuring the world's most feared prisons. SENTENCED TO HELL is a series that is not for the faint hearted describing the last place on earth you would want to find yourself.

Taylor then entered into the turbulent world of killer wives with.. KILLER WIVES...DEADLIER THAN THE MALE 1.... 15 examples of spousal murder committed by women in the UK and USA. First of a series featuring, not only evil personified, but women who kill for self protection.

Next came a fascinating study into "EVERY WOMAN EXECUTED IN THE USA SINCE 1900" The first in a series of 2 books documenting almost 60 female executions conducted in the since 1900.

KILLER WIVES...DEADLIER THAN THE MALE 2 (Volume 2) follows on from volume one with a further 15 cases of husbands killed off by their deadly spouses.

Followed By .....EXECUTED 2 Second volume of 3 featuring every woman executed in the USA since 1900

Taylor then turned his pen to the crimes committed by German female prison camp guards during World War 2, and the consequences that placed them on the gallows in NAZI FEMALE CAMP GUARD EXECUTIONS: JUSTIFIABLE EXECUTIONS

KILLER WIVES 5 is a continuation of Taylor's successful KILLER WIVES series with another 9 cases where unfortunate husbands fell victim to their evil wives.

ALSO BY MATTHEW KELL TAYLOR

50 Crimes That Rocked The World

Another 25 Crimes That Rocked The World

40 Deadly Women

25 Killer Kids

Kids Who Kill Kids

21 Deadly Inmates

The Worlds Most Prolific Serial Killers

Sentenced To Hell : Worlds Scariest Prisons

Killer Wives: "Deadlier Than The Male"

Killer Wives 2: More Deadly Wives---More Dead Husbands

Killer Wives 3: 10 More Deadly Wives : 10 More Dead Husbands

EXECUTED! : Every Woman Executed In The USA Since 1900

EXECUTED 2 Every Woman Executed In The USA Since 1900

Nazi Female Camp Guard Executions: Justifiable Executions

Killer Wives 3: 10 More Deadly Wives : 10 More Dead Husbands

Killer Wives 4: 10 Deadly Dames - 10 Dead Dudes

Disclaimer

While every effort has been made to ensure the factual accuracy of the information presented in this book, due to the nature of criminal investigations, details may vary depending on sources and available records. This work is based on publicly available information, including court documents, news reports, and interviews. Where factual details are scarce, a limited use of AI research has been employed to further the narrative without guesswork or improvisation. Some names and certain personal details may have been altered to protect privacy. The author and publisher do not claim to have provided an exhaustive account of every case and acknowledge that interpretations of events may differ.

Copyright © 2025 Matthew Kell Taylor
All rights reserved.

Printed in Dunstable, United Kingdom